NUTSHELLS

Contract Law

SECOND EDITION

Round Hall's Nutshell Series

NUTSHELL TITLES

Specially written for students of Irish law, each title in the **Nutshell Series** from Round Hall is an accessible review of key principles, concepts and cases. Nutshells are both the ideal introductory text and the perfect revision aid.

- **Administrative Law** – 2nd edition by Matthew Holmes
- **Company Law** – 4th edition
- **Constitutional Law** – 3rd edition by Fergus Ryan
- **Contract Law** – 2nd edition by Shauna Colgan
- **Criminal Law** – 4th edition by Cecilia Ní Choileáin
- **Employment Law** – 3rd edition by Dorothy Donovan
- **Equity and Trusts** – 2nd edition by Miriam Dowling
- **EU Law** by Matthew Holmes
- **Evidence** by Ross Gorman
- **Family Law** – 2nd edition by Marianne Joyce
- **Immigration, Free Movement of Persons, and Citizenship Law** by John M. Stanley
- **The Irish Legal System** by Dorothy Donovan
- **Land Law** – 3rd edition by Ruth Cannon
- **Succession Law** by Karl Dowling and Robert Grimes
- **Tort** – 3rd edition by Irene Fisher

NUTSHELLS

Contract Law

SECOND EDITION

by

SHAUNA COLGAN
BCL, LL.M., Barrister at Law

ROUND HALL

Published in 2024 by
Thomson Reuters (Professional) Ireland Limited
(Registered in Ireland, Company No. 80867.
Registered Office and address for service:
Spaces, Office 313, 77 Sir John Rogerson's Quay,
Block C, Dublin 2, D02 VK60)
trading as Round Hall.

Typeset by Carrigboy Typesetting Services

Printed and bound in the UK by
CPI Group (UK) Ltd, Croydon, CR0 4YY

ISBN (Print): 9780414071773
ISBN (ProView): 9780414121300
ISBN (Print & ProView): 9780414121294
ISBN (eBook): 9780414099234

A catalogue record for this book is available from the British Library.

All rights reserved. No part of this publication may be reproduced or transmitted in any form or by any means, or stored in any retrieval system of any nature, without prior written permission.

Thomson Reuters and the Thomson Reuters Logo are trademarks of Thomson Reuters. Round Hall is a registered trademark of Thomson Reuters (Professional) Ireland Limited.

© Thomson Reuters (Professional) Ireland Limited, 2024

Preface

The *Contract Law Nutshell Second Edition* aims to provide students and practitioners with an accessible overview of Irish contract law.

Since the first edition of this book was published in 2006, there have been some significant developments in the study and practice of contract law. These are noted with emphasis in the following text. Notwithstanding these changes, contract law remains a subject firmly rooted in the past, as evidenced by its reliance on Victorian case law. Given the antiquated nature of much of the jurisprudence referred to herein, modern, practical examples are used throughout in order to illustrate clearly the rules and exceptions discussed.

Given its nature and size, this text is not intended to be an exhaustive review of the subject matter. Notwithstanding this, it is my hope that readers will find this to be an instructive starting-point in their examination of the area, its principles and case law.

Sincere thanks are due to a number of people, in particular:

Donough Cassidy, Siobhán Mulholland and the staff of Thomson Reuters: Thank you for your tireless help and encouragement.

Dr. Fergus Ryan: Your incomparable first edition was my benchmark throughout the writing process. If the second edition is a fraction as effective as your first, I will consider it a roaring success. I so appreciate your support and well wishes throughout the process.

My family, in particular: Deborah Colgan, John Colgan, Maureen Dunne and Tom Dunne: Thank you for your love, example and patience.

Alexander Wahlrab: Who was with me every step of the way.

Finally, and most of all: Ivan Wahlrab: Thank you for your kindness and often blind championing of my efforts. This text could not have been completed without you.

Sole responsibility for errors and omissions herein lies with the author. However, every effort has been made to ensure the accuracy of this text as of 18 June 2024.

Shauna Colgan

Contents

Table of Cases xiii
Table of Legislation. xxix

1. **Introduction.** 1
   Introduction. 1
   A Contract as a Bargain 1
   Sources of Contract Law. 2
   The Right to Enter into a Bad or Foolish Bargain. 2
   Caveat Emptor 2
   Objective Approach to Interpretation 3
   Recording an Agreement in Writing 3

2. **Offer.** 4
   Introduction. 4
   Bilateral Offer 4
   Unilateral Offer 5
   Distinguishing Offers from Other Phenomena 5
   Termination of an Offer. 12

3. **Acceptance** 19
   Introduction. 19
   Preliminary Points on Acceptance 19
   Methods of Acceptance. 20
   Indicating Acceptance. 24
   Mode of Acceptance. 27
   Acceptance Must Be Communicated 27
   Exceptions to the Communication Rule 28
   The Postal Rule 28
   Cases Where the Postal Rule Does Not Apply. 30

4. **Intention to Create Legal Relations.** 33
   Presumptions against an Intention to Create Legal Relations 33
   Family Arrangements 34
   Commercial Agreements 36

5.	**The Requirement of Certainty**..........................**45**
	Introduction..45
	Methods of Clarification 46

6.	**Consideration** **48**
	Introduction..48
	Consideration as a Concept.............................48
	Consideration Must Move from the Promisee 49
	Consideration Need Not Move to the Promisor 49
	Consideration Must Have Some Tangible Value 50
	Insufficient Consideration................................52

7.	**Promissory Estoppel** **59**
	Introduction..59
	The *High Trees* Principle 59
	Conditions Attached to the Creation of an Estoppel............61
	Distinguishing Promissory Estoppel from Other Similar Concepts... 68

8.	**Privity of Contract**......................................**70**
	Introduction..70
	Examples of the Privity Rule.............................70
	Comparison with Consideration 71
	Exceptions to the Privity Requirements 72
	Law Reform Commission Proposals 76

9.	**Capacity to Contract** **77**
	Introduction..77
	Infancy: General.......................................77
	Contracts Void under the Infants Relief Act 1874.............78
	Contracts that Are Valid unless Repudiated..................80
	Contracts that Are Binding on the Infant....................81
	Reform 83
	"Mental Incapacity".....................................84
	Intoxication 85
	Convicts 86

10.	**Formalities of Contract** **87**
	Introduction..87
	Contracts that Must Be Evidenced in Writing.................87
	Statute of Frauds (Ireland) 1695..........................87

	Requirements of the 1695 Statute and Section 51 of the
	2009 Act 92
	Joinder of Documents. 94
	"Subject to Contract". 96
	Part Performance of a Contract—Equitable Means of
	Enforcing a Contract. 96

11. Electronic Commerce 100
Introduction. 100
Formation of a Contract 100
Consumer Rights Arising from Electronic Contracts. 103

12. Express Terms. 105
Introduction. 105
Can Oral Statements Form Part of a Contract? 105
Warranty or Representation? 105
Collateral Contracts 116
Conditions Precedent/Subsequent. 118
The Relevant Importance of Contract Terms 119
General Principles in Relation to the Interpretation of Terms 122

13. Implied Terms 123
Introduction. 123
Terms Implied in Fact 123
Terms Implied by Reference to Custom or Trade Usage 125
Terms Implied by Common Law 126
Terms Implied by Legislation 128
Terms Implied by the Constitution 128

14. Exclusion Clauses 129
Introduction. 129
Incorporation of Exclusion Clauses 130
Interpreting Exclusion and Limitation Clauses 138

15. Consumer Rights under Contract. 142
Introduction. 142
Sale of Goods Act 1893, Sale of Goods and Supply of
Services Act 1980, and the History of Consumer Law
in Ireland 143
Consumer Rights Act 2022. 144
Other Consumer Protections of Recent Note. 159

16.	**Misrepresentation**	160
	Introduction	160
	When Does Misrepresentation Arise?	160
	Can Silence Amount to Misrepresentation?	164
	Types of Misrepresentation	169
	Remedies	173
	Exclusion for Liability	175
17.	**Mistake**	176
	Did the Mistake Exist at the Time the Contract Was Entered Into?	176
	Mistake of Law	177
	Common Mistake of Fact	178
	Common Mistake of Fact in Equity	181
	Mutual Mistake	182
	Unilateral Mistake	183
	Errors as to Identity	184
	Remedies for Mistake	185
18.	**Duress, Undue Influence and Unconscionability**	188
	Duress at Common Law	188
	Duress in Equity	191
	Undue Influence	191
	Undue Influence and Third Parties	197
	Unconscionability	201
19.	**Illegal and Void Contracts**	204
	Introduction	204
	Illegal Contracts under Legislation	204
	Illegal Contracts at Common Law	207
	Consequences of Illegality	210
	Void Contracts	212
	Severability	216
20.	**Discharge of a Contract**	217
	Introduction	217
	Agreement	217
	Performance	217
	Frustration	222
	Discharge by Breach	226

21.	**Remedies.** **229**
	Damages 229
	Mitigation 233
	Types of Damages 234
	Other Matters Relating to Damages. 239
	Remedies other than Damages 240

Appendix: Answering Exam Questions **242**
    General Points to Note 242
    Essay Questions 242
    Problem Questions 244

Index 247

Table of Cases

ACC Bank plc v Dillon [2012] IEHC 474. 188
ACC Loan Management Ltd v Connolly [2017] IECA 119 200
ACC Loan Management Ltd v Sheehan [2015] IEHC 818. 194
Actionstrength Ltd v International Glass Engineering SpA [2003] 2 A.C. 541 89
Adams v Lindsell (1818) 1 B. & Ald. 681 28
Addis v Gramophone Co Ltd [1909] A.C. 488 . . . . 236, 237
Afton v Film Studios of Ireland (unreported, High Court, 12 July 1971). 234
Aga Khan v Firestone [1992] I.L.R.M. 31. 125
AGM Londis plc v Gorman's Supermarket Ltd and Kerrigan [2014] IEHC 95 . . . 131
Ailsa Craig Fishing Co v Malvern Fishing and Securicor [1983] 1 All E.R. 101 . . 139
Ajayi v Briscoe [1964] 1 W.L.R. 1326. 65
Allcard v Skinner (1887) 36 Ch. D. 145 . . . . 193, 195
Allied Irish Bank plc v Cuddy [2020] IECA 211. 118
Allied Irish Bank plc v Griffin [2020] IECA 221 62
Allied Irish Banks plc v Galvin Developments (Killarney) Ltd
    [2011] IEHC 314. . . . . .117, 118
Amalgamated Investment & Property Co Ltd v John Walker & Sons Ltd
    [1977] 1 W.L.R. 164. 177
Analog Devices BV v Zurich Insurance Co Ltd [2005] 1 I.R. 274. 122
Anderson v Backlund 159 Minn. 423 (1924) 5, 107
Anderson v Ryan [1967] I.R. 34 174
Andrews v Singer [1934] 1 K.B. 17. 138
Anglia Television v Reed [1972] 1 Q.B. 60. 234
Apicella v Scala (1931) 66 I.L.T.R. 33 40
Appleby v Myers (1867) L.R. 2 C.P. 651 225
Armhouse Lee Ltd v Chappell (*The Times*, 7 August 1996). 207
Aro Road and Land Vehicles Ltd v Insurance Corporation of Ireland Ltd
    [1986] I.R. 403 . . . . 166, 167
Arterial Drainage v Rathangan River Drainage Board (1880) 6 L.R. (Ir.) 513 . . . 220
Association of General Practitioners v Minister for Health
    [1995] 2 I.L.R.M. 481 63
Astley Industrial Trust v Grimley [1963] 2 All E.R. 33. 140
Athlone RDC v A.G. Campbell and Son (No. 2) (1912) 47 I.L.T.R. 142 227
Atlas Express v Kafco [1989] 1 All E.R. 641. 190
Attwood v Lamont [1920] 3 K.B. 571 216
Attwood v Small (1838) 7 E.R. 684 162

B. & S. Contracts v Victor Green Publications [1984] 1 I.C.R. 419 190
Bacon v Kavanagh (1908) 42 I.L.T.R. 120 93

Baker v Jones [1954] 1 W.L.R. 1005 212
Balfour v Balfour [1919] 2 K.B. 571 34
Bank of Australasia v Palmer [1897] A.C. 540 111
Bank of Credit and Commerce International v Aboody [1990] 1 Q.B. 923 195
Bank of Ireland v Curran [2016] IECA 399 200
Bank of Ireland v Lennon (unreported, High Court, 17 February 1998) 172
Bank of Ireland v Smith [1966] I.R. 646 .... 108, 171
Bank of Nova Scotia v Hogan [1996] 3 I.R. 239 .... 196, 197
Bannerman v White (1861) 10 C.B. (N.S.) 844 109
Barclay's Bank v O'Brien [1993] 3 All E.R. 417 .... 192, 195, 197
Barry v Davies [2001] 1 All E.R. 944 10
Barry v Ennis Property Finance DAC [2018] IEHC 766 201
Barton v Armstrong [1975] 2 All E.R. 465 188
Bell v Lever Bros Ltd [1932] A.C. 161 180
Beresford v Royal Insurance Co Ltd [1937] 2 K.B. 197 207
Beswick v Beswick [1968] A.C. 59 71
Billings v Arnott (1945) 80 I.L.T.R. 50 .... 11, 23, 24
Bissett v Wilkinson [1927] A.C. 177 161
Black v Grealy (unreported, High Court, 10 December 1977) 116
Black v Kavanagh (1973) 108 I.L.T.R. 91 94
Blackpool and Flyde Aero Club v Blackpool Borough Council
    [1990] 3 All E.R. 25 234
Blake v Concannon (1870) I.R. 4 C.L. 323 81
Blomley v Ryan (1956) 99 C.L.R. 362 202
Bolton v Mahadeva [1972] 2 All E.R. 1322 219
Boone v Eyre (1779) 1 Hy. Bl. 273n 218
Bord Iascaigh Mhara v Scallan (unreported, High Court, 8 May 1973) 228, 233
Bowley Logging v Domtar (1982) 135 D.L.R. (3d) 179 235
Bowman v Secular Society [1917] A.C. 406 208
Boyers & Co v Duke [1905] 2 I.R. 617 6
Boyle and Boyle v Lee and Goyns [1992] I.L.R.M. 65 .... 42, 96
Brace v Calder [1895] 2 Q.B. 253 233
Bradbury v Morgan (1862) 1 H. & C. 249 14
Bradford v Roulston (1858) 8 I.R.C.L. 468 53
Brady v Flood (1841) 6 Circ. Cases 309 208
Bridgman v Green (1755) 2 Ves. Sen. 627 192
Brikom Investments v Carr [1979] Q.B. 467 66
Brinkibon Ltd v Stahag Stahl GmbH [1983] 2 A.C. 34 31
British Road Services v Crutchley Ltd [1968] 1 All E.R. 811 21
Brogden v Metropolitan Railway Co (1877) 2 App. Cas. 666 24
Brown v Wood (1864) 6 Ir. Jur. 221 220
Browne v Iarnród Éireann (No. 2) [2014] IEHC 117 237
Bunge Corp (New York) v Tradax Export SA (Panama) [1981] 2 All E.R. 513 ... 119
Burke v Dublin Corporation [1991] I.R. 341 126
Burrows v Subsurface Surveys Ltd (1968) 68 D.L.R. (2d) 354 64

Butler Machine Co v Ex-cell-O Corp Ltd [1979] 1 W.L.R. 401 22
Butler v McAlpine [1904] 2 I.R. 445 125
Byrne v Martina Investments Ltd (unreported, High Court, 30 January 1984) . . . 127
Byrne v Van Tienhoven (1880) 49 L.J.Q.B. 316 .... 16, 29

Cadbury Ireland Ltd v Kerry Co-operative Creameries Ltd
   [1982] I.L.R.M. 77. .... 37, 73
Canary Wharf (BP4) T1 Ltd v European Medicines Agency
   [2019] EWHC 921 (Ch) 225
Carbin v Somerville [1933] I.R. 227 170
Carey v Independent Newspapers [2004] 3 I.R. 52 109
Carlill v Carbolic Smokeball Co [1893] 1 Q.B. 256 .... 7, 38, 161, 242
Carlo Tassara Assets Management SA v Éire Composites Teoranta
   [2018] IEHC 182. 191
Carna Foods v Eagle Star Insurance [1997] 2 I.L.R.M. 499. 124
Carroll v An Post National Lottery Co [1996] 1 I.R. 443 125
Carroll v Carroll [1998] 2 I.L.R.M. 218 201
Carroll v Carroll [2000] 1 I.L.R.M. 210 .... 194, 196, 202
Carroll v Dublin Bus [2005] IEHC 278 126
Carthy v O'Neill [1981] I.L.R.M. 443. 96
Carvill v Irish Industrial Bank [1968] I.R. 325 127
Casey v Irish Intercontinental Bank [1979] I.R. 364 .... 42, 93
Cehave NV v Bremer Handelsgesellschaft (The Hansa Nord)
   [1975] 3 W.L.R. 447 121
Central London Property Trust Ltd v High Trees House Ltd
   [1947] K.B. 130 .... 59, 60, 62, 68
Central Meat Products v Carney (1944) 10 Ir. Jur. Rep. 34 45
Centrovincial Estates v Merchant Investors Insurance [1983] Com. L.R. 158 . . . 183
CF v JDF [2005] 4 I.R. 154. 63
Chambers v Kelly (1873) 7 I.R.C.L. 231. 112
Chapleton v Barry UDC [1940] 1 All E.R. 356 135
Chaplin v Leslie Frewin Publishers (Ltd) [1966] Ch. 71 83
Chappell and Co Ltd v Nestlé Ltd [1960] A.C. 87. 51
Chapple v Cooper (1844) 13 M. & W. 252 79
Chariot Inns Ltd v Assicurazioni Generali SpA [1981] I.L.R.M. 173 .... 166, 167
Charles Rickards Ltd v Oppenhaim [1950] 1 K.B. 616. 68
Chartered Trust (Ireland) v Healy (unreported, High Court,
   10 December 1985) 63, 67
City and Westminster Properties v Mudd [1959] Ch. 129. 116
Clayton Love & Sons (Dublin) Ltd v The British and Irish Steam
   Packet Co Ltd (1970) 104 I.L.T.R. 157 .... 114, 140, 141
Clifton v Palumbo [1944] 2 All E.R. 497 5
Clitheroe v Simpson (1879) 4 L.R. (Ir.) 59 71
Cohane v Cohane [1968] I.R. 176 213
Coleman v New Ireland Assurance plc [2009] IEHC 173 167

Collins v Godefroy (1831) 1 B. & Ad. 950. 53
Colthurst v La Touche Colthurst [2000] IEHC 14 160
Combe v Combe [1951] 2 K.B. 215 . . . . 62, 67
Commane v Walsh (unreported, High Court, 3 May 1983). 17
Commodity Broking Co Ltd v Meehan [1985] I.R. 12. 89
Continental Oil v Moynihan (1977) 111 I.L.T.R. 5 215
Cooper v Phibbs (1867) L.R. 2 H.L. 149 . . . . 177, 180, 181
Couchman v Hill [1947] 1 All E.R. 103 . . . . 109, 114
Coughlan v Moloney (1905) 39 I.L.T.R. 153. 218
Courtney v Courtney (1923) 57 I.L.T.R. 42. . . . . 34, 35
Couturier v Hastie (1856) 5 H.L.C. 673 179
Cowan v Milbourn (1867) L.R. 2 Exch. 230 208
Cowan v O'Connor (1888) 20 Q.B.D. 640 28
Craddock Bros v Hunt [1923] 2 Ch. 136. 186
Crean v Drinan [1983] I.L.R.M. 82 221
Cundy v Lindsay (1878) 3 App. Cas. 459. 184
Curling v Walsh (unreported, High Court, 23 October 1987) 127
Currie v Misa (1875) L.R. 10 Ex. 153. 48
Curtis v Chemical Cleaning & Dyeing Co Ltd [1951] 1 K.B. 805 . . . . . 131, 141, 165
Cutter v Powell (1795) 6 Term Rep. 320 . . . . 218, 219

D & C Builders Ltd v Rees [1966] 2 Q.B. 617. 67
Da Silva v Miranda [2017] IECA 252 237
Dakota Packaging Ltd v APH Manufacturing BV t/a Wyeth Medica Ireland
    (unreported, High Court, 10 October 2003); [2005] 2 I.R. 54 (SC) 99, 125
Daly v Minister for the Marine [2001] 3 I.R. 513. . . . . 65, 66
Darlington Properties Ltd v Meath County Council [2011] IEHC 70 171
Daulia v Four Milbank Nominees [1978] Ch. 231. . . . . 16, 23
Davis Contractors v Fareham UDC [1956] A.C. 696 223
De Francesco v Barnum (1890) 45 Ch. D. 430 82
Derry v Peek (1889) 14 App. Cas. 337. 169
Devine v Scott (1931) 66 I.L.T.R. 107. 207
Dick Bentley Productions v Harold Smith Motors [1965] 2 All E.R. 65. . . . . 106, 108
Dickinson v Dodds (1876) 2 Ch. D. 463. . . . . 15, 243
Dimmock v Hallett (1866) 2 Ch. App. 21 161
Dinnegan v Ryan [2002] 3 I.R. 178 237
Dodds v Millman (1964) 45 D.L.R. (2d) 472. 172
Doheny v Bank of Ireland (*Irish Times*, 12 December 1997) 161
Doherty v Gallagher (unreported, High Court, 9 June 1975) 93
Dolan v Nelligan [1967] I.R. 247. 178
Doolan v Murray (unreported, High Court, 21 December 1993). 162, 172
Dooley v Egan (1938) 72 I.L.T.R. 155 . . . . 6, 18, 21, 29
Doran v Delaney [1998] 2 I.L.R.M. 1 172
Doyle v Irish National Insurance Co plc [1998] 1 I.L.R.M. 502. 228
Doyle v White City Stadium [1935] 1 K.B. 110 . . . . 82, 83

Drimmie v Davies [1899] 1 I.R. 176 73
Dublin and Wicklow Railway Co v Black (1852) 8 Exch. 181 81
Dublin Corporation v Trinity College Dublin [1985] I.L.R.M. 283 178
Dundalk Shopping Centre v Roof Spray Ltd (unreported, High Court,
  21 March 1979) 227
Dunlop Pneumatic Tyre v New Garage and Motor Co [1915] A.C. 79 238
Dunlop v Selfridge [1915] A.C. 847 71
Durkan New Homes v Minister for the Environment, Heritage and Local
  Government [2012] IEHC 265 239

Early v Great Southern Railway [1940] I.R. 414 .... 133, 136
eBay International AG v Creative Festival Entertainment Pty Ltd
  (2006) 170 F.C.R. 450 102
Ecay v Godfrey (1947) 80 Lloyd's Rep. 286 110
Edgington v Fitzmaurice (1855) 29 Ch. D. 459 162
Edwards v Skyways Ltd [1964] 1 All E.R. 494 40
Ennis v Butterly [1997] 1 I.L.R.M. 28 .... 213, 214
Entores Ltd v Miles Far East Corp [1955] 2 Q.B. 327 .... 27, 31
Errington v Errington [1952] 1 K.B. 290 24
ESB v Newman (1933) 67 I.L.T.R. 124 46
Esso Petroleum Co Ltd v Mardon [1976] Q.B. 801 161
Esso Petroleum v Commissioner of Customs and Excise
  [1976] 1 All E.R. 117 37
Esso Petroleum v Harper's Garage [1968] A.C. 269 .... 214, 215
Evans v Merzario [1976] 1 W.L.R. 1078 115
Everet v Williams (1725) see (1893) 9 L.Q.R. 197 207

Farina v Fickus [1900] 1 Ch. 331 6
Farley v Skinner [2001] 3 W.L.R. 899 237
Farrington v Donohoe (1866) I.R. 1 C.L. 675 90
Fawcett v Smethurst (1914) 84 L.J.K.B. 473 80
Felthouse v Bindley (1862) 11 C.B. (N.S.) 869 25
Fenton v Schofield (1966) 100 I.L.T.R. 69 169
Fibrosa Spolka Akeyjna v Fairbairn Lawson Combe Barbour
  [1943] A.C. 32 .... 223, 225
Filmer v Gott (1774) 4 Bro. P.C. 230 203
Financings Ltd v Stimson [1962] 1 W.L.R. 1184 18
First Charter Financial Corp Ltd v Musclow 49 D.L.R. (3d) 138
  (B.C. Sup. Ct, 1974) 79, 80
Fitch v Snedaker (1868) 38 N.Y. 248 19
Fitzsimons v O'Hanlon [1999] 2 I.L.R.M. 551 180
Fletcher v Krell (1873) 42 L.J.Q.B. 55 164
Foakes v Beer (1884) 9 App. Cas. 605 57
Folens v Minister for Education [1984] I.L.R.M. 265 63
Foley v Classique Coaches [1934] 2 K.B. 1 46

Foot Locker Retail Ireland Ltd v Percy Nominees Ltd [2021] IEHC 749. 225
Forshall v Walsh (unreported, High Court, 18 June 1997). 170
Foster v Driscoll [1929] 1 K.B. 470. 210
Fraser v Buckle [1996] 2 I.L.R.M. 34 209
Fry v Lane (1888) 40 Ch D. 312. 202

Gahan v Boland (unreported, Supreme Court, 20 January 1984) 163, 173
Galloway v Galloway (1914) 30 T.L.R 267 179
Garvey v Ireland (1979) 113 I.L.T.R. 61 238
Geryani v O'Callaghan (unreported, High Court, 25 January 1995). 166
Gibson v Manchester City Council [1979] 1 All E.R. 972 6
Gill v McDowell [1903] 2 I.R. 463 165
Glasbrook Bros v Glamorgan County Council [1925] A.C. 270 54
Glover v B.L.N. [1973] I.R. 388. 128
Glynn v Margotson [1893] A.C. 351 139
Godley v Power (1961) 95 I.L.T.R. 135 . . . . .93, 117
Goldsworthy v Brickell [1987] Ch. 378 195
Goodlife Foods Ltd v Hall Fire Protection Ltd [2018] EWCA Civ 1371. 136
Grainger & Sons v Gough [1896] A.C. 325. 7
Gray v Cathcart (1899) 33 I.L.T.R. 35. 205
Grealish v Murphy [1946] I.R. 35 . . . . 84, 202, 203
Great Peace Shipping Ltd v Tsavliris Salvage (International) Ltd
 [2002] 4 All E.R. 689 181
Great Southern and Western Railway v Robertson (1878) 2 L.R. (Ir.) 548 191
Green Park Properties v Dorku [2001] H.K.L.R.D 139. 164
Gregg v Kidd [1956] I.R. 183 . . . . 194, 196
Griffith v Griffith [1944] I.R. 35 189
Grist v Bailey [1967] Ch. 532 181
Grogan v Robin Meredith Plant Hire (1996) 15 Tr. L.R. 371. 130
Guardian Builders Ltd v Patrick Kelly & Park Avenue Ltd (unreported,
 High Court, 31 March 1981). 93, 94

Hadley v Baxendale (1854) 9 Exch. 341 230–232
Hall v Woolston Hall Leisure Ltd [2001] 1 W.L.R. 225 210
Hamer v Sidway 124 N.Y. 538 (1891) 50
Harris v Nickerson (1873) L.R. 8 Q.B. 286. 10
Harris v Sheffield United Football Club [1988] Q.B. 77 54
Hart v O'Connor [1985] 1 A.C. 1000, [1985] 2 All E.R. 880 . . . . 84, 202
Hartley v Ponsonby (1857) 7 E. & B. 872. 54
Hartog v Colin and Shields [1939] 3 All E.R. 566 183
Harvela Investments v Royal Trust of Canada [1985] 2 All E.R. 966 11
Harvey v Facey [1893] A.C. 552. 5
Hassard v Smith (1872) I.R. 6 Eq. 429. 84
Hawkins v Rogers (1951) 85 I.L.T.R. 129. 234
Hayden v Sean Quinn Properties Ltd (unreported, High Court,
 6 December 1993) 209

Healy v Ulster Bank Ireland Ltd [2020] IECA 332. 62
Hearn and Matchroom Boxing v Collins (unreported, High Court,
   3 February 1998) 75
Hedley Byrne v Heller & Partners [1964] A.C. 465. 171–173
Henderson v Arthur [1907] 1 K.B. 10 111
Herman v Owners of S.S. Vicia [1942] I.R. 304 224
Hermann v Charlesworth [1905] 2 K.B. 123. 213
Herne Bay Steam Boat v Hutton [1903] 2 K.B. 683 223
Hickey & Co Ltd v Roches Stores (Dublin) Ltd (No. 1) (unreported,
   High Court, 14 July 1976) 235
Hickman v Haynes (1875) L.R. 10 C.P. 598. 68
Hillas v Arcos (1932) 147 L.T. 503 47
Hirachand Punamchand v Temple [1911] 2 K.B. 330. 58
Hochster v De La Tour (1853) 2 E. & B. 678 227
Hoenig v Isaacs [1952] 2 All E.R. 176 218
Hollier v Rambler Motors [1972] 2 Q.B. 71. 137
Hollingworth v Southern Ferries Ltd [1977] 2 Lloyd's Rep. 70 134
Holwell Securities v Hughes [1974] 1 W.L.R. 155 30
Hong Kong Fir Shipping Co v Kawasaki [1962] 1 All E.R. 474. 121
Houghton v Trafalgar Insurance [1954] 1 Q.B. 247 138
Household Fire Insurance v Grant (1879) L.R. 4 Ex. 216 29
Howden v Ulster Bank [1924] I.R. 117 114
Howlin v Power (unreported, High Court, 5 May 1978) 98
Hughes v Metropolitan Railway Co (1877) 2 App. Cas. 439 . . . . 60, 66
Hummingbird Motors v Hobbs [1986] R.T.R. 276. 107
Hyde v Wrench (1840) 3 Beav. 334 13
Hynes v Hynes (unreported, High Court, 21 December 1984). 35, 36, 90

Imperial Loan Co v Stone [1892] 1 Q.B. 599 84
Inche Noriah v Shaik Allie Bin Omar [1929] A.C. 127. . . . . 194, 196
Ingram v Little [1961] 1 Q.B. 31 184
Interfoto Picture Library Ltd v Stiletto Visual Programmes Ltd
   [1988] 1 All E.R. 348 135
Intrum Justitia BV v Legal and Trade Financial Services Ltd
   [2005] IEHC 190. 163
Investors Compensation Scheme v West Bromwich Building Society
   [1998] 1 W.L.R. 896 122
Irish Mainport Holdings Ltd v Crosshaven Sailing Centre Ltd (unreported,
   High Court, 14 October 1980) 44

J. Evans & Son (Portsmouth) Ltd v Andrea Merzario Ltd [1976] 2 All E.R. 930 . . . 37
James Elliott Construction Ltd v Irish Asphalt Ltd [2014] IESC 74 136
Jarvis v Swan Tours [1973] 2 Q.B. 233 . . . . 236, 237
JLT Financial Services Ltd v Gannon [2017] IESC 70 . . . . 43, 96
JN Hipwell & Son v Szurek [2018] EWCA Civ 674. 127
Johnson v Longleat Properties (unreported, High Court, 19 May 1976) 237

Jones v Daniel [1894] 2 Ch. 332 13
Jones v Padavatton [1969] 1 W.L.R. 328 . . . . 35, 50
Jones v Vernon's Pools Ltd [1938] 2 All E.R. 626 40

K v K [2018] IEHC 615 . . . . 35, 36
Karsales (Harrow) v Wallis [1956] 1 W.L.R. 936. 140
Kavanagh v Gilbert (1875) I.R. 9 C.L. 136 123
Keating v Keating [2009] IEHC 405 202
Keays v Great Southern Railway [1941] I.R. 534. 83
Keegan and Roberts v Comhairle Chontae Átha Cliath (unreported,
    High Court, 12 March 1981). 63
Keena v Coughlan [2019] IEHC 12 . . . . 95, 96
Keir v Leeman (1846) 9 Q.B. 371. 208
Kelleher v Irish Life Assurance (unreported, High Court, 16 December 1988). . . 167
Kelly v Crowley (unreported, High Court, 5 March 1985). 236
Kelly v Cruise Catering [1994] 2 I.L.R.M. 394 29
Kelly v Irish Landscape Nursery Ltd [1981] I.L.R.M. 433 96
Kelly v Morrisroe (1919) 53 I.L.T.R. 145. 203
Kelly v Park Hall School [1979] I.R. 340. . . . . 42, 94, 96
Kelly v Ross & Ross (unreported, High Court, 29 April 1980) 95
Kemp v Intasun Holidays [1987] 2 F.T.L.R. 234 231
Kennedy v Hennessy (1906) 40 I.L.T.R. 84 166
Kennedy v Kennedy (unreported, High Court, 12 January 1984). 97
Kenny v An Post [1988] J.I.S.L.L. 187 55
Kenny v Kelly [1988] I.R. 457. 61
Kincora Builders v Cronin (unreported, High Court, 5 March 1973). 219
King's Norton Metal Co v Edridge, Merrett & Co (1897) 14 T.L.R. 98 184
Kingswood Estate v Anderson [1963] 2 Q.B. 169. 97
Kinlen v Ennis UDC [1916] 2 I.R. 299 113
Kiriri Cotton Co Ltd v Dewani [1960] A.C. 192 . . . . 177, 178
Kirkham v Marter (1819) 2 B. & Ald. 613 89
Kirwan v Cullen (1856) 4 Ir. Ch. Rep. 322). 196
Kleinwort Benson Ltd v Malaysia Mining Corp Bhd [1989] 1 All E.R. 785 40
Kleinwort Benson v Lincoln City Council [1998] 3 W.L.R. 1095 178
Krell v Henry [1903] 2 K.B. 740 . . . . 223, 225

L. Schuler A.G. v Wickman Machine Tool Sales Ltd [1973] 2 All E.R. 39. 120
L'Estrange v Graucob [1934] 2 K.B. 394 . . . . 130, 140
Lampleigh v Braithwait (1615) Hob. 105 . . . . 52, 53
Law Society of Ireland v Motor Insurers' Bureau of Ireland [2017] IESC 31. 122
Law v Roberts [1964] I.R. 292 . . . . 93, 94
Lawless v Mansfield (1841) 1 Dr. & War. 557) 193
Leaf v International Galleries [1950] 2 K.B. 86. 174
Leahy v Rawson (unreported, High Court, 14 January 2003) 34, 35, 235
Lecky v Walter [1914] I.R. 378 174

Lee and Donoghue v Rowan (unreported, High Court, 17 November 1981) 231
Leeds United Football Club v Chief Constable of West Yorkshire Police
    [2013] EWCA Civ 115. 54
Leeson v North British Oil and Candle Co (1874) 8 I.R.C.L. 309 227
Lefkowitz v Great Minneapolis Surplus Store 86 N.W. 2d 689 (Minn., 1957)...... 11
Leonard v Pepsico, Inc 88 F. Supp. 2d 116 (S.D.N.Y., 1999) 38, 39
Lessee of Blackwood v Gregg (1831) Hayes 277 188
Lewis v Avery [1972] 1 Q.B. 198 184
Lewis v Squash Ireland Ltd [1983] I.L.R.M. 363. 209
Lipkin Gorman v Karpnale [1991] 3 W.L.R. 10. 51
Liverpool City Council v Irwin [1977] A.C. 239 126
Loftus v Roberts (1902) 18 T.L.R. 532 45
Lord Mayor, Aldermen and Burgesses of Dublin v Hayes (1876)
    10 I.R.C.L. 226. 209
Lowe v Lombank Ltd [1960] 1 W.L.R. 196 66
Lowe v Peers (1768) 4 Burr. 2225 213
Lumley v Wagner (1852) 1 De G.M. & G. 604 240
Luxor (Eastbourne) Ltd v Cooper [1941] 1 All E.R. 33 23
Lynch Roofing Systems (Ballaghaderreen) Ltd v Bennett and Son
    (Construction) Ltd [1999] 2 I.R. 450. .... 47, 137
Lynch v Governors of St Vincent's Hospital (unreported, High Court,
    31 July 1987) 18
Lynch v O'Meara (unreported, High Court, 23 October 1973) 94
Lyndel v Mobil (1997) 37 I.P.R. 599 .... 17, 24

Macken v O'Reilly [1979] I.L.R.M. 791. 215
Mackey v Jones (1959) 93 I.L.T.R. 177 34
Mackie v Wilde and Longin [1998] 2 I.R. 578. .... 45, 91, 97
Macklin and McDonald v Greacen & Co [1983] I.R. 61 .... 111, 112
Malcomson v Morton (1847) 11 Ir. L.R. 230. 113
Malik v Bank of Credit and Commerce International SA [1997] 3 W.L.R. 95 127
Malone v Malone (unreported, High Court, 9 June 1982) 233
Maloney v O'Connor [2015] IEHC 678. 93
Maritime National Fish Ltd v Ocean Trawlers Ltd [1935] A.C. 524. 224
Marles v Philip Trant & Sons Ltd (No. 2) [1954] 1 Q.B. 29. 211
Marquess of Westmeath v Marquess of Salisbury (1830) 5 Bli. (n.s.) 339. 213
Martin v Galbraith [1942] I.R. 37. 211
Maye v Merriman (unreported, High Court, 13 February 1980) 230
MC (A Ward) v FC [2013] IEHC 272. 202
McAleenan v AIG (Europe) Ltd [2013] 3 I.R. 202. 170
McCambridge v Winters (unreported, High Court, 28 August 1984) 66
McCann v Brinks Allied Ltd [1997] 1 I.L.R.M. 461 127
McCarron v McCarron (unreported, Supreme Court, 13 February 1997). 35
McCaughey v Irish Bank Resolution Corp [2013] IESC 17 163
McCormack v Bennett (1973) 107 I.L.T.R. 127 203

McCoubray v Thompson (1868) 2 I.R.C.L. 226 .... 49, 71, 72
McCrystal v O'Kane [1986] N.I. 123 195
McCutcheon v MacBrayne [1964] 1 W.L.R. 125. 137
McEllistrem v Ballymacelligott Co-op [1919] A.C. 548 215
McElroy v Flynn [1991] I.L.R.M. 294 208
McGonigle v Black (unreported, High Court, 14 November 1988) 194
McGuill v Aer Lingus and United Airlines (unreported, High Court,
   3 October 1983)... 224
McGuinness v Hunter (1853) 6 Ir. Jur. 103. 107
McHugh v Kildare County Council [2006] 1 I.R. 100 55
McMackin v Hibernian Bank [1905] 1 I.R. 296 .... 193, 196
McNeill v Miller [1907] 2 I.R. 328 68
McQuaid v Lynam [1965] I.R. 564 93–96
McRae v Commonwealth Disposals Commission (1951) 84 C.L.R. 377 179
McSweeney v Bourke (unreported, High Court, 24 November 1980) 172
Megaw v Molloy (1878) 2 L.R. Ir. 530................................. 182
Mendelssohn v Normand [1970] 1 Q.B. 177 141
Merritt v Merritt [1969] 2 All E.R. 760 34
Meskell v CIÉ [1972] I.R. 121... 128
Mespil Ltd v Capaldi [1986] I.L.R.M. 373 183
Miley v McKechnie (1949) 84 I.L.T.R. 89 137
Minister for Industry and Commerce v Pim Bros Ltd [1966] I.R. 154 9
MK (McC) v McC [1982] I.L.R.M. 277................................. 189
Morgan v Rainsford (1845) 8 Ir. E.R. 299. 52
Mulcahy v Mulcahy [2011] IEHC 186 161
Mulhall v Haren [1981] I.R. 364 .... 42, 96
Mulhallen v Marum (1843) 3 Dr. & War. 317. 193
Mulligan v Browne (unreported, Supreme Court, 23 November 1977) 224
Munster Base Metals v Bula Ltd (unreported, High Court, 27 July 1983) 166
Murphy & Co v Crean [1915] 1 I.R. 111 210
Murphy & Co v O'Donovan [1939] I.R. 457 215
Murphy v Bower (1868) I.R. 2 C.L. 506 71
Murphy v Joe O'Toole & Sons Ltd [2014] IEHC 486. 3

Nash & Co v Hartland (1840) 2 Ir. L.R. 190 218
Nash v Inman [1908] 2 K.B. 1.. 80
National Asset Loan Management Ltd v McMahon [2014] IEHC 71 64
National Westminster Bank v Morgan [1985] A.C. 686 195
Nature Resorts Ltd v First Citizens Bank Ltd [2022] UKPC 10. 191
Naughton v Limestone Land Co [1952] Ir. Jur. Rep. 19................... 90
New Zealand Shipping Co Ltd v A.M. Satterthwaite and Co Ltd
   (The "Eurymedon") [1975] A.C. 154............................... 74
Nicholson & Venn v Smith-Marriott (1947) 177 L.T. 189................... 180
Nolan v Driscoll (unreported, High Court, 25 April 1978) 221
Nolan v Shiels (1926) 60 I.L.T.R. 143................................. 208

Noonan (A Ward of Court) v O'Connell (unreported, High Court,
    10 April 1987).. 51
Nordenfelt v Maxim Nordenfelt & Co [1894] A.C. 535 214
North Down Hotels v Province Wide Filling Stations [1993] N.I. 261 66
North Ocean Shipping Co v Hyundai Construction Co Ltd (The Atlantic Baron)
    [1978] 3 All E.R. 1170, [1979] Q.B. 705 .... 50, 55, 189, 190
Nunin Holdings v Tullamarine Estates Property [1994] 1 V.R. 74............... 30

Ó Conaill v Gaelic Echo (1958) 92 I.L.T.R. 156 126
Ó Cruadhlaoich v Minister for Finance (1934) 68 I.L.T.R. 174 224
O'Connor v Coady [2004] 3 I.R. 271 118
O'Connor v Potts [1897] 1 I.R. 534.. 174
O'Donnell v Truck and Machinery Sales [1998] 4 I.R. 191.................... 239
O'Flaherty v Arvan Property (unreported, High Court, 3 November 1976)....... 42
O'Flanagan v Ray-Ger Ltd [1963–1993] Irish Co. Law Reports 289 (1983)..... 192
O'Keeffe v Ryanair Holdings plc [2003] 1 I.L.R.M. 14 .... 49, 72
O'Kelly v Glenny (1846) 9 Ir. Eq. R. 25.................................... 174
O'Leary v Irish National Insurance Co Ltd [1958] Ir. Jur. Rep. 1 73
O'Loghlen v O'Callaghan (1874) I.R. 8 C.L. 116 177
O'Mahony v Promontoria (Gem) DAC [2020] IECA 30...................... 13
O'Neill v Murphy [1936] N.I. 16.. 50, 194
O'Neill v Ryan [1991] I.L.R.M. 672.. 181
O'Neill v Ryan [1992] 1 I.R. 166... 240
OB v R [2000] 1 I.L.R.M. 306... 189
Oblique Financial Services Ltd v The Promise Production Co Ltd
    [1994] 1 I.L.R.M. 74 75
Odyssey Pavilion LLP v Marcus Ward Ltd [2011] NICh 10.................... 65
Olley v Marlborough Court [1949] 1 K.B. 532........................110, 134
Osborne v Amalgamated Society of Railway Servants [1910] A.C. 87......... 209
Oscar Chess Ltd v Williams [1957] 1 W.L.R. 370........................ 106, 108

Page One Records v Britton [1968] 1 W.L.R. 157 240
Paget v Paget (1882) 11 L.R. Ir. 26 80
Pao On v Lau Yiu Long [1980] A.C. 614................................... 53
Paradine v Jane (1647) Aleyn 26 222
Parker v South Eastern Railway Co (1877) 2 C.P.D. 416.................... 132
Parkgrange Investments v Shandon Park Mills (unreported, High Court,
    2 May 1991).. 17, 27
Parkinson v College of Ambulance Ltd [1925] 2 K.B. 1 209
Partridge v Crittendon [1968] 2 All E.R. 421............................... 7
Pearce v Brooks (1866) 1 Ex. 213 207
Pearson v Dublin Corporation [1907] A.C. 351.................. 139, 169, 175
Pernod Ricard v FII Fyffes plc (unreported, High Court, 21 October 1988)...... 87
Pharmaceutical Society of Great Britain v Boots Cash Chemists
    [1953] 1 Q.B. 401... 9

Phelps v White (1881) 5 L.R. Ir. 318. 163
Phillips v Brooks [1919] 2 K.B. 243 184
Photo Production Ltd v Securicor [1980] 2 W.L.R. 283 . . . . 140, 141
Pinnel's Case (1602) 5 Co. Rep. 117a. 57
Pitts v Jones [2008] Q.B. 706. 89
Planché v Colburn (1831) 8 Bing. 14 220
Power v Barrett (1887) 19 L.R. (Ir.) 450 165
Prendergast v Joyce [2009] 3 I.R. 519. . . . . 202, 203
Proform Sports Management Ltd v Proactive Sports Management Ltd
   [2007] 1 All E.R. 542 83
Provincial Bank of Ireland v O'Donnell (1932) 67 I.L.T.R. 142 52
Provincial Bank v McKeever [1941] 1 I.R. 471. . . . . 195, 196
Prunty v Crowley [2016] IEHC 293. 42
Pym v Campbell (1856) 6 E. & B. 370 . . . . 115, 118

Quadling v Robinson (1976) 137 C.L.R. 192 23
Quinn v Irish Bank Resolution Corp Ltd (In Special Liquidation)
   [2015] IESC 29. . . . . 206, 212

R. v Clarke (1927) 40 C.L.R. 227 20
Radmacher v Granatino (No. 4) [2010] UKSC 42 213
Raffles v Wichelhaus (1864) 159 E.R. 375. 182
Ramsgate Victoria Hotel v Montefiore (1866) L.R. Exch. 109 17
Rawlinson v Ames [1925] Ch. 96 97
Re Article 26 of the Constitution and in the Matter of the Health
   (Amendment) (No. 2) Bill 2004 [2005] 1 I.R. 105. 178
Re Irvine [1928] 3 D.L.R. 268. 15
Re Mahmoud and Ispahani [1921] 2 K.B. 716 210
Re Moore & Co v Landauer [1921] 2 K.B. 519. 218
Re Selectmove [1995] 2 All E.R. 531 . . . . 26, 57
Re Whelan [1897] 1 I.R. 575 14
Redgrave v Hurd (1881) 20 Ch. D. 1 163
Revenue Commissioners v Moroney [1972] I.R. 372. . . . . 60–62, 112
Richardson Spence & Co v Rowntree [1894] A.C. 297 132
Roberts v Gray [1913] 1 K.B. 520. 82
Rogers v Smith (unreported, Supreme Court, 16 July 1970) 33–35
Ronan v Midland Railway Co (1883) 14 L.R. (Ir.) 157 139
Roscorla v Thomas (1842) 3 Q.B. 234. . . . . .52, 110
Rose and Frank Co v Crompton Bros [1923] 2 K.B. 261 39
Ross v Shaw [1917] 2 I.R. 367. 224
Rourke v Mealy (1879) 13 I.L.T.R. 52. . . . . 191, 208
Routledge v Grant (1828) 4 Bing. 653 15
Routledge v McKay [1954] 1 W.L.R. 615 . . . . .109, 110
Royal Bank of Scotland v Etridge (No. 2) [2001] 3 W.L.R. 1021 . . . 195, 198, 199, 200
Royal Trust Co of Canada v Kelly (unreported, High Court,
   27 February 1989) 127

RTS Flexible Systems Ltd v Molkerei Alois Müller GmbH [2010] UKSC 14 37
Russell & Baird v Hoban [1922] 2 I.R. 159 25
Ruxley Electronics v Forsyth [1995] UKHL 8 236
Ryan v Great Southern & Western Railway (1898) 32 I.L.T.R. 108 133
Ryanair Ltd v Billigfluege.de GmbH/Ticket Point Reiseburo GmbH
  [2015] IESC 1 103
Ryanair Ltd v On the Beach Ltd [2013] IEHC 124 103
Ryder v Wombwell (1868) L.R. 4 Ex. 32 79

Sanderson v Cunningham [1919] 2 I.R. 234 29
Scaife v Falcon Leisure Group [2007] IESC 57 237
Scammell v Ouston [1941] A.C. 251 45
Scarborough v Sturzaker (1905) 1 Tas. L.R. 117 79
Schawel v Reade (1912) 46 I.L.T.R. 281 .... 106, 107, 110
Schiesser International (Ireland) v Gallagher (1971) 106 I.L.T.R. 22 239
Scotson v Pegg (1861) 6 H. & N. 295 57
Scott v Avery (1856) 5 H.L.C. 811 213
Scott v Coulson [1903] 2 Ch. 249 179
Scriven Bros v Hindley & Co [1913] 3 K.B. 564 182
Scruttons Ltd v Midland Silicones Ltd [1962] A.C. 446 .... 74, 75
Scully v Corboy [1950] I.R. 140 91
Securities Trust v Hugh Moore & Alexander Ltd [1964] I.R. 417 172
Seddon v North Eastern Salt [1905] 1 Ch. 326 174
Shadwell v Shadwell (1860) 9 C.B. (N.S.) 159 56
Shanklin Pier Ltd v Detel Products Ltd [1951] 2 K.B. 854 76
Shea v Great Southern Railway [1944] Ir. Jur. Rep. 26 133
Shears v Mendeloff (1914) 30 T.L.R. 342 82
Sheehy v Ryan [2008] IESC 14 127
Sheppard v Murphy (1867) 1 I.R. Eq. 490 74
Sherwood v Walker 66 Mich. 568 (1887) 180
Shirlaw v Southern Foundries [1939] 2 K.B. 206 124
Shogun Finance v Hudson [2004] 1 All E.R. 215 184
Silver Wraith v Siúicre Éireann (unreported, High Court, 8 June 1989) 43, 97
Simpkin v Pays [1955] 1 W.L.R. 975 .... 35, 36
Siney v Dublin Corporation [1980] I.R. 400 126
Skerry's College v Moles (1907) 42 I.L.T.R. 46 216
Skrine v Gordon (1875) I.R. 9 C.L. 479 79
Smart Telecom plc v Radio Telefís Éireann [2007] 1 I.R. 732 12
Smelter Corp v O'Driscoll [1977] I.R. 305 .... 174, 191
Smith v Chadwick (1884) 9 App. Cas. 187 .... 162, 163
Smith v Halpin [1997] 3 I.L.R.M. 38 68
Smith v Hughes (1871) L.R. 2 Q.B. 597 182
Smith v Land and House Property Corp (1884) 28 Ch. D. 7 161
Smith v Lynn (1954) 85 I.L.T.R. 57 .... 38, 163
Smith v Mawhood (1845) 14 M. & W. 452 205
Smith v Wilson (1832) 3 B. & Ad. 728 113

Smyth v Morrison 10 Ir. Law Rep. 213 52
Solle v Butcher [1950] 1 K.B. 671................................. 181, 182
South Australia Asset Management Corp v York Montague Ltd
    [1997] A.C. 191 233
Spencer v Harding (1870) L.R. 5 C.P. 561................................11
Spice Girls Ltd v Aprilia World Services [2002] E.M.L.R. 478 164
Spring v Guardian Assurance plc [1994] 3 W.L.R. 354 127
Spring v National Amalgamated Stevedores and Dockers Society
    [1956] 1 W.L.R. 585... 124
Sproule v Triumph Cycle [1927] N.I. 83 138
Spurling v Bradshaw [1956] 1 W.L.R. 461, [1956] 2 All E.R. 121........... 47, 137
St John Shipping Corp v Joseph Rank Ltd [1957] 1 Q.B. 267 205
Stafford v Keane Mahony Smith [1980] I.L.R.M. 53........................ 171
Stapleton v Prudential Insurance (1928) 62 I.L.T.R. 56 .... 80, 81, 187
Startup v MacDonald (1843) 6 Man. & G. 593 220
Steadman v Steadman [1976] A.C. 536.................................... 98
Stevenson, Jacques and Co v McLean (1880) 5 Q.B.D. 340............... 13, 21
Stilk v Myrick (1809) 2 Camp. 317 .... 54, 55
Stock v Urey [1955] N.I. 71.. 231
Stoney v Foley (1897) 3 I.L.T. 165 235
Storer v Manchester City Council [1974] 3 All E.R. 824..................... 4, 6
Strickland v Turner (1852) 7 Exch. 208 179
Sugar v LMS Railway [1941] 1 All E.R. 172 135
Supershield Ltd v Siemens Building Technologies FE Ltd
    [2010] EWCA Civ 7 232
Swan v Miller [1919] 1 I.R. 151... 20
Sweeney v Duggan [1997] 2 I.L.R.M. 211 124

Tansey v College of Occupational Therapists (unreported, High Court,
    27 August 1986)... 20
Taylor v Caldwell (1863) 3 B. & S. 826.................................. 222
Taylor v Laird (1856) 25 L.J. Exch. 329 20
Ted Castle McCormack and Co v McCrystal (unreported, High Court,
    15 March 1999) 186
The Amer Energy [2009] 1 Lloyd's Rep. 293 232
The Barge Inn Ltd v Quinn Hospitality Ireland Operations 3 Ltd
    [2013] IEHC 387.. 61, 62
The Heron II [1969] 1 A.C. 350... 230
The Lisheen Mine v Mullock and Sons (Shipbrokers) Ltd [2015] IEHC 50....... 44
The Moorcock (1889) 14 P.D. 64 .... 47, 124, 125
Thomas v Thomas (1842) 2 Q.B. 851 51
Thompson v The King [1920] 2 I.R. 365................................. 41
Thornton v Shoe Lane Parking [1971] 1 All E.R. 686..................... 134
Thoroughgood's case (1584) 2 Co. Rep. 9a 131
Tinn v Hoffman (1873) 29 L.T. 271................................. 21, 27

Tinsley v Milligan [1993] 3 All E.R. 65 211
Tokn Grass Products v Sexton & Co Ltd (unreported, High Court,
    13 October 1983)... 141
Tomlinson v Dick Evans "U" Drive [1978] I.C.R. 638..................... 209
Tomlinson v Gill (1756) Amb. 330....................................... 73
Tradax (Ireland) Ltd v Irish Grain Board Ltd [1984] I.R. 1............. 92, 95, 123
Transfield Shipping Inc v Mercator Shipping Inc (The Achilleas)
    [2009] 1 A.C. 61.. 231–233
Trans-Pacific Trading v Rayonier Canada Ltd (1998) 39 B.L.R. (2d) 306....... 30
Traynor v Fegan [1985] I.R. 586....................................... 67
Treacy v Corcoran (1874) I.R. 8 C.L. 40............................... 219
Truck and Machinery Sales Ltd v Marubeni Komatsu Ltd (unreported,
    High Court, 23 February 1996) 57
Tsakiroglou & Co Ltd v Noblee Thorl GmbH [1962] A.C. 93................. 222
Tully v Irish Land Commission (1961) 97 I.L.T.R. 174 10
Tweddle v Atkinson (1861) 1 B. & S. 393........................... 49, 70

Ulster Bank (Ireland) Ltd v De Kretser [2016] IECA 371 200
Ulster Bank Ireland Ltd v Deane [2012] IEHC 248.........................117
Ulster Bank Ireland Ltd v Roche and Buttimer [2012] IEHC 166 198–201
Ulster Bank v Fitzgerald (unreported, High Court, 9 November 2001)..... 198, 199
Ulster Bank v Synnott (1871) 5 I.R. Eq. 595.............................113
United Scientific Holdings v Burnley Borough Council [1978] A.C. 904 221
Universe Tankships Inc of Monrovia v International Transport Workers
    Federation (The Universe Sentinel) [1983] A.C. 366 190
Uppington v Bullen (1842) 2 Dr. & War. 184............................ 208

Verolme Cork Dockyard Ltd v Shannon Atlantic Fisheries Ltd
    (unreported, High Court, 31 July 1978) 220
Victoria Laundry v Newman Industries [1949] 2 K.B. 528 230
Vigers v Pike (1842) 8 E.R. 220....................................... 174

W.J. Alan v El Nasr Export and Import Co [1972] 2 Q.B. 189................. 66
Wadlow v Samuel [2007] EWCA Civ 155............................... 196
Walker v Glass [1979] N.I. 129...................................... 15, 16
Wallis v Russell [1902] 2 I.R. 585..................................... 143
Walsh v Jones Lang LaSalle Ltd [2017] IESC 38........................ 172
Walton Stores v Maher (1988) 76 A.L.R. 513............................ 63
Ward v Byham [1956] 2 All E.R. 318 55
Warlow v Harrison (1859) 1 E. & E. 309................................ 10
Warner Bros Pictures Inc v Nelson [1937] 1 K.B. 209 240
Watts v Morrow [1991] 1 W.L.R. 1421 237
Webster v Higgin [1948] 2 All E.R. 127 116
Western Electric v Welsh Development Agency [1983] Q.B. 796.............. 24
Western Meats v National Ice and Cold Storage [1982] I.L.R.M. 101 141

Western Potato Co-Operative Ltd v Durnan [1985] I.L.R.M. 5 180
White v Bluett (1853) 23 L.J. Ex. 36 .... 50, 51
White v John Warrick & Co Ltd [1953] 2 All E.R. 1021 138
White v McCooey (unreported, High Court, 24 June 1976) 86
White v Meade (1840) 2 Ir. Eq. R 420 193
Whitecross Potatoes v Coyle [1978] I.L.R.M. 31 211
Williams v Carwardine (1833) 4 B. & Ad. 621 20
Williams v Roffey Bros & Nicholls (Contractors) Ltd [1990] 1 All E.R. 512 55–57
Williams v Stern (1879) 5 Q.B.D. 409 67
Williams v Williams [1957] 1 W.L.R. 148 55
Wilson Strain v Pinkerton (1897) 3 I.L.T.R. 86 113
Wilson v Belfast Corporation (1921) 55 I.L.T.R. 205 11
Wilson v Dunville (1879) 6 L.R. (Ir.) 210 231
With v O'Flanagan [1936] 1 All E.R. 727 165
Wood v Scarth (1855) 2 K. & J. 33 183
Woodhouse A.C. Israel Cocoa v Nigerian Produce Marketing [1972] A.C. 741 . . . 63

Yates Building Co v Pulleyn & Sons (1975) 119 S.J. 370 27

Table of Legislation

IRELAND

CONSTITUTION OF IRELAND

Constitution of Ireland 1937 .... 123, 128, 214
    Art.40.6.1°iii 128
    Art.40.6.2° 128

ACTS OF THE OIREACHTAS

Age of Majority Act 1985... 77
Arbitration Act 2010 87
Assisted Decision-Making (Capacity) Act 2015 .... 84, 85
    s.3(1)–(3) 84
    s.3(2)–(6) 84
    s.3(4)–(6) 85
    s.137(1).. 85

Civil Partnership and Certain Rights and Obligations of Cohabitants Act 2010
    s.202.. 214
Companies Act 1963
    s.60 .... 206, 212
Consumer Information Act 1978
    s.25.. 204
Consumer Insurance Contracts Act 2019....................... 167, 168, 175
    s.1... 168
    s.2(1), (2) 168
    s.8(2).. 168
    s.8(6).. 168
    s.8(7)(a), (b) 167
    s.9... 168
    s.9(2), (3) 168
    s.9(4).. 169
    s.9(5).. 168
Consumer Protection Act 2007....................................... 159
    Pt 3 7
Consumer Rights Act 2022....... 2, 72, 88, 92, 100, 103, 104, 142, 144, 243, 244
    s.11(1)... 144
    s.14 .... 145, 150, 152

s.15(1)	145
ss.16–19	145, 146
s.16	145
s.17	145, 146
s.18	145–147
s.18(3)	147
s.18(7)	147
s.18(8)	148
ss.19, 20	145
s.23(2)	148
s.23(3)	149
s.24	148
s.24(2)	148
s.24(4)	148
s.25	148, 149
s.26	148, 149
s.26(3)	150
s.27	150
s.28	145, 148, 150, 151
s.29	150
s.30	145, 148, 150, 151
s.32	148, 151
s.32(2)	151
s.35	151
s.36	151
s.36(4)	151
s.39	151
s.46	72, 76, 152
s.47	72, 76, 152
s.50	152
s.51	152
ss.52–55	152
ss.53–55	104, 152
s.66	152, 153
s.67	152, 153
s.71	153
s.78	153
ss.80–83	153
ss.88, 89	153
s.94	153
s.98	154
s.99	158
s.101	155
ss.103–105	157
s.103	146, 156, 157

s.104	146, 156, 158
ss.106–109	157
s.106	103, 146, 157
ss.107, 108	158
s.111	157, 158
s.112	156
s.113	158
s.115	158
ss.117, 118	158
s.119	157
ss.123, 124	158
s.125	25, 158
s.125(1)	25
s.129	158
ss.132, 133	158
Pt 2	72, 120, 142–146, 152, 153
Pt 2, Chap.3	146, 148
Pts 3–6	144
Pt 3	104, 142, 145, 152, 153
Pt 3, Chap.3	152
Pt 4	142, 153
Pt 4, Chap.3	153
Pt 5	142, 146, 154
Pt 5, Chaps 5, 6	158
Pt 6	142, 158
Sch.2	155
Sch.3	103, 156, 158

Criminal Law Act 1997
- s.16 86
- Sch.3 86

Digital Services Act 2024 159

Electronic Commerce Act 2000 . . . . 101, 102
- s.2(2) 87
- s.10 102
- s.19(1), (2) 100

Equal Status Acts 2000–2018 . . . . 13, 15

Family Home Protection Act 1976
- s.3(1) 204

Family Law Act 1981 . . . . 90, 213

Income Tax Acts 209

Land and Conveyancing Law Reform Act 2009 .... 87, 88
    s.51 92
    s.51(1), (2) 91
    s.74 212

Married Women's Status Act 1957
    ss.7, 8 72

Protection of Young Persons (Employment) Act 1996 82

Representative Actions for the Protection of the Collective Interests of
    Consumers Act 2023 159

Sale of Goods and Supply of Services Act 1980 .... 2, 142, 143, 175
    s.44 .... 174, 175
    s.45 175
    s.45(1), (2) 175
    s.46 175
    s.47 26
    Pt IV 153
    Pt V 175
Social Welfare Acts 209
Statute of Limitations 1957 67

Pre-1922 Acts

Belfast Corporation Acts 205

Forfeiture Act 1870 86
    s.8 86

Infants Relief Act 1874 .... 77, 78, 81
    s.2 78

Marine Insurance Act 1906 166
    s.18(1) 166
    s.18(2) 166, 168
Married Women's Property Act 1882
    s.11 72
Merchandise Marks Acts 1887–1970 205

Sale of Goods Act 1893 .... 2, 92, 142–144, 152
    s.2 .... 78, 80, 86
    s.4 92
    s.6 179

s.11	119, 120
s.13	143
s.14(3)	143
s.15	143
s.58(2)	10
Statute of Frauds (Ireland) 1695	87–92, 96, 98, 116
s.2	87, 88, 91
s.13	92
Statute of Fraudulent Conveyances 1634	212

Statutory Instruments

Consumer (Information and Cancellation Rights) Regulations 2013 (S.I. No. 484 of 2013)	154
Electronic Commerce Act 2000 (Application of Sections 12 to 23 to Registered Land) Regulations 2022 (S.I. No. 55 of 2022)	102
European Communities (Directive 2000/31/EC) Regulations 2003 (S.I. No. 68 of 2003)	32
Regulation 14	32
European Communities (Unfair Terms in Consumer Contracts) Regulations 1995 (S.I. No. 27 of 1995)	158
Hire Purchase and Credit Sale (Advertising) Order 1961 (S.I. No. 183 of 1961)	9
Market Abuse (Directive 2003/6/EC) Regulations 2005 (S.I. No. 342 of 2005)	206, 212
Prison Rules 2007–2020	86

European Union

Regulations

Regulation (EU) No 910/2014 of the European Parliament and of the Council of 23 July 2014 on electronic identification and trust services for electronic transactions in the internal market and repealing Directive 1999/93/EC	101, 102
Recital 49	101
art.3	101
art.26	101
Regulation (EU) 2022/2065 of the European Parliament and of the Council of 19 October 2022 on a Single Market For Digital Services and amending Directive 2000/31/EC (Digital Services Act)	159

DIRECTIVES

Council Directive 93/13/EEC of 5 April 1993 on unfair terms in consumer contracts. 144
Directive 98/6/EC of the European Parliament and of the Council of 16 February 1998 on consumer protection in the indication of the prices of products offered to consumers 144
Directive 1999/44/EC of the European Parliament and of the Council of 25 May 1999 on certain aspects of the sale of consumer goods and associated guarantees. 143
   art.2(1), (2) 143
Directive 2005/29/EC of the European Parliament and of the Council of 11 May 2005 concerning unfair business-to-consumer commercial practices in the internal market and amending Council Directive 84/450/EEC, Directives 97/7/EC, 98/27/EC and 2002/65/EC of the European Parliament and of the Council and Regulation (EC) No 2006/2004 of the European Parliament and of the Council ('Unfair Commercial Practices Directive'). 144
Directive 2011/83/EU of the European Parliament and of the Council of 25 October 2011 on consumer rights, amending Council Directive 93/13/EEC and Directive 1999/44/EC of the European Parliament and of the Council and repealing Council Directive 85/577/EEC and Directive 97/7/EC of the European Parliament and of the Council 144
Directive (EU) 2015/2302 of the European Parliament and of the Council of 25 November 2015 on package travel and linked travel arrangements, amending Regulation (EC) No 2006/2004 and Directive 2011/83/EU of the European Parliament and of the Council and repealing Council Directive 90/314/EEC 237
Directive (EU) 2019/770 of the European Parliament and of the Council of 20 May 2019 on certain aspects concerning contracts for the supply of digital content and digital services 144, 152
Directive (EU) 2019/771 of the European Parliament and of the Council of 20 May 2019 on certain aspects concerning contracts for the sale of goods, amending Regulation (EU) 2017/2394 and Directive 2009/22/EC, and repealing Directive 1999/44/EC 144
Directive (EU) 2019/2161 of the European Parliament and of the Council of 27 November 2019 amending Council Directive 93/13/EEC and Directives 98/6/EC, 2005/29/EC and 2011/83/EU of the European Parliament and of the Council as regards the better enforcement and modernisation of Union consumer protection rules 144, 154

INTERNATIONAL

Convention on the International Sale of Goods (the Vienna Convention) art.19. 22

Introduction

INTRODUCTION

The study of contract law involves an examination of the formation, construction, interpretation and enforceability of an agreement, along with the remedies available to parties following any breach of said agreement.

The principles and rules that underpin contract law are almost always subject to a number of exceptions, caveats and nuances. This reality is often cited as the bane of the contract law scholar and is something to keep in mind throughout this review. There are also a number of seminal concepts that should be kept in mind in any examination of the jurisprudence in this area.

A CONTRACT AS A BARGAIN

In order to be valid under law, a contract must satisfy certain requirements:

1. There must be a valid offer, i.e. a clear and unambiguous statement upon which the offeror is willing to contract.
2. This offer must be accepted, unconditionally, by the offeree.
3. There must be consideration for the contract.
4. The parties must have the capacity and intention to enter legal relations.
5. Any relevant formal and evidentiary requirements must be complied with.

These requirements will be examined more fully in the chapters that follow.

Before embarking on said review, however, and by way of introduction, it is helpful to think of a contract as a bargain or an agreement. The words "bargain" and "agreement" here indicate the involvement of two or more people and an exchange of promises between them. In this way, a contract cannot be made by one person acting alone (thus, a will is not a contract). The words also presuppose accord between the parties. A contract cannot arise between parties who are fundamentally at variance regarding the content of the proposed agreement.

Sources of Contract Law

The sources of the principles, rules and exceptions discussed in this text have developed from common law, equity and legislation. Certain specialisations rely more heavily on these sources than others.

Legislation as a source of law has become increasingly important in the area of consumer protection, for example, over the past 130 years. The Sale of Goods Act 1893 codified certain judge-made common law principles and introduced standard terms that would be implied into all contracts for the sale of goods. Initially, these terms were intended only as default measures (i.e. to be included in the absence of agreement to the contrary). However, the Sale of Goods and Supply of Services Act 1980 rendered many of these terms mandatory (i.e. they could not be excluded from contracts), in particular where consumers are involved. The Consumer Rights Act 2022 introduced new protections and implemented a number of EU Directives aimed at protecting consumers. As such, many of the usual terms found in consumer contracts are determined by legislation rather than by agreement.

The Right to Enter into a Bad or Foolish Bargain

The law is concerned with holding parties to their bargain, however ill-advised or foolish. As such, if it is established that both Ailbhe and Deirdre agreed that Ailbhe would sell her car to Deirdre for €2.00, the court will not seek to interpret the contract in such a way as to assist Ailbhe in attaining a better price for her car or otherwise relieve her of the consequences of this bad bargain. The court must give effect to the mutual intentions of the parties as they were at the time the contract came into being.

Caveat Emptor

Following on from the preceding paragraph, it should be noted that parties to an agreement assume the responsibility of ensuring that the contract gives them what they want. The Latin phrase "caveat emptor" translates to "let the buyer beware". This has become so established as a guiding principle of contract law that it has trickled into layman's vernacular as a proverb. The applicability of the principle may be affected by, for example, misrepresentation on the part of one or more of the parties to a contract (see Chapter 16). Furthermore, it is accepted that certain contractual terms should not be permitted, for example, a term proposed by a trader that allows it to avoid its statutory obligations to a consumer under consumer law. It is acknowledged that due to the disparity in bargaining power between an ordinary consumer and a commercial entity, greater protection must be afforded to the former against any sharp practice of the latter.

OBJECTIVE APPROACH TO INTERPRETATION

As stated, the courts must give effect to what the parties have agreed to—their "manifest intentions"—at the time of entering the contract. In assessing the intentions of the contracting parties, contract law generally takes an objective approach. In this way, the courts do not attempt to read the minds of parties. Rather, the courts look to objective evidence of their intentions at the time the contract was entered into, e.g. their actions and/or words. The law asks what the "ordinary reasonable person" observing these actions and/or words would assume was the intention of the particular party.

Let us return to our previous example: Ailbhe offers to sell her car to Deirdre for €2.00 as a joke. Notwithstanding Ailbhe's subjective intention, she may be bound to sell her car for the price agreed if it is established that her objective conduct was such that an ordinary reasonable person would have believed the offer was a serious one.

RECORDING AN AGREEMENT IN WRITING

It is not *generally* necessary to have an agreement recorded in writing for it to be considered legally binding.

Consider the following example: Ivan silently presents a packet of crisps to a cashier in a supermarket and hands them a €5.00 note. The cashier, who is too busy scrolling on their phone to utter a word to Ivan, takes the money and presents him with his change. No written contract has been signed evidencing this transaction. Indeed, no words have been exchanged at all. Notwithstanding this, an enforceable contract has been concluded.

In *Murphy v Joe O'Toole & Sons Ltd* [2014] IEHC 486, the plaintiff bought from the first defendant, Joe O'Toole & Sons Ltd, a piece of agricultural machinery. It was held that this bargain was legally enforceable notwithstanding the fact that the deal had been completed by way of handshake.

There are some categories of contract that are required by law to be recorded in writing in order to ensure enforceability thereof, however. These categories are explored in Chapter 10.

2 Offer

Introduction

An offer may be defined as a clear and unambiguous statement of the terms upon which the offeror is willing to contract. As observed in *Storer v Manchester City Council* [1974] 3 All E.R. 824, an offer "empowers the persons to whom it is addressed to create a contract by their acceptance".

An offer may be converted into a contract by the unconditional acceptance of the offer by the person to whom it is made (i.e. the offeree). An offer may be made orally or in writing, or may be inferred from the gestures or conduct of an offeror. It should be noted that an offer may be made to one or more persons. There is no upper limit on the number of persons to whom a single offer may be made. Nor is it necessary that an offer be made to any specified or named persons for it to be valid. It is possible, for instance, to make an offer to the world at large.

For instance, if Fatima were to offer to pay €1,000 to anyone who reads *War and Peace* by Leo Tolstoy, from beginning to end, within 30 days, it would be open to any number of people who accepted the challenge to collect the sum offered. The fact that Fatima might not be able financially to satisfy all completed contracts is irrelevant.

Two categories of offer are worth describing: a bilateral offer and a unilateral offer. The key differences between the categories involve:

1. the *manner* in which the offer may be accepted; and
2. *who* is bound by the resulting contract.

Bilateral Offer

Acceptance of a bilateral offer usually takes the form of a promise. In this way, there are two promises at play (hence the term "bilateral").

Consider the following example: Karen offers Marcus €5,000 in exchange for Marcus' promise to sell her his car. Here, Karen is the offeror and she has tendered a bilateral offer. If a bilateral offer is accepted, the contract crystallises and both the offeror and offeree(s) are obliged to complete the promised actions.

Unilateral Offer

Acceptance of a unilateral offer requires the performance of a specified act (or, in some cases, refraining from a particular act).

Consider this example: Alex offers Archer €1,000 if he runs 10km a day for one week. This is a unilateral offer that is accepted not by *promising* to run the 10km, but by the *performance* of the act. Initially, no one is obliged to perform either task. However, once the contemplated act (Archer running 10km a day for one week) is performed, the contract is deemed to have been created and is enforceable. It is clear from this example that once the contract is accepted (via performance), only one of the parties is still required to do something: Alex is still required to act (i.e. give Archer €1,000).

Another good example of a unilateral offer is the offer of a reward for the return of an item, such as a lost wallet. Acceptance occurs not by promising to return the item to the offeror but by the performance of that act. Upon returning the lost item to the offeror, it is only the offeror that is bound to do something under the crystallised contract, i.e. pay the reward money.

Distinguishing Offers from Other Phenomena

Not everything that appears to be an offer is considered to be so under law. The following guides may prove useful in drawing the distinction between what is and is not an offer in law.

A Statement of Opinion or Quotation of Price

A statement setting out one's opinion, hope or expectation is not an offer. The case of *Harvey v Facey* [1893] A.C. 552 concerned the sale of a property in Jamaica, called "Bumper Hall Pen". The plaintiff sent a telegram to the defendant vendor which read: "Will you sell us Bumper Hall Pen? Telegraph lowest cash price-answer paid." The vendor replied: "Lowest price for Bumper Hall Pen £900." The plaintiff then sent the following statement of purported acceptance: "We agree to buy Bumper Hall Pen for the sum of nine hundred pounds asked by you. Please send us your title deed in order that we may get early possession." The Privy Council held that there was no contract here. The statement that £900 was the lowest cash price that would be accepted for the property could not constitute an offer to sell at that price. Rather, it amounted to an opinion as to the likely price the owners would accept if they were minded to sell. (See also *Anderson v Backlund* 159 Minn. 423 (1924); *Clifton v Palumbo* [1944] 2 All E.R. 497).

Generally speaking, quotations and/or estimates of a likely price for goods do not amount to an offer. In *Boyers & Co v Duke* [1905] 2 I.R. 617, for instance, the plaintiff wrote asking for the lowest quotation the defendant would give for 3,000 yards of canvas. The defendant replied with its lowest price and the plaintiff made an order at this price, purportedly accepting this "offer". It came to the defendant's attention that the quotation was excessively low due to a clerical error. It therefore refused to supply the canvas at the price originally quoted. The plaintiff sued for breach of contract. Madden J. held that the initial statement of the lowest price at which canvas would be sold was merely a quotation or estimate and not an offer to sell at that price.

It should be noted that the wording of a quotation might cause a quotation to be interpreted as an offer. In *Dooley v Egan* (1938) 72 I.L.T.R. 155, the plaintiff wrote to the defendant and stated that it could supply a medical cabinet and six sterilising drums at a fixed price. The quotation was issued for "immediate acceptance only". The plaintiff relied on *Boyers v Duke* to argue that the quotation did not constitute an offer but rather a statement of the terms upon which it might be willing to sell. The court interpreted the wording of the quotation to have been intended to offer the goods for sale for "immediate acceptance". This demand changed the tenor of the statement from quotation to offer.

LETTER OF INTENT / STATEMENT OF INTENTION

An offer must also be distinguished from a statement of intention.

In *Gibson v Manchester City Council* [1979] 1 All E.R. 972, the plaintiff, who lived in a house owned by the defendant council, wanted to buy his home. In reply to an enquiry, the defendant wrote to the plaintiff indicating that it "may be prepared to sell the house" for £2,180. The letter further stated that if he wished to make a formal application to buy the house, the plaintiff should complete and return the enclosed application form. The House of Lords concluded that although there was a specified price mentioned in the letter, it was otherwise relatively non-committal (a point underlined by use of the phrase "may be prepared" and the suggestion that the plaintiff would have to make a formal application to purchase the house). This was taken not to constitute an offer. (See also *Farina v Fickus* [1900] 1 Ch. 331. See, however, *Storer v Manchester City Council* [1974] 3 All E.R. 824 where a more definitive letter regarding the sale of a council house was interpreted as containing an offer.)

ADVERTISEMENTS

As stated above, an offer is defined as a clear and unambiguous statement of the terms upon which the offeror is willing to contract should the offeree decide to accept. An invitation to treat may be described as an expression of willingness to *consider offers* from other persons.

The classic example of an invitation to treat is an advertisement. An advertisement generally invites the customer to make an offer to purchase an item. For instance, in *Partridge v Crittendon* [1968] 2 All E.R. 421, a magazine advertised "Bramblefinch cocks and hens" for sale at 25 shillings each. This, the court ruled, did not constitute an offer to sell wildlife, which was an offence under British law. Similarly, in *Grainger & Sons v Gough* [1896] A.C. 325, the distribution by a wine merchant of a price list for various wines was deemed not to be an offer.

It should be noted that it is a criminal offence under consumer protection legislation to invite offers by way of false or misleading advertisements or displays as to price (see Part 3 of the Consumer Protection Act 2007).

The general approach, that advertisements constitute invitations to treat and not offers, is protectionist and rooted in the theory of "limited stocks". Consider a stadium with a 10,000-seat capacity that advertises tickets for a concert. If the advertisement were taken to constitute an offer, accepted by any member of the public who presents themselves at the stadium with the ticket price in hand, the stadium could potentially be liable in contract to many more persons than can safely fit in the stadium. If the stadium refused entry on foot of capacity concerns, it could be liable to thousands of disappointed fans.

This is not to say that advertisements can never constitute an offer. The more explicit and unconditional the advertisement, the more likely it is that the court will consider that it was seriously intended to be binding should persons come forward prepared to act on it. In this regard, the court will look at the offeror's intention. In particular, if the advertisement states that if a person performs a particular act, she will receive a particular specified benefit, it is likely that the advertisement will be interpreted as a unilateral offer.

The decision in *Carlill v Carbolic Smokeball Co* [1893] 1 Q.B. 256 is instructive in this regard. This case concerned a newspaper advertisement placed by the defendant company for the sale of a "smokeball". The advertisement claimed that, if used correctly, the smokeball would protect the user from contracting influenza. The manufacturer was so confident in its product, it promised that anyone who used it in accordance with the instructions provided and still contracted the flu would be paid £100 in compensation. Having used the smokeball as instructed, Mrs Carlill nonetheless caught the flu. She sued for the promised sum. Despite the manufacturer's claim that the advertisement in question did not constitute an offer, the court interpreted it as a unilateral offer which had been accepted by Mrs Carlill when she satisfied the conditions of performance outlined—contracting influenza while using the smokeball in accordance with the instructions. Particular emphasis was placed on the advert's statement that as proof of the company's sincerity, £1,000 had been lodged in a bank to pay for any claims made. Thus, the company was bound to pay Mrs Carlill £100.

In *Lefkowitz v Great Minneapolis Surplus Store* 86 N.W. 2d 689 (Minn., 1957), the defendant had placed an advertisement for fur coats (worth $100) in a Minneapolis newspaper, indicating that on a specified Saturday it would sell the coats for $1 each on a first come, first served basis. A week later, the defendant published a second advertisement offering two mink scarves (worth $89.50) for $1 each and a lapin stole (worth $139.50) for sale on a particular Saturday, on a first come, first served basis. On each of these Saturdays, Mr Lefkowitz was the first person to present at the shop and willing to pay $1 for the advertised items. On both occasions, the shop owner refused to sell to him, explaining that there was a "house rule" that the deals advertised were meant for women only. This was notwithstanding the fact that the advisement made no mention of gender. The court concluded that the advertisement, being sufficiently "clear, definite, and explicit" and having left "nothing open for negotiation", constituted an offer and not an invitation to treat. This offer was not explicitly conditional on the gender of the purchaser and, as such, Mr Lefkowitz was entitled to performance on the part of the defendant.

The following cases have similar facts but different outcomes and provide an interesting comparison. In *Wilson v Belfast Corporation* (1921) 55 I.L.T.R. 205, an unauthorised newspaper report indicated that the defendant council would pay half wages to any employee who signed up to serve in the Defence Forces during World War I. The court looked at the intention of the defendant and concluded that the newspaper report was not the medium through which the defendant intended to communicate with its employees. As such, this was not held to constitute an offer. In *Billings v Arnott* (1945) 80 I.L.T.R. 50, the defendant published an advertisement offering any of its employees who joined the Defence Forces one-half of their salaries up to the sum of £2 per week. The plaintiff, an employee of the defendant, informed the defendant that he intended to accept this offer. The plaintiff was informed that this would not be possible as another employee from the his department had already signed up to the Defence Forces and the plaintiff could not be spared. Nonetheless, the plaintiff signed up to the Defence Forces and subsequently attempted to enforce the contract. The offer was deemed to be a clear and precise one, accepted through performance (i.e. being an employee of the defendant company and signing up for the Defence Forces).

Displays

Similarly, where a shop displays goods for sale, this does not generally constitute an offer to sell but rather an invitation to treat. Thus, in most consumer transactions it is usually the buyer who makes the offer and the seller who accepts.

Take the following example: while shopping at her local grocery store, Orla notices a display of her favourite brand of crisps and picks up two packets to purchase. She presents them to the cashier, a health food enthusiast, who refuses to sell the crisps to her on principle, citing something about artificial flavourings. Because the crisp display constitutes an invitation to treat and not an offer, it is open to the cashier to reject Orla's offer on behalf of the shop.

The UK case of *Pharmaceutical Society of Great Britain v Boots Cash Chemists* [1953] 1 Q.B. 401 is instructive in this regard. At the time of this case, it was illegal to contract for the sale of certain pharmaceutical products otherwise than in the presence of a qualified pharmacist. The defendant pharmacist had stocked its open shelving with such items. The key question in this case was whether the display of goods was an offer which the customer accepted by taking the goods off the shelf, in which case the contract would have been completed otherwise than in the presence of a qualified pharmacist. The court ruled that it was not. The offer in such a scenario was made not by the shop but by the customer, who offered to buy the items by presenting them to the pharmacist, thus empowering the pharmacist to accept or reject the customer's offer. As such, no offence had been committed, the contract having been completed in the presence of the pharmacist.

In the Irish case of *Minister for Industry and Commerce v Pim Bros Ltd* [1966] I.R. 154, the defendants displayed a coat for sale accompanied by a statement that listed its price as being 24 guineas. The statement indicated that periodic payments in respect of this aggregate sum would be permitted at 5s 10d per week. The Hire Purchase and Credit Sale (Advertising) Order 1961 dictated that it was an offence to offer goods for sale on credit terms without simultaneously indicating what those terms were. The plaintiff prosecuted the defendants for breach of these rules but the High Court held that the display of the coat was an invitation to treat and not an offer. The court stated:

> "In one sense it could be described as an offer to sell. In popular terms the coat could properly be said to be on offer to the public. In the strictly legal sense, however, the advertisement was merely a statement of the cash price at which the defendants were prepared to sell the goods, with an indication that certain credit facilities, the exact nature of which were unspecified, would be available. This would not constitute an offer to sell which could be made a contract of sale by acceptance."

Again, the rationale underpinning this result has public policy roots. A shop will invariably have limited stocks of an item. The rule protects shop owners who might otherwise be required to sell to anyone who saw the display if same was taken to constitute an offer. This would cause issues if, for example, the shop owner had already sold the items in a display to another customer.

AUCTION

Section 58(2) of the Sale of Goods Act 1893 states that a sale by auction is complete when the auctioneer announces its conclusion. This is usually communicated by the fall of the hammer. In this way, it is the *bidder* who generally makes the offer to purchase goods at auction and that offer may be accepted or rejected by the auctioneer. *Harris v Nickerson* (1873) L.R. 8 Q.B. 286 is authority for the proposition that an advertisement stating that an auction will take place at a specified place and time is a declaration of intention only and not an offer to hold the auction.

In this case, the auctioneer advertised that furniture would be auctioned on a particular day. The plaintiff travelled to the auction to participate but discovered that the furniture advertised had been withdrawn from the auction. It was held that potential bidders who arrive at an auction intending to bid cannot claim that they have accepted the auctioneer's offer to hold an auction. In this context, it is generally said that the advert is an invitation to the public to attend and make a bid.

At an auction, a reserve price might be set for an item (i.e. a price below which the item will not be sold) or it may be sold "without reserve" (i.e. there is no minimum price). Where an auction is commenced "without reserve", the auctioneer will be considered to have made a unilateral offer to all of the bidders attending the sale that they will sell to the highest bona fide bidder. Anyone who attends and bids at such auction is deemed to have accepted the offer; however, it is only the highest bona fide bidder that may sue the auctioneer for damages if the auctioneer refuses to subsequently sell the item to them (see *Tully v Irish Land Commission* (1961) 97 I.L.T.R. 174 and *Warlow v Harrison* (1859) 1 E. & E. 309). As such, it is not open to the auctioneer, where an item is to be sold "without reserve", to withdraw the lot from sale because it has not attracted a high enough offer. In *Barry v Davies* [2001] 1 All E.R. 944, the plaintiff was the only bidder at a "without reserve" sale of engineering equipment with a list price of £28,000. The plaintiff bid £400 and the auctioneer attempted to withdraw the goods rather than knock them down at such a discount. The English Court of Appeal measured the damages owed to the plaintiff at £27,600.

Clark in his seminal text *Contract Law in Ireland*, 9th edn (Dublin: Round Hall, 2022) posits at para.1-11 that where an auctioneer has been authorised to sell "without reserve" and the subsequent refusal to sell to the highest bidder is due to the owner's change of mind, the auctioneer should in all fairness be indemnified by the owner from liability, the auctioneer acting as the owner's agent.

Tenders

Tendering involves the process of choosing a company or individual to purchase/supply goods/services or to perform works, by inviting bids or "tenders" for same. A request for tenders, then, is not generally deemed to be an offer; instead, those who respond are usually deemed to be making an offer to supply the goods or services or perform the work, and these offers may be accepted or rejected by the organisation requesting tenders. In this way, the advertisement seeking tenders is generally regarded as an invitation to treat.

It should be noted that, in general, there is no obligation to accept the highest or lowest tender bid, unless the advertisement/statement promised to accept the lowest figure. In fact, the organisation requesting tenders is usually free to decline all bids. An organisation inviting tenders from prospective contractors might shore up their position by including a privilege clause, reserving the right to decline all offers.

In *Spencer v Harding* (1870) L.R. 5 C.P. 561, the defendant had invited tenders for the purchase of stock. The highest bidder, whose bid was declined, sued claiming that his bid constituted an acceptance of an offer to sell. The Court of Common Pleas concluded that the invitation for tenders did not amount to an offer, and in particular that there was no obligation on the defendant to accept the highest bid. Willes J. held that if there is no undertaking to sell to the highest bidder, an invitation for tenders is "a mere attempt to ascertain whether an offer can be obtained within such margin as the sellers are willing to adopt".

Where an invitation to tender expressly indicates that the best bid (e.g. the highest offer to buy items or the lowest offer to supply goods or services) will be accepted, the position changes and the advertisement might be held to be an offer rather than simply an invitation to treat. In *Harvela Investments v Royal Trust of Canada* [1985] 2 All E.R. 966, the defendant invited two parties to tender for the purchase of shares, indicating that it bound itself to accept the highest offer. In such a case, the House of Lords ruled, the invitation was in fact a unilateral offer that was accepted by the party making the highest bid. The judgment in *Harvela* also concerned the topic of "referential tenders" or "referential bids", i.e. a tender that promises to top the best bid received by the inviter by a specified amount (e.g. an offer to pay €10,000 more than any higher bid). In this case, the second defendant made a bid that was lower than that of the plaintiff, but added a referential clause that promised $101,000 more than any higher bid submitted. The first defendant accepted this referential bid. The House of Lords held that by stating that they would accept the highest bid, the first defendant had made an offer that they would accept the highest *genuine* bid. A referential tender, the House concluded, was not a genuine bid. If each party were able to make a referential bid, it might not be possible to determine the identity of the best bid.

This approach received strong endorsement in *Smart Telecom plc v Radio Telefís Éireann* [2007] 1 I.R. 732. The case concerned a tender advertised by RTÉ for sponsorship of its weather forecast. The plaintiff submitted a referential bid of "5% above the highest priced bid received". Although RTÉ had not expressly excluded referential bids, Kelly J. held that it was clear from the advertisement that RTÉ did not intend to permit referential bids, noting:

> "[E]ach bidder was asked to state clearly what price it would commit to per annum and in total for the two year period. Not merely that, but the best offer was to be a gross figure inclusive of agency commission. This suggests to me that the first defendant wished to have *actual figures quoted*. This is entirely consistent with the idea that each bidder should make its best offer" (emphasis added).

That is not to say that referential bids are never permitted in the tendering process. However, it should be noted that Kelly J. was of the opinion in *Smart Telecom plc* that "where referential bids are sought there ought to be an express provision in the invitation permitting such bids to be made".

TERMINATION OF AN OFFER

An offer, once made, may come to an end in a number of ways:

(a) rejection;
(b) making a counter-offer;
(c) death;
(d) revocation;
(e) lapse of time;
(f) failure of a precondition.

Termination of an offer in any of the above ways must take place *before* acceptance in order to be valid. Once it has been terminated, an offer can no longer be accepted.

REJECTION

If an offeree rejects an offer, the offer terminates and it cannot subsequently be accepted even if the offeree changes their mind. Such rejection may be express or implied. It is important, however, to distinguish between the rejection of an offer and an enquiry as to the offeror's openness to alter or amend the terms of the offer. In *Stevenson, Jacques and Co v McLean* (1880) 5 Q.B.D. 340, the plaintiff was an iron merchant that purchased iron for resale. The defendant possessed several warrants for iron. He wrote to the plaintiff and offered to sell a quantity of iron for 40 shillings per tonne. The plaintiff sent a telegram asking if the defendant would agree to delivery over two months, and if not, how long could he give. The defendant did not respond and sold the iron to another buyer. The enquiry was deemed to be a request for further information only and not an outright rejection of the offer.

An offer may be rejected for almost any reason, but is subject to the restrictions provided by the Equal Status Acts 2000–2018. The Acts prohibit discrimination on specific grounds, e.g. gender, civil status, family status, sexual orientation, religion, age, disability, race, being a member of the Traveller community, and housing assistance status. As a result, the rejection of an offer on one of these grounds is not permitted under the Acts.

Making a Counter-offer

A counter-offer is a response to an offer that does not meet the terms of the offer. It is treated as a new offer and has the effect of terminating the original offer. For instance, in *Hyde v Wrench* (1840) 3 Beav. 334, the defendant offered to sell property to the plaintiff for £1,000. The plaintiff responded indicating that he would only pay £950, a counter-offer that terminated the original offer. In such circumstances, it was not possible for the offeree subsequently to accept the original offer.

A counter-offer is also made where a person purports to accept an offer but in fact adds new terms. For instance, in *Jones v Daniel* [1894] 2 Ch. 332, the defendant had offered to purchase land from the plaintiff for £1,450. The plaintiff agreed to the price but presented the defendant with a contract containing terms that the defendant had not previously seen. This attempt to introduce new terms meant that the plaintiff had not accepted the offer but had made, instead, a counter-offer.

In *O'Mahony v Promontoria (Gem) DAC* [2020] IECA 30, the first respondent, Mr O'Mahony, had substantial borrowings with Allied Irish Banks plc. The second and third respondents provided certain guarantees in relation to these liabilities. The fifth respondent, Mrs O'Mahony, was the wife of the first respondent. Mr O'Mahony's loans were transferred to the National Asset Management Agency in 2009 and subsequently to the appellant, Promontoria (Gem) DAC. Mr O'Mahony entered settlement talks for the discharge of the loans, offering a sum of €4 million in full and final settlement of his debt. The appellant rejected this and invited him to make an offer of, or in excess of, €6 million. Mr O'Mahony duly offered €6 million. The appellant's agent replied and informed Mr O'Mahony that the approval request for the deal was processing and that a 10% deposit would be required "upon signing to demonstrate your commitment to the deal". Some weeks later, the appellant responded to Mr O'Mahony's offer with an email dated 20 June 2017, entitled "Heads of Terms and KYC". There was disagreement between the parties as to whether the said email amounted to an acceptance or merely a counter-offer introducing new terms (e.g. the need for a deposit). The High Court did not accept Promontoria's argument that the email of 20 June 2017 amounted to a counter-offer and emphasised the fact that the prospect of a 10% deposit had been mentioned earlier in negotiations without objection from Mr O'Mahony. The court held that the email indicated agreement between the parties of all essential terms and that the language used in the email evidenced this:

> "Words used such as 'terms', 'Promontoria approve', 'this deal has been approved' all connote and demonstrate the finality of the agreement and this was their bargain. There was no need for further acceptance, or any further need for discussion or negotiation. The wording used and the circumstances of this case are such as to lead me to conclude that there is a binding contract."

The Court of Appeal agreed with the findings of the High Court.

DEATH

Unfortunately, there is a dearth of Irish case law dealing with the impact that death has on an offer. In *Re Whelan* [1897] 1 I.R. 575, Whelan had guaranteed the current account of his firm. When he died in April, no notice of his death was given to the bank. In November, the bank manager learned of Whelan's death in casual conversation. Despite this, the bank did not close the account until the following January. The issue to be decided was whether Whelan's estate was liable for any amounts overdrawn in the current account after his death. The court held that the mere death of Whelan did not terminate the operation of the guarantee. However, the knowledge of Whelan's death was sufficient to put the bank on notice. Therefore, any advances made after his death but before the bank became aware of his death were recoverable but those made after the bank became aware of his death were not. This case has been cited as authority for the proposition that if the offeree was not aware of the offeror's death, the offer may still be accepted if the contract can be performed by the estate. The outcome seems to be quite different if *personal* performance is required by the deceased offeror, e.g. *Bradbury v Morgan* (1862) 1 H. & C. 249. If an offeree dies before the offer has been accepted, the offer to that offeree lapses automatically. Surviving offerees, if the offer was made to more than one person, may still accept the offer, however.

In the Canadian case of *Re Irvine* [1928] 3 D.L.R. 268, a father received an offer to purchase some of his property. He executed an acceptance of the offer but died before the acceptance could be posted to the offeror by his son. The acceptance was therefore not executed before the father's death and the offer lapsed.

Revocation

An offer, once made, may be withdrawn at any time prior to acceptance. The offeror need not give any reason for the withdrawal of the offer (though a revocation based on grounds set out in the Equal Status Acts 2000–2018 (see above) might constitute discrimination and would not be permissible).

Revocation is permissible even where the offer was promised to be kept open for a specific period, unless there is a separate enforceable contract to keep the offer open. *Walker v Glass* [1979] N.I. 129 is authority for this and concerned the defendant's offer to sell the plaintiff's house. The offer was to remain open until a specified date but was revoked before that date. The court held that the defendant was permitted to revoke his offer at any time prior to acceptance. (See also *Routledge v Grant* (1828) 4 Bing. 653.)

A revocation will only be effective when it is communicated to the offeree. Such communication may be explicit (using words) or implicit (by actions). In the latter instance, a revocation may be communicated where the offeree is informed of behaviour or events that are inconsistent with the continuance of the offer. In *Dickinson v Dodds* (1876) 2 Ch. D. 463, the defendant had offered to sell his house to the plaintiff for an agreed sum and the offer was to remain open until Friday, 12 June at 9am. On Thursday afternoon, the plaintiff was informed by a third party that the house might have been sold to someone else. This third party was not authorised by the defendant to communicate this news. On Thursday evening, notwithstanding the news received, the plaintiff furnished the defendant with a letter of acceptance. Although the offeror had not personally informed the plaintiff of the revocation, the third party's information was deemed to amount to effective communication to the offeree of the fact of revocation. James L.J. held:

> "It must, to constitute a contract, appear that the two minds were at one, at the same moment of time, that is, that there was an offer continuing up to the time of the acceptance. If there was not such a continuing offer, then the acceptance comes to nothing."

In Chapter 3, we will discuss the "postal rule" and how it affects acceptance. Although acceptance is usually said to occur when it is *communicated* to the offeror, the postal rule dictates that acceptance crystallises as soon as the letter of acceptance is *mailed*. However, the postal rule does *not* apply to letters of revocation and, as such, a letter of revocation terminates the offer only when it arrives at its destination and is read, i.e. the revocation is communicated. For example, in *Byrne v Van Tienhoven* (1880) 49 L.J.Q.B. 316, on 1 October the defendants (based in Wales) posted a letter to the plaintiff (located in New York) offering to sell the latter 1,000 boxes of tinplates. The letter arrived on 11 October and on the same day the plaintiff telegrammed its acceptance, following this up with a letter posted on 15 October. However, on 8 October, the defendant had posted a letter withdrawing the original offer. This did not reach New York until 20 October. While the postal rule dictated that acceptance of the offer occurred at the point of postage on 11 October (telegrams being subject to the postal rule by their nature), it was held that revocation did not occur until it was communicated to the offeree (20 October). Lindley J. held that the revocation of the offer was not permissible as a complete contract had crystallised on 11 October by telegram, upon acceptance by the plaintiff who had no reason to suppose that it had been withdrawn by letter dated 8 October.

An offer can be revoked if the stated method of acceptance is not completed. In the case of *Walker v Glass* [1979] N.I. 129, the defendant offered to sell an estate to the plaintiff for £400,000 with a deposit of £40,000. The defendant stated that in order to accept, the plaintiff had to sign a form of acceptance and forward him the deposit before 13 March. On 2 March, the plaintiff signed the acceptance form and telephoned the defendant's solicitors to let them know. Later that day, the defendant's solicitors informed the plaintiff that the offer was withdrawn. The court held that the plaintiff had not accepted the offer before the defendant revoked it because the acceptance had not been in the form described. Oral acceptance (unaccompanied by payment of the deposit and without delivery to the defendant) was not complete performance.

As discussed above, a unilateral offer may be accepted through performance. It would seem that while an offeror may withdraw a unilateral offer if performance has not yet begun, where the offeree has begun to perform, revocation will no longer be permissible. In *Daulia v Four Milbank Nominees* [1978] Ch. 231, the court held:

> "Whilst I think that the true view of a unilateral contract must in general be that the offeror is entitled to require full performance of the condition which he has imposed and short of that he is not bound, that must be subject to one important qualification, which stems from the fact that there must be an *implied obligation on the part of the offeror not to prevent the condition becoming satisfied, which obligation it seems to me must arise as soon as the offeree starts to perform.* Until then the

offeror can revoke the whole thing, but once the offeree has embarked on performance it is too late for the offeror to revoke his offer" (emphasis added).

The rule that a unilateral offer may not be revoked if performance has commenced was also discussed in *Lyndel v Mobil* (1997) 37 I.P.R. 599. The defendant here ran a Circle of Excellence programme for its franchises and promised that those franchises that achieved a score of 90% each year for the next six years in the programme would be guaranteed a renewal of their franchise for another nine years with no associated fees. The plaintiff incurred significant expense in order to meet the requisite standards to score 90% in the programme (e.g. increased wages, associated maintenance and equipment expenditure). The defendant abandoned the programme, purporting to have revoked the offer before completion of the act. The plaintiff successfully sued for breach of contract.

If performance has not yet commenced and the unilateral offer has been made to the world at large, reasonable steps must be taken to inform the public of the revocation. In principle, this means that the revocation must be communicated by a method equally as effective as that by which the original offer was advertised. For instance, if an offer is made in a prominent newspaper advertisement, its withdrawal may need to be similarly publicised.

Lapse of Time

As noted, if a deadline has been set for acceptance of an offer, it may be possible to terminate the offer before the deadline has passed. Further, providing that an offer has not been revoked before a designated deadline, the offer will lapse once this deadline expires. As Carroll J. noted in *Parkgrange Investments v Shandon Park Mills* (unreported, High Court, 2 May 1991), "[a] purchaser who ignores a time limit for accepting an offer runs the risk that it will lapse". This case concerned the sale of property. After a series of offers and counter-offers, the vendor made a final offer that was only valid for a limited time. In circumstances where the offer was not accepted within that time, the offer lapsed. If a time limit for acceptance is not provided, acceptance must take place within a reasonable time (see *Commane v Walsh* (unreported, High Court, 3 May 1983)). What amounts to a "reasonable time" is construed on a case-by-case basis and will be informed by the facts and circumstances at play, e.g. an offer by a restaurant to purchase a consignment of freshly harvested organic vegetables would presumably have to be accepted by the seller in a matter of days.

In *Ramsgate Victoria Hotel v Montefiore* (1866) L.R. Exch. 109, the defendant applied to purchase shares in the plaintiff company. He received a response five months later, which was deemed too long to wait to accept, given the nature of the commodity. In *Dooley v Egan* (1938) 72 I.L.T.R. 155, the plaintiff wrote to the defendant and stated that it could supply a medical cabinet and six sterilising drums at a fixed price. The quotation was issued for "immediate acceptance only". Meredith J. held that this quotation constituted an offer and anything less than immediate acceptance of it was not sufficient.

In *Lynch v Governors of St Vincent's Hospital* (unreported, High Court, 31 July 1987), the plaintiff was offered a new contract of employment by the defendant in February. The hospital left a blank space under the heading "service requirement". A second copy of the contract was sent in September which listed the service requirement as 21 hours. The defendant requested that the plaintiff sign this new contract and return it. The plaintiff became aware, via an internal circular, that acceptance of the contract had to be made by 31 December. He decided to accept the offer in December after seeking legal advice. Unable to find the September version of the contract, he inserted the 21-hour service requirement into the February contract, executed it, and returned it to the hospital. The hospital claimed that this did not constitute valid acceptance and was instead a counter-offer. Costello J. held that the plaintiff's acceptance was valid notwithstanding that it had taken nine months to effectuate. The existence of the internal circular seemed to have convinced the court that the offer remained open at the time of acceptance.

FAILURE OF A PRECONDITION

If an offer is predicated on the satisfaction of a condition, which fails prior to acceptance, the offer cannot be accepted.

For example, Kayla offers Kelsie €100 for a festival ticket. Before Kelsie can accept, the festival is cancelled. The offer is therefore terminated, given that a precondition to its purchase—that the festival proceeds as planned—has failed.

In *Financings Ltd v Stimson* [1962] 1 W.L.R. 1184, the defendant offered to buy a car on hire-purchase terms. Before the offer was accepted, the car was stolen and, when recovered, was found to be badly damaged. The court implied a condition into the contract that the car be sold in good condition—a precondition that had failed before acceptance. As such, the offer was terminated before acceptance.

Acceptance

Introduction

Acceptance may be defined as the final and unconditional expression of agreement to the terms of an offer. A contract comes into being where an offer is unequivocally accepted by the person to whom it is made. Acceptance, once communicated, causes a contract to crystallise. The *enforceability* or *validity* of a contract, on the other hand, will depend on a number of factors that we will explore in the coming chapters.

Preliminary Points on Acceptance

An Offer May Only Be Accepted by a Person to Whom It Is Made

A person may only accept an offer where, under the terms of the offer, it has been made to that person. For example, if the offer is made to an individual, it cannot be accepted by a company owned by that individual, given their separate legal personalities. Of course, it is possible to make an offer to more than one person, or to the public at large—anyone who meets the conditions of the offer may thus reap the benefits of a contract.

Consider the following: if Thomas offers €100 to any red-haired person who climbs the Sugar Loaf Mountain, any red-haired person who did so could collect the promised money. A blond man who climbed the Sugar Loaf Mountain would not be able to collect the money, as the offer was not made to him; he does not meet the conditions of the offer.

It is a question of fact whether an offer made collectively to several people can be accepted by only one of those persons alone. For instance, if a magazine offers to give €10,000 to a charity if *all* the members of a boyband run the marathon, it would not be liable if only one member did so. Liability would arise, however, if the offer stipulated that it would pay the money if *any* member runs the marathon.

An Offer Cannot Be Accepted in Ignorance of the Offer

There can be no acceptance where the offeree acts in ignorance of the offer. In *Fitch v Snedaker* (1868) 38 N.Y. 248, the defendant had offered a reward for the return of his lost dog. The plaintiff was not aware of this reward but upon finding the dog, returned it to the defendant. He was not permitted to claim the money subsequently.

In the Australian case of *R. v Clarke* (1927) 40 C.L.R. 227, a reward was offered for information that would lead to the arrest and conviction of the person or persons who committed two murders. Clarke was arrested and charged with committing one of the two murders. Whilst in custody, he provided information that led to the arrest and conviction of another person for the second murder. The trial judge held that although the defendant had initially been aware of the offer of reward, he was held to have subsequently panicked and forgotten about it at the time of his confession, giving information simply "to save his own skin".

That is not to say that a person acting with a *motive* other than reward is thereby prejudiced. In *Williams v Carwardine* (1833) 4 B. & Ad. 621, the plaintiff had supplied information about a murder to the police. Although the plaintiff was fully aware of the reward at the time of the offer, her primary motive for providing information was to ease her conscience before she died. Being aware of the offer at the time of acceptance, she was nonetheless entitled to claim the award. The court held: "[t]he motive was the state of her own feelings. My opinion is, the motive is not material." A somewhat similar principle arises from *Taylor v Laird* (1856) 25 L.J. Exch. 329. Taylor, the captain of a ship, mid-voyage had resigned his position, but unbeknownst to the defendant had continued to do work on the ship. This offer of work could not therefore be accepted by the defendant as it was not communicated thereto. Taylor was therefore unable to sue for services rendered during this time.

Methods of Acceptance

Acceptance Must Be Unconditional

In order to give rise to a contract, the acceptance must be made unconditionally, that is, in precisely the same terms as the offer. If the response to an offer is anything other than a clear and unconditional acceptance of the exact terms of the offer, it is said to be a counter-offer and does not constitute acceptance. This is sometimes called the "mirror image" effect: the acceptance must match the terms of the offer (see *Tansey v College of Occupational Therapists* (unreported, High Court, 27 August 1986)). Where a counter-offer is made, it acts as a rejection of the original offer which can no longer be accepted.

In *Swan v Miller* [1919] 1 I.R. 151, in response to an offer to sell land for £4,750 plus a ground rent, the plaintiff responded stating that they would pay

£4,750, with no mention of the ground rent. As the plaintiff's response did not match the offer, the plaintiff was deemed to have made a counter-offer.

In *Dooley v Egan* (1938) 72 I.L.T.R. 155, the plaintiff provided a quotation for the sale of a medical cabinet and six sterilising drums. This quotation was for "immediate acceptance only". The court held that this constituted an offer. The defendants subsequently ordered two medical cabinets. The court held that response did not amount to acceptance of the original offer but rather a counter-offer. Similarly, in *Tinn v Hoffman* (1873) 29 L.T. 271, an offer to sell 1,200 tons of iron received a response ordering 800 tons. The response, being in terms different from the offer, was held to be a counter-offer and not an acceptance.

A counter-offer must be distinguished from a request for more information about or an enquiry as to the terms of an original offer, if it is clear that there will or may be acceptance regardless of the response to such inquiries. In *Stevenson, Jacques and Co v McLean* (1880) 5 Q.B.D. 340, the plaintiff was an iron merchant that purchased iron for resale. The defendant possessed several warrants for iron. He wrote to the plaintiff and offered to sell the plaintiff a quantity of iron for 40 shillings per ton. The plaintiff sent a telegram asking if the defendant would agree to delivery over two months, and if not, how long could he give. The defendant did not respond and sold the iron to another buyer. The enquiry was deemed to be a request for further information only and not an outright rejection of the offer.

Negotiations often involve the cyclical exchange of printed or digital forms that set out each party's terms and conditions. If a dispute occurs, each party will claim that it is their terms and conditions that govern the contract. These are often called "Battle of the Forms" cases. The basic rule is that until one party accepts the other party's terms without conditions, there is no contract. In essence, "the last shot wins the battle": the offer (including associated terms and conditions) that is last made immediately before unconditional acceptance is given governs the terms of the contract.

In *British Road Services v Crutchley Ltd* [1968] 1 All E.R. 811, a driver working for the plaintiff company had delivered whisky to the defendant for the purpose of storage. On delivery, the driver presented a delivery note to the defendant's agent which set out the plaintiff's standard "conditions of carriage". This note was in turn stamped by the defendant's agent, the stamp indicating that the goods were "[r]eceived under [Crutchley's standard] conditions". The driver accepted this note. The court concluded that by placing the stamp on the note, Crutchley had issued a counter-offer, asserting that its terms (and not the plaintiff's) would apply to the contract. Since the driver, an agent of the plaintiff, accepted the stamped note, the contract was held to have been accepted on the defendant's conditions.

In *Butler Machine Co v Ex-cell-O Corp Ltd* [1979] 1 W.L.R. 401, the plaintiff company offered to sell a machine for £75,535. The terms of the offer included a clause allowing the plaintiff to increase the sale price should its costs rise before delivery (a price variation clause). The defendant purchaser placed an order using its own form, which did not allow for any price variation and which contained additional terms, e.g. costs of carriage and installation and a delivery date. The plaintiff, having signed and returned an acknowledgement slip confirming that it accepted the defendant's terms, was held to be bound by those terms. The purchaser's response was held to be a counter-offer that was accepted by returning the acknowledgement slip. Lord Denning M.R. held that in "Battle of the Forms" cases, it was important to consider all exchanged documents in the round, and:

> "... glean from them, or from the conduct of the parties, whether they have reached agreement on all material points – even though there may be differences between the forms and the conditions printed on the back of them."

Applying this test, it may be that a response that seemingly deviates from the terms of an offer may not constitute a rejection/counter-offer of this offer if the deviation does not *materially* alter its terms. The guidance offered in Article 19 of the Convention on the International Sale of Goods (the Vienna Convention) concerning "Battle of the Forms" scenarios is worth considering, given Lord Denning M.R.'s judgment:

> "(1) A reply to an offer which purports to be an acceptance but contains additions, limitations or other modifications is a rejection of the offer and constitutes a counter-offer.
>
> (2) However, a reply to an offer which purports to be an acceptance but contains additional or different terms which do not materially alter the terms of the offer constitutes an acceptance, unless the offeror, without undue delay, objects orally to the discrepancy or dispatches a notice to that effect. If he does not so object, the terms of the contract are the terms of the offer with the modifications contained in the acceptance.
>
> (3) Additional or different terms relating, among other things, to the price, payment, quality and quantity of the goods, place and time of delivery, extent of one party's liability to the other or the settlement of disputes are considered to alter the terms of the offer materially."

A deviation in the form of a new term may also be treated as acceptance rather than a counter-offer if the new term is suggested by the offeree and will benefit the offeror (see *Quadling v Robinson* (1976) 137 C.L.R. 192 where the offeree promised to pay on a date earlier than stipulated in the offer; the offeror could hardly complain that it was to receive an early payment). Similarly, a deviation may be taken as acceptance rather than a rejection of the offer if the new terms would be inserted by law regardless of the wishes of the party, e.g. terms implied into all consumer contracts under legislation.

When Is a Unilateral Offer Accepted?

As discussed in Chapter 2, acceptance of a unilateral offer is made by performing (or refraining from performing, depending on the offer) a specified act. For example, in *Billings v Arnott* (1945) 80 I.L.T.R. 50, the defendant published an advertisement offering any of its employees who joined the Defence Forces one half of their salaries up to the sum of £2 per week. The plaintiff, an employee of the defendant, informed it that he intended to accept this offer. The plaintiff was told that this would not be possible as another employee from his department had already signed up to the Defence Forces and the plaintiff could not be spared. Nonetheless, the plaintiff signed up to the Defence Forces and subsequently attempted to enforce the contract. His acceptance was held to have been effected not by stating "I agree" or "I accept" but by *performance* (i.e. being an employee of the defendant company and signing up for the Defence Forces).

It would seem that while an offeror may withdraw a unilateral offer if performance has not yet begun, where the offeree has begun to perform, revocation will no longer be permissible. This was not the traditional view, however. In *Luxor (Eastbourne) Ltd v Cooper* [1941] 1 All E.R. 33, an estate agent was offered £10,000 if it found a buyer for a house. After the estate agent began making serious efforts to sell the property, but before a purchaser was found, the landowner revoked the offer. The House of Lords ruled that the estate agent had no claim over the £10,000 as the owner was entitled to revoke the offer at any time before the completion of performance.

It would seem, however, that this traditional approach has changed over time. As discussed above, in *Daulia v Four Milbank Nominees* [1978] Ch. 231, the court held:

> "[T]here must be an implied obligation on the part of the offeror not to prevent the condition becoming satisfied, which obligation it seems to me must arise as soon as the offeree starts to perform. Until then the offeror can revoke the whole thing, but once the offeree has embarked on performance it is too late for the offeror to revoke his offer."

The case of *Lyndel v Mobil* (1997) 37 I.P.R. 599, discussed in Chapter 2, is also evidence of this.

In *Errington v Errington* [1952] 1 K.B. 290, a father had promised his son and daughter-in-law that once they paid off the mortgage on his house, the house would be theirs. Before the mortgage was fully cleared, the father's executors attempted to revoke the offer. As performance had already commenced, the court ruled that the offer could not be withdrawn, even though it had not yet technically been accepted (performance had yet to have been fully completed).

Indicating Acceptance

An unexpressed mental intention to accept an offer, without more, is not sufficient to make a valid contract. In other words, acceptance cannot occur simply in the mind of the offeree. There must be some outward indication of acceptance. This may occur either expressly (by words) or implicitly (by conduct). The court places great emphasis on the objective intention of the parties. A person may indicate acceptance by their conduct if, objectively speaking, the conduct would indicate to a reasonable person that they intend to be bound by their words or conduct.

Subjective intent is therefore not relevant and will not convince a court that no contract exists.

Express Acceptance

A person may indicate acceptance expressly, that is, by making a definitive statement, either orally or in writing, to the effect that they accept the offer without condition. Such acceptance must explicitly indicate an intention to accept the offer in the terms in which the offer is made.

Implied Acceptance

Acceptance may also be implied, or inferred from certain conduct. As we have seen above, acceptance by conduct is a regular response to unilateral offers (see *Billings v Arnott* (1945) 80 I.L.T.R. 50).

In *Western Electric v Welsh Development Agency* [1983] Q.B. 796, the defendant, by letter, offered work to the plaintiff. Instead of responding to the letter, the plaintiff, with the defendant's knowledge, began to perform the contemplated work. This action was deemed to constitute acceptance: though words had not been exchanged, the conduct of the plaintiff could only have been consistent with his implicit acceptance of the offer. Likewise, in *Brogden v Metropolitan Railway Co* (1877) 2 App. Cas. 666, a contract was deemed to have been accepted by the defendant's conduct in ordering coal and accepting receipt of it.

Acceptance by Silence

The general rule is that silence will not normally amount to acceptance. This means that while a person may communicate acceptance through conduct, silent inactivity in the face of an offer does not typically denote agreement. If the offeree neither speaks nor acts in apparent acceptance of the offer then there can be no contract.

It should be noted that the offeror is not permitted to impose a unilateral condition that the offeree's silence will be taken as acceptance. This practice is known as "inertia selling". The classic example of this principle arises from *Felthouse v Bindley* (1862) 11 C.B. (N.S.) 869. In this case, an uncle wrote to his nephew offering £30 and 15 shillings for the nephew's horse. In the letter, the uncle indicated that "if I hear no more about him, I consider the horse mine at that price". The nephew did not respond. A court held that the uncle had not been entitled to the horse as the nephew had not accepted his offer. Mere silence on the part of the nephew was not sufficient to give rise to a contract.

In *Russell & Baird v Hoban* [1922] 2 I.R. 159, the plaintiff had sent a sale note to the defendant offering to supply 42 tons of oatmeal. In the correspondence, the plaintiff had indicated that "if this sale note be retained beyond three days after this date, it will be held to have been accepted by the buyer." The court ruled that there was no contract, as silence did not denote consent.

Section 125 of the Consumer Rights Act 2022 deals with inertia selling in consumer contracts. It states:

"(1) Where—
    (a) goods are supplied by a trader to a consumer without any request by or on behalf of the consumer, or
    (b) a service, digital service, digital content, or (where not supplied in a limited volume or set quantity) water, gas or electricity, is supplied by a trader to a consumer without any request by or on behalf of the consumer,

the consumer is exempted from any requirement to pay or provide any consideration to the trader and may treat the goods, service, digital service, digital content, water, gas or electricity as an unconditional gift.

(2) The absence of a response from the consumer following the supply as mentioned in subsection (1) of goods, a service, digital service, digital content, water, gas or electricity does not constitute consent to—

(a) the provision of consideration for the goods, service, digital service, digital content, water, gas or electricity, or
(b) the return or safekeeping of any goods so supplied."

Section 47 of the Sale of Goods and Supply of Services Act 1980 deals with inertia selling in the context of commercial (business-to-business) contracts.

As with so many aspects of contract law, the general rule that silence does not denote acceptance is subject to a number of exceptions.

(a) If the parties agree that silence may be interpreted as consent, a contract may form as the result of silence

In particular, if it is the offeree who suggests that silence on their part will denote acceptance, they thus assume the risk that acceptance will occur unless they expressly reject the offer.

In *Re Selectmove* [1995] 2 All E.R. 531, Gibson L.J. described this exception as follows:

> "Where the offeree himself indicates that an offer is to be taken as accepted if he does not indicate to the contrary by an ascertainable time, he is undertaking to speak if he does not want an agreement to be concluded. I see no reason in principle why that should not be an exceptional circumstance such that the offer can be accepted by silence."

(b) Where past dealings give rise to a legitimate expectation that silence will suffice

Past dealings between the parties may also give rise to an expectation that silence indicates acceptance. Industry practice may also dictate that silence denotes consent, a good example being the insurance industry practice whereby a contract will often be renewed automatically unless the offeree expressly contacts the insurer to cancel the cover.

(c) Where there is an implied contract for services

Silence can denote acceptance where a contract involves a service that cannot be returned once given, where the recipient of the service, having a reasonable opportunity to object, does not object to the performance of the act. For example, if a van broke down on the side of a road and a passing mechanic stopped to fix the car. If the van driver had a reasonable opportunity to reject the service but instead was silent, it may be that he would be required to pay for the service.

Mode of Acceptance

If the offeror requires as a term of the offer that acceptance occurs in a particular manner, that condition must be complied with. For instance, if the offeror stipulates that the offer must be accepted in writing by post, a phone call indicating acceptance may not suffice. However, if an equally effective method or better method is used, this will suffice as acceptance. In *Tinn v Hoffman* (1873) 29 L.T. 271, Honeyman J. stated in obiter that a telegram, communication verbally or any other kind of communication that was at least as fast as a letter (the required method of acceptance in this case) would have sufficed. Furthermore, if the method of acceptance is stipulated for the benefit of the offeree (the person accepting the offer) rather than the offeror, the offeree is not obliged to use the stipulated method of acceptance (see *Yates Building Co v Pulleyn & Sons* (1975) 119 S.J. 370). However, as discussed above, a stipulation for silence cannot bind the offeree.

Acceptance Must Be Communicated

Acceptance must be communicated to the person who made the offer in order to be valid. Exceptions to this rule are set out below. The policy reason for this appears to be that the law wishes to avoid a situation where a person becomes bound by a contract without knowing it. It is suggested, for instance, that even where two people simultaneously post each other offers in the same terms ("cross-offers"), each made in ignorance of the other, there can be no acceptance as each party is ignorant of the other's acceptance. A contract cannot form, therefore, until acceptance is received.

In *Entores Ltd v Miles Far East Corp* [1955] 2 Q.B. 327, Lord Denning put forward a hypothetical example of this rule. Suppose A and B are standing on opposite sides of a river. A shouts an offer across the river to B. B shouts his acceptance in response, but due to a plane flying overhead, A does not hear B's message of acceptance. In such a case, because A is unaware of the acceptance, there is no contract. There can be no contract until the offeror is aware that the offeree has accepted. Lord Denning provided another example: where an offer is made over the telephone and the line goes dead in the middle of the offeree's reply. In such circumstances, the acceptance must be repeated before the contract is complete.

Parkgrange Investments v Shandon Park Mills (unreported, High Court, 2 May 1991) provides a good Irish example of such a scenario. Here, a contract signed by the defendant vendor of property did not constitute acceptance of the plaintiff's offer to buy it. The defendant only signed the contract to obtain tax clearance in case the sale actually went ahead. No acceptance was ever communicated to the purchaser and they remained ignorant of the acceptance until after litigation commenced and the document appeared in discovery. Carroll J. ruled that there had been no contract, partly because the defendant lacked the intention to accept, partly owing to the defendant's failure to communicate the acceptance to the other side.

Exceptions to the Communication Rule

Unilateral Contracts

Unilateral offers are accepted through the performance of an act. As such, communication of acceptance is generally unnecessary. The acceptance occurs when the act is completely performed.

The Offer Permits Acceptance without Communication

If the offer itself states that communication of acceptance is not required, an uncommunicated acceptance will bind the offeror. The offeror is deemed to have accepted the risk of becoming bound by a contract without their knowledge.

Offeror's Own Fault

It is generally accepted that where the offeror fails to hear of the acceptance because of their own conduct, the offer may nonetheless be accepted. An example might include a situation where a note of acceptance is received but not read.

The Postal Rule

The general rule discussed above (that a contract crystallises only when the offeror learns of acceptance) does *not* apply where communication of that acceptance is sent by post or by telegram. The so-called "postal rule" posits that when a letter (or telegram: see *Cowan v O'Connor* (1888) 20 Q.B.D. 640) of acceptance is sent through the post, the acceptance is deemed in law to have been made (a) at the time it was *posted* and (b) in the *place* it was posted. The policy reason underpinning this rule is one of convenience: historically, it was easier to verify the fact of postage as compared to the arrival or non-arrival of a letter. The postal rule was first established in the English case of *Adams v Lindsell* (1818) 1 B. & Ald. 681. Some Irish examples usefully demonstrate the operation of this rule.

In *Sanderson v Cunningham* [1919] 2 I.R. 234, a Dublin-based plaintiff had offered to purchase insurance from a London insurer. The insurer accepted the plaintiff's offer by issuing an insurance policy by letter from London. The Irish Court of Appeal ruled that because the acceptance had been posted from London, the contract had been concluded in London.

In *Dooley v Egan* (1938) 72 I.L.T.R. 155, the plaintiff, in Dublin, wrote to the defendant, in Cork, on 22 June and stated that it could supply a medical cabinet and six sterilising drums at a fixed price. The quotation was for "immediate acceptance only". The defendant, on 24 June, ordered two medical cabinets, not one. The plaintiff, on 26 June, agreed to supply said two medical cabinets. The court held that the letter of 22 June was an offer notwithstanding the fact that it was posed as a quotation. The reply of 24 June was a counter-offer and not acceptance as it sought to order two medical cabinets and not the one cabinet offered. This counter-offer was accepted in Dublin on 26 June by the plaintiff. As such, it was confirmed that the contract was formed in Dublin.

In *Kelly v Cruise Catering* [1994] 2 I.L.R.M. 394, an Irish employee was injured while working on a boat en route from Mexico to Texas. The Irish courts would only have the power to hear the case if the contract of employment was concluded in Ireland. In this case, the contract of employment was drafted in Oslo but was signed by the plaintiff in Dublin and returned to Norway by post. This being the case, the courts ruled that the contract was concluded in Ireland because the acceptance had occurred at the point of postage, not at the point of receipt.

Remarkably, the postal rule takes effect even if the letter in question is lost or delayed in the post, the offeror assuming the risk that the acceptance will be lost in the post. In *Household Fire Insurance v Grant* (1879) L.R. 4 Ex. 216, the defendant made an offer to take out an insurance policy. The plaintiff posted its acceptance. The letter never arrived. Notwithstanding this, the court held that the defendant was required to pay the insurance premiums. The rationale for this seemed to be that a letter handed to a postal worker constitutes communication to an agent of the offeror. This rationale clearly ignores the fact that the so-called agent is unaware of the contents of an envelope that they accept for postage. Where the loss or delay results from the fault of the offeree, as, for instance, where the offeree has misaddressed the letter, or paid insufficient postage, it would seem that acceptance will not occur at the point of postage.

As discussed above, where a letter of acceptance is put in the post before notification of a revocation is received, revocation will not be effective. In *Byrne v Van Tienhoven* (1880) 49 L.J.Q.B. 316, the defendants posted a letter offering to sell tin plates to the plaintiff on 1 October. The letter arrived on 11 October and on the same day the plaintiff telegrammed its acceptance, following this up with a letter posted on 15 October. However, on 8 October the defendant had posted a letter withdrawing the original offer. This did not reach the plaintiff until 20 October. While the postal rule dictated that acceptance of the offer occurred at the point of postage (the telegram was placed with the post office on 11 October and, failing that, a letter of acceptance was posted on 15 October, it was held that revocation did not occur until it was communicated to the offeree (20 October).

CASES WHERE THE POSTAL RULE DOES NOT APPLY

EXPRESS EXCLUSION OF RULE

It is possible to exclude the application of the postal rule by stipulating as a term of the offer that the offeror's *receipt* of acceptance is a precondition to the formation of a valid contract. This was successfully achieved by the defendant in *Holwell Securities v Hughes* [1974] 1 W.L.R. 155 who stipulated acceptance had to be made "by notice in writing" within six months of the offer. "Notice" here was held to mean that the defendant had to have knowledge of the acceptance. In *Nunin Holdings v Tullamarine Estates Property* [1994] 1 V.R. 74, the plaintiff stated in the offer that he would be bound "upon receipt by us of an identical contract". After the acceptance was posted but before the acceptance was received, the defendant telephoned revoking the posted acceptance. The rejection of the offer was deemed effective as it occurred before acceptance was received.

STIPULATION THAT ANOTHER MODE OF DELIVERY BE USED

The postal rule will not apply where the offeror has stipulated for a method of delivery other than the post, e.g. by telephone or courier. In *Trans-Pacific Trading v Rayonier Canada Ltd* (1998) 39 B.L.R. (2d) 306, the purchaser made an offer that required a faxed reply. The vendor accepted the offer by post. Before this letter arrived, the purchaser sent a fax revoking the offer. The vendor relied on the postal rule at trial. However, the court noted that the parties had been communicating entirely by telephone and fax throughout negotiations and the purchaser specifically limited the methods of acceptance in its offer to fax transmission.

MANIFEST INCONVENIENCE AND ABSURDITY

If the application of the postal rule would result in manifest inconvenience and absurdity, it will not apply. For example, where a postal strike was occurring.

Instantaneous Communication

Although the postal rule applies to telegrams, it does not apply where the method of communication is instantaneous, e.g. fax or telephone.

Entores Ltd v Miles Far East Corp [1955] 2 Q.B. 327 is authority for the proposition that the postal rule does not apply to a communication by telex (a form of electronic communication, similar to fax, whereby a message is typed into a special typewriter and conveyed via telephone lines to the recipient). In this case, a telex was sent from Amsterdam to London indicating acceptance of an offer. The court ruled that because telexes offered the possibility of virtually instantaneous communication, the postal rule did not apply. Acceptance, thus, was only concluded on *receipt* of the telex message, i.e. in England as opposed to at the point of dispatch in Amsterdam.

In *Brinkibon Ltd v Stahag Stahl GmbH* [1983] 2 A.C. 34, the House of Lords approved the *Entores* decision but noted that the rule therein (that where the postal rule does not apply, the formation of a contract occurs in the place and at the time that the acceptance is *received*, as opposed to at the point of dispatch) would not apply in circumstances where the "condition of simultaneity" was not met. Several examples were given by Lord Wilberforce where a telex dispatched by the sender may not be received instantaneously:

> "[M]essages may be sent out of office hours, or at night ... There may be some error or default at the recipient's end which prevents receipt at the time contemplated and believed in by the sender. The message may have been sent and/or received through machines operated by third persons."

Lord Wilberforce said that in such scenarios, "[n]o universal rule can cover all such cases; they must be resolved by reference to the intentions of the parties, by sound business practice and in some cases by a judgment where the risks should lie."

Modern Methods of Communication

It is likely that offers made while instant messaging or by using the "click-wrap method" (where an internet user clicks on a box to indicate acceptance of certain terms and conditions) are sufficiently instantaneous that they follow the same rule applicable to fax, telex and phone: that acceptance occurs at the time of receipt and not dispatch (i.e. the postal rule does not apply).

It is not clear whether the postal rule applies to email. Its application turns on whether or not email can be considered instantaneous. Email communication certainly can be quicker than regular post and several authors have described it as a form of instantaneous communication to be governed by the general rather than the postal rule. However, it may be argued that email is a "mediated" form of delivery. After all, there is no direct line of communication between sender and receiver, unlike with telephone, telex and fax. The moment an email is sent, it is routed from server to server via the Simple Mail Transfer Protocol (SMTP) until it makes its way to the recipient's email server. The incoming mail then sits on the server until the recipient accesses their email. There are also a number of issues that may impact successful receipt of an email that do not affect telex or fax correspondence, e.g. network failure, server downtime, a large attachment being blocked by the messaging service, and other technological and infrastructure issues.

There is no clear Irish decision on the applicability of the postal rule to emails. Applicability may well hinge on the facts of a case and reference should always be made to "how the communications are phrased, whether prescribed modes of acceptance exist and whether any statutory rules are in place" (Clark, *Contract Law in Ireland*, 9th edn (Dublin: Round Hall, 2022), para.1-65).

Where a party is negotiating *not* via email but through, for example, an interactive website, the European Communities (Directive 2000/31/EC) Regulations 2003 apply. Regulation 14 thereof provides that the relevant service provider shall "acknowledge" the receipt of an "order" without undue delay and by electronic means. Further, the order and acknowledgement of receipt are deemed to be received when the parties to whom they are addressed have access to them. It should be noted that the phrases used ("order" and "acknowledgement") are not necessarily the same as "offer and "acceptance".

Intention to Create Legal Relations

While negotiations may include an offer and purported acceptance, the resulting agreement may nonetheless fail to be enforceable if the parties did not intend to create legal relations. It is essential that parties have demonstrated through their actions or words the intention or belief that their contract should be legally binding. In other words: is it clear that the parties intended, objectively speaking, that if broken or otherwise in contention, the contract could be enforced in a court of law?

Take the following example: Harry invites Archie to go to the park to play football. Archie is delighted and accepts this invitation. It might be argued that there is both an offer and acceptance of a promise here. However, it is unlikely that the parties would reasonably be taken to have intended to have their agreement attract legal consequences. It is also notable that no consideration supports this contract, a topic that we shall discuss more fully in Chapter 6.

PRESUMPTIONS AGAINST AN INTENTION TO CREATE LEGAL RELATIONS

- There is a presumption (rebuttable if the contrary is proven) in law that where the agreement springs from a family, social or domestic relationship, it was *not* intended to attract legal relations.
- There is a presumption (rebuttable if the contrary is proven) in law that where the agreement is of a commercial nature, it *was* intended to attract legal relations.

As Budd J. noted in *Rogers v Smith* (unreported, Supreme Court, 16 July 1970):

> "[I]n social and family matters agreements may come to be which do not give rise to legal relations because such a consequence is not the intention of the parties, and in family matters, an intention to remain free of legal obligations will be readily implied whereas in business matters the opposite result would ordinarily follow."

Family Arrangements

According to O'Sullivan J. in *Leahy v Rawson* (unreported, High Court, 14 January 2003), the presumption that agreements between family members are not intended to create legal relations "appears to apply only to the closest family kinships such as parent and child and spouses." Where the presumption applied, it was held to be "only a presumption of fact which can be rebutted". In *Leahy* the relationship between the plaintiff and her non-marital partner's brother was deemed insufficiently close to attract the presumption.

Agreements between Spouses

The key decision in this area is *Balfour v Balfour* [1919] 2 K.B. 571, an English case where an agreement by a husband to the effect that he would maintain his wife was deemed not to be legally enforceable as there was presumed to be no intent to create legal relations. It is important to note, however, that at the time of the agreement, the marriage was still intact and the couple were on good terms. Such a conclusion would *not* apply where the parties made the agreement in the context of a relationship breakup, for example, where the parties were no longer living together. It would seem that the less amicable the relationship at the time of the agreement, the easier it will be to displace the presumption. It has also been suggested that if the parties in *Balfour* had asked a solicitor to draw up the agreement, this would have gone some way towards rebutting the presumption.

In *Courtney v Courtney* (1923) 57 I.L.T.R. 42, a contract between spouses to live separate and apart was upheld as enforceable. (See also *Merritt v Merritt* [1969] 2 All E.R. 760.)

Agreements between Other Family Members

Two Irish cases involving family property arrangements are instructive in this regard. In the Irish Supreme Court case of *Rogers v Smith* (unreported, Supreme Court, 16 July 1970), a mother promised her son that if he maintained her, the cost of supporting her would be recoverable when she died from her estate: "any money that I owe you when I am dead and gone you will probably take it from my estate." The Supreme Court held that this promise was made in the most general terms and therefore not seriously intended. Further, the son had given evidence that if the promise had not been made, he would have supported his mother regardless. This seemed to bolster the court's view that there was no intention to create legal relations here.

In *Mackey v Jones* (1959) 93 I.L.T.R. 177, the plaintiff had worked on his uncle's farm for some years without payment and claimed that his uncle had promised him the farm upon his death in return. When the farm was bequeathed to another relative, the plaintiff sued for breach of contract. Deale J. ruled, however, that no contract had crystallised. The uncle's representation amounted to a statement of intention or wish only, with no binding effects. In contrast, the Supreme Court in *McCarron v McCarron* (unreported, Supreme Court, 13 February 1997) recognised that a contract existed between the parties where the plaintiff (the defendant's first cousin) had worked long hours for the deceased without reward for 16 years. Here, compensation had been promised to the plaintiff by the defendant: "You will be a rich man after my day." The court was convinced that the plaintiff was telling the truth as to the nature and extent of the work completed and accepted his evidence as to the conversations that took place between the plaintiff and deceased. This rebutted the presumption that there was no intention to enter legal relations between the parties.

In *Jones v Padavatton* [1969] 1 W.L.R. 328, a mother and daughter entered into an agreement under which the mother agreed to maintain and accommodate her daughter if the daughter undertook studies for the Bar. The presumption that family arrangements did not attract legal relations was not, on the facts, displaced. Salmon L.J. indicated that the test for determining whether the presumption should be rebutted is objective: would a reasonable person, given the agreement and surrounding circumstances, have intended to create a legally binding agreement?

Rebutting the Presumption

The presumption that legal relations were not intended to be created between family members may be rebutted by evidence that legal relations *were* intended. A number of factors may be considered by the court in this regard:

- The degree of closeness between the parties (husband and wife relationships, for example, are very compelling: see *Leahy v Rawson*).
- The extent to which the promisee has relied on the promise (see *Rogers v Smith* where the son would have maintained his mother regardless of the promise; see also *K v K* below).
- The more vague and/or general the promise, the more likely that an absence of legal intent might be inferred (however, see *Simpkin v Pays* below).
- The less amicable the relationship between the parties, the more likely it is that there was an intention to create legal relations (see *Courtney v Courtney*).
- The more business-like the agreement, the more likely it is that the intention to create legal relations will arise, even between family members (see *Hynes v Hynes* below or *McCarron v McCarron* above).

On the final point, the case of *Hynes v Hynes* (unreported, High Court, 21 December 1984) is instructive. Here, an agreement between two brothers was held to amount to a contract notwithstanding the blood relationship that existed between the two. The agreement concerned the transfer of a business, owned and run by the plaintiff, to the defendant. It is notable that the subject matter of the contract, therefore, was commercial in nature. This seems to have provided added weight to the argument that the presumption should be displaced.

In the case of *K v K* [2018] IEHC 615, the plaintiff alleged that he was promised by his father and subsequently by his mother that a third of the family farm (approximately 90 acres) would be left to him upon his mother's death. The plaintiff had left school at the age of 15 to work on the farm and worked there without remuneration for 20 years. He also started, along with his mother and brothers, a successful family business on the farm. A rift in the family occurred and the plaintiff was asked to leave the family business in 2007. Upon her passing, it became clear that the mother did not make the provision promised to the plaintiff in her will. McDonald J. held that the promises made to the plaintiff could be upheld. Particular emphasis was placed on the plaintiff's reliance on the promise and the "substantial detriment" suffered by him in tying:

> "… himself to the family farm and the family business little knowing that he would subsequently find himself expelled from that business at a stage in his life when, as is well known, it is much more difficult to strike out into a new career. Equally, the plaintiff little knew that he would be expelled from the family business at a time when he had significant commitments, in particular the need to provide for his wife and two school-going children".

In several cases, agreements between friends regarding the sharing of competition winnings have been upheld, notwithstanding the relatively informal nature of the arrangements. For instance, in *Simpkins v Pays* [1955] 1 W.L.R. 975, a lodger living in the defendant's house won £750 in a Sunday newspaper competition. The defendant and her granddaughter, who had helped the lodger complete and pay for the entry, were held to be entitled to a share in the prize money.

COMMERCIAL AGREEMENTS

Contract law generally assumes that unless there is a clear statement to the contrary, parties to a commercial or business contract intended to create a legal relationship.

In fact, it is quite unusual to find a commercial contract where there was no intention to attract legal relations. The UK Supreme Court provided the following statement of the law as it pertains to legal intent cases in its judgment in *RTS Flexible Systems Ltd v Molkerei Alois Müller GmbH* [2010] UKSC 14:

> "The general principles are not in doubt. Whether there is a binding contract between the parties and, if so, upon what terms depends upon what they have agreed. It depends not upon their subjective state of mind, but upon a consideration of what was communicated between them by words or conduct, and whether that leads objectively to a conclusion that they intended to create legal relations and had agreed upon all the terms which they regarded or the law requires as essential for the formation of legally binding relations. Even if certain terms of economic or other significance to the parties have not been finalised, an objective appraisal of their words and conduct may lead to the conclusion that they did not intend agreement of such terms to be a pre-condition to a concluded and legally binding agreement."

It is clear, therefore, that an objective analysis will be required of the parties' words or conduct to ascertain whether the commercial contract was intended to attract legal relations. The fact that some economically essential terms or clauses are not present may not be detrimental to a finding that, objectively speaking, the parties intended for an enforceable contract to arise. This is also the case even where the negotiations leading to the contract were quite informal. It is possible, for instance, to make a binding agreement over a round of golf, or between cocktails at a business lunch. For instance, in *J. Evans & Son (Portsmouth) Ltd v Andrea Merzario Ltd* [1976] 2 All E.R. 930, an impromptu visit by a sales representative, making a courtesy call to a client, led to the conclusion of a binding contract, notwithstanding the informality of the arrangement. Likewise, in *Esso Petroleum v Commissioner of Customs and Excise* [1976] 1 All E.R. 117, a binding contract was deemed to arise from a transaction in which football tokens were offered to anyone who purchased four gallons of the plaintiff's petrol. According to Lord Simon, "the whole transaction took place in a setting of business relations", the purpose of the offer being commercial: Esso wanted the public to buy its petrol. In the case of *Cadbury Ireland Ltd v Kerry Co-operative Creameries Ltd* [1982] I.L.R.M. 77, the defendant acquired a creamery that had previously supplied milk to the plaintiff. The plaintiff claimed that the defendant had agreed to continue to supply milk to the plaintiff in a binding contract. Barrington J., however, held that the agreement was non-contractual despite the presumption viz. commercial agreements. The clause in question essentially amounted to an intention to draw up a clear and binding agreement at some time in the future.

In the absence of a subsequent agreement, this provision by itself was held to lack legal status. While informality may not be detrimental to a finding of legal intent, it is clearly important, from *Cadbury Ireland Ltd*, that the intention to create legal relations is objectively ascertainable from the alleged contract.

There are some exceptions to the general rule that commercial agreements attract legal relations.

Exaggerated Statements

Certain statements made in the course of contractual dealings may, by their very nature, not be intended to give rise to contractual liability. In particular, some statements made in the course of advertising cannot realistically be interpreted as having contractual force. For instance, a representation that a deodorant or cologne will have women or men (or both) chasing after you in romantic adulation or that a washing powder will clean your whites to the point that they are visible from space, would not reasonably be interpreted as a contractual promise. Such representations amount to "trader's puff", obvious exaggerations designed to draw in the punters but not meant to be taken seriously. (See *Smith v Lynn* (1954) 85 I.L.T.R. 57.)

Whether such statements give rise to legal relations is a matter of fact. The question to be asked is not whether the person making the representation *intended* it to be binding. The question is instead based on objective criteria: would the ordinary reasonable person take this statement as a serious promise? In *Carlill v Carbolic Smokeball Co* [1893] 1 Q.B. 256 (see Chapter 2), for instance, the court concluded that a promise that the use of a smokeball would prevent the user from contracting the flu was a genuine offer. The fact that the defendant had laid aside £1,000 to pay to users who did contract the flu was deemed to confirm the defendant's seriousness in making this offer.

The case of *Leonard v Pepsico, Inc* 88 F. Supp. 2d 116 (S.D.N.Y., 1999) is instructive. The case was initiated in the United States District Court for the Southern District of New York and related to a promotional loyalty programme launched by the defendant company in which customers could earn Pepsi Points by purchasing Pepsi products and could exchange these points for prizes. A television advertisement for the programme included the following examples: T-shirt 75 Pepsi Points, Leather Jacket 1,450 Pepsi Points, Shades 175 Pepsi Points. The advertisement concluded with the image of a young programme participant arriving at school in a Harrier Fighter Jet with the following message: "Harrier Fighter 7,000,000 Pepsi Points". The participant was shown laughing from the cockpit of the jet and remarking "sure beats the bus!". The plaintiff in this case discovered a loophole in the programme rules which allowed him to purchase Pepsi Points at 10c per point. He delivered a cheque for $700,008.50 to the plaintiff and attempted to purchase the Harrier Jet advertised for 7,000,000 Pepsi Points. The court denied recovery on several grounds including that the promise of a Harrier Fighter Jet to eligible programme participants was an example of trader's puff; no reasonable person would have believed the offer was seriously intended. The court noted as evidence of this that the jet itself was "the prized aircraft of the United States Marine Corps" and "[t]he teenager's comment that flying a Harrier Jet to school 'sure beats the bus' evinces an improbably insouciant attitude toward the relative difficulty and danger of piloting a fighter plane in a residential area."

Joke Offer

A similar principle applies to contracts made in jest, that is, as a result of what the parties intended to be a joke. The contract will not be enforceable if (but only if) it would have been clear to a reasonable bystander that agreement was meant to be a joke. The fact that one or other party to the contract did not seriously contemplate a sale will not be conclusive in this regard. The question is whether or not, from an objective standpoint, the parties can reasonably be deemed to have made a serious contract. In this regard, context is crucial. *Leonard v Pepsico, Inc* is also instructive here, as the court commented that the advertisement was "evidently done in jest".

Honour Clauses / Gentlemen's Agreements

Even in a commercial context, the presumption in favour of the intention to create legal relations can be displaced by a very clear expression of lack of legal intention. In other words, the parties may exclude the possibility of legal consequences by expressly stating that a breach of contract will not result in legal liability. A clause ousting legal jurisdiction in this way is sometimes called an "honour clause". The resulting agreement is often known as a "gentlemen's agreement": an agreement that is binding only as a matter of honour and not as a matter of law. A classic example of such a clause arose in *Rose and Frank Co v Crompton Bros* [1923] 2 K.B. 261. In this case, the parties had agreed that the plaintiff would be permitted to distribute the defendants' goods in the United States. The agreement, however, contained an "honourable pledge clause" based on past business which was "not entered into ... as a formal or legal agreement". Such confidence had clearly been misplaced, the defendants having withdrawn from the agreement. The English Court of Appeal concluded, however, that because of the honour clause set out above, the agreement could not be enforced. By this clause the parties had, the court ruled, unequivocally ruled out an intention to create a legally binding contract, and thus had agreed that a breach would not result in legal liability.

A similar clause served to exclude legal consequences in *Jones v Vernon's Pools Ltd* [1938] 2 All E.R. 626, a case involving a football pools coupon. The coupon contained a statement to the effect that any agreement or transaction in that case "shall not be attended by or give rise to any legal relationship, rights, duties or consequences whatsoever or be legally enforceable or the subject of litigation". Any agreement arising would be "binding in honour only", a condition that excluded the creation of a legal relationship.

In *Apicella v Scala* (1931) 66 I.L.T.R. 33, an agreement between parties regarding sweepstake tickets to be purchased by the defendant was described as a "conditional or revocable decision". As such, no contract arose.

It is evident, however, from *Edwards v Skyways Ltd* [1964] 1 All E.R. 494 that those wishing to avoid the creation of a legal relationship in a business context must express that intention clearly and unambiguously. In other words, in a commercial context, a very explicit statement is required to prevent a contract from giving rise to legal relations. Megaw L.J. stated in this case: "the onus is on the party who asserts that no legal effect was intended and the onus is a heavy one."

LETTERS OF COMFORT

A "letter of comfort" is similar in many respects to an honour clause. In short, a letter of comfort is a document designed to reassure its recipient regarding certain matters, without subjecting the writer to a contractual liability. Often, it is an assurance that the writer intends to maintain or adopt a particular position. Such a letter, in summary, simply sets out the current state of mind of the writer; it does not amount to an enforceable promise. While it may be useful in reassuring the recipient, the terms of the letter are not intended to give rise to a legal relationship.

Whether or not a statement amounts to a letter of comfort depends on the wording of the letter. A good example of the effects of a letter of comfort arose in *Kleinwort Benson Ltd v Malaysia Mining Corp Bhd* [1989] 1 All E.R. 785. In this case, the defendant owned a subsidiary company that traded in tin on the London Metal Exchange. It sought a credit facility from the plaintiff bank for the benefit of the subsidiary. In the course of negotiations for the loan, the defendant provided the following undertaking to the bank:

> "[I]t is our policy to ensure that the business of our subsidiary is at all times in a position to meet its liabilities to you."

The tin market collapsed and the plaintiff bank sued on this assurance. The English Court of Appeal concluded that this undertaking was drafted in such a way that it did not give rise to any promissory intent. As such, the statement did not bind the defendant. The letter was not purporting to make a binding promise. It was simply stating the company's policy, a policy that might be changed or adjusted in response to novel circumstances.

Clark in his text *Contract Law in Ireland*, 9th edn (Dublin: Round Hall, 2022) at para.3-27 notes that "[t]here is a considerable degree of uncertainty surrounding letters of comfort". Whether or not such a letter creates a legally binding promise is a matter to be discerned primarily from the language used. The simple fact that the words "letter of comfort" have been used, while evidentially relevant, may not conclusively prevent the agreement from having legal implications.

Letters of Intent

In contrast to a letter of comfort, this is issued to indicate the intention of a party to enter into a contract with the person to whom it is issued at some future point. The effect of such a letter will depend on its wording. The mere use of the phrase "letter of intent" will not necessarily be conclusive. A letter of intent might be issued when the parties are at negotiation stage, in order to induce the recipient to expend money or begin the contract work before the negotiations are finalised. In such cases, the courts will be positively disposed to finding that a contract exists. Reliance on the promise of reimbursement is key here. Where a letter of intent contains detailed terms and induces the expenditure of money by the recipient, it will be difficult to assert that it has no legal effect.

"Subject to Contract"

This phrase is used prevalently in relation to negotiations for the sale of land and is best viewed as a statement to the effect that the relevant arrangement is *not* a binding contract and is conditional on a final contract being concluded and signed by both parties. The vendor may wish to stipulate that an agreement is "subject to contract" in order to reserve the right to accept a better offer. The purchaser may want to invoke the phrase to keep the status quo in order to ensure that they have the requisite funds before committing in contract to the deal.

The leading Irish authority on this is *Thompson v The King* [1920] 2 I.R. 365 where, after significant negotiations, the plaintiff received a telegram from the defendant that read "will accept subject to contract ... £24,200 for Waterford factory". The plaintiff in response sent the following telegram: "we accept your offer ... at £24,200". The negotiations subsequently broke down and the plaintiff attempted to enforce his rights under contract. The King's Bench Divisional Court held that there was no concluded contract here and that the words used ("subject to contract") by the defendant indicated that no contractual obligation arose until a formal contract was settled, accepted and executed. In *Mulhall v Haren* [1981] I.R. 364, Costello J. likewise suggested that the phrase "subject to contract" precluded the enforcement of a contract, the parties having indicated that the matter was still subject to negotiation.

For a while, the courts drifted from this view. In *O'Flaherty v Arvan Property* (unreported, High Court, 3 November 1976), for example, the purchasers of property were given a receipt for the deposit they paid which contained all the material terms of the agreement, adding that same were "subject to contract". It was argued that during negotiations, nothing was said about the sale being "subject to contract". The High Court ruled that because the parties had not used this phrase during their negotiations, it had no effect now. This meant that agents of the parties (solicitors, auctioneers, etc.) could not add the "subject to contract" caveat after oral negotiations had concluded, if the parties had not themselves used this phrase during negotiations.

In *Casey v Irish Intercontinental Bank* [1979] I.R. 364, an auctioneer concluded an oral agreement with the plaintiff for the sale of certain lands to him by the defendants. The auctioneer prepared a document that purported to be a summary of the oral agreement, which stated that the oral agreement had been made "subject to contract and title". The High Court ordered specific performance of the oral agreements. The Supreme Court disallowed the defendants' appeals, holding as significant the fact that the words "subject to contract and title" had not been part of the oral agreements between the parties to date. (See also *Kelly v Park Hall Schools* [1979] I.R. 340.)

The Supreme Court decision in *Boyle and Boyle v Lee and Goyns* [1992] I.L.R.M. 65 re-examined the decisions in *Casey* and *Kelly*. Finlay C.J., Hederman J. and McCarthy J. doubted the soundness of the conclusions in these cases. Ultimately, it was found that the use of the phrase "subject to contract" in a note evidencing a contract is conclusive, and that a contract cannot be enforced where a note of the contract contains these words. The court observed that both *Kelly* and *Casey* turned on their own special facts. Therefore, it would seem that the Supreme Court has reverted back to the original position and that a note of an agreement, containing the words "subject to contract", cannot be contradicted by oral evidence that the parties in fact intended their contract to be conclusive and not subject to any further negotiation. There is a ring of sense to this conclusion: a note denying the existence of a final contract could hardly be fairly used to enforce the very contract it denies.

However, two more recent cases have demonstrated that equity may intervene if one party tries to *unconscionably* rely on the "subject to contract" verbiage. In *Prunty v Crowley* [2016] IEHC 293, for example, a landowner and a developer had entered a contract for the sale of a piece of land. When relations broke down, specific performance proceedings were initiated by the landowner. The developer wrote to the landowner and stated, "subject to contract", that if the proceedings were discontinued, he would discharge the balance of monies and complete the transaction. The proceedings were discontinued but the developer did not complete. The court held that despite the use of the phrase "subject to contract", the letter was an:

> "... unequivocal inducement to the plaintiff to surrender his claim against [the developer] on the basis that, once he did so, he could have the €99,000. That, in my view, could only be seen as amounting to an implicit promise ... and that the 'subject to contract' phrase would not be relied upon."

In the Supreme Court case of *JLT Financial Services Ltd v Gannon* [2017] IESC 70, two landowners carried out businesses from adjoining premises. Both were seeking to expand their businesses and so proposed to enter into transactions whereby landowner A would acquire the neighbouring site from landowner B and landowner B would be granted a lease over land owned by landowner A elsewhere. Although the latter lease was successfully concluded, landowner A sought to terminate negotiations on the acquisition of the neighbouring site from B. Correspondence between the parties was marked "subject to contract". The court held that these two agreements amounted to a "package" and that it would be unconscionable and a breach of good faith to allow landowner A to avoid his contractual liability when landowner B had executed his obligations.

In summation then, recent case law seems to indicate that equity will not allow the terms "subject to contract" to protect a party if:

(a) the letter containing the words amounts to an "unequivocal inducement" for the other party to act to its detriment and is relied upon as such; or
(b) if the correspondence concerns a "package" of agreements such that it would be "unconscionable" or a "breach of good faith" to allow one party to rely on the "subject to contract" formulation to avoid liability.

This is particularly so, it would seem, where the court has found that there was a clear intention to contract between the parties or where there has been some part performance of the obligations under that contract.

Other phrases have been taken to have the same effect as "subject to contract" when used instead. For instance, in *Silver Wraith v Siúicre Éireann* (unreported, High Court, 8 June 1989), the defendants sent the plaintiff a letter setting out the terms of agreement and stating that "the following terms are acceptable subject to full lease terms being agreed." On the facts, the court concluded that there was no final contract. In *The Lisheen Mine v Mullock and Sons (Shipbrokers) Ltd* [2015] IEHC 50, the court held that emails identifying the agreed terms but adding the words "subject to details" amounted to the same thing as the inclusion of the words "subject to contract", namely that no agreement existed until a contract was finalised and executed. In *Irish Mainport Holdings Ltd v Crosshaven Sailing Centre Ltd* (unreported, High Court, 14 October 1980), however, the words "my Board have agreed in principle" were held not to have the same effect as the words "subject to contract".

The Requirement of Certainty

Introduction

A contract will not be enforced unless its terms are sufficiently clear and certain. Thus, the terms of a contract should generally not be vague, ambiguous or insusceptible to clarification.

For instance, in *Scammell v Ouston* [1941] A.C. 251, a contract agreeing that the balance for the purchase of a van would be paid "on hire-purchase terms" was deemed too vague to be enforced. Given the diversity of hire-purchase arrangements that might be entered into, it was ultimately unclear to the court what was meant in this context by the phrase "hire-purchase terms".

Similarly, in *Loftus v Roberts* (1902) 18 T.L.R. 532, a contract promising to pay an actor a "West End salary to be mutually agreed between us" was held to be uncertain as to the salary (as it was again unclear that there was any such thing as a standard "West End salary"—a leading actress and a chorus girl would receive significantly different rates) and thus unenforceable.

In *Mackie v Wilde* [1998] 2 I.R. 578, the plaintiff had agreed to issue the defendant 25 annual fishing permits and "a few day tickets" for fishing. The Supreme Court ruled that as the quantity of day tickets available was uncertain, the contract could not be enforced. The promise to supply annual fishing permits, moreover, could not be severed from the agreement regarding the day tickets: thus the whole contract was rendered unenforceable.

Likewise, in *Central Meat Products v Carney* (1944) 10 Ir. Jur. Rep. 34, an action was brought to prevent the sale of cattle by the defendant to third parties. The plaintiff argued that an agreement existed between the parties whereby all cattle acquired by the defendant for canning purposes would be sold to the plaintiff. The court held there was no contract capable of being enforced here as it was clear that there had been no agreement on issues that were important to this specific contract, e.g. price variation clauses and insurance arrangements.

At a minimum, there should be clarity as to the three Ps: the "parties" (who is contracting), the "price", and the "property" (the subject matter) of the agreement. That is not to say, however, that unless every contingency is provided for, the contract will be doomed. It may not always be feasible, especially in a contract that is intended to endure for an indefinite time, to provide for every possible eventuality. Some flexibility may be required.

METHODS OF CLARIFICATION

Notwithstanding the above, the courts in general have proved quite reluctant to rule that a contract is unenforceable. If the courts can clarify ambiguous aspects of the contract, then they will make every effort to do so. Over the years, a variety of techniques have been developed by which judges may avoid a finding of uncertainty.

WHERE THERE IS A PROVISION FOR CLARIFICATION

It may be that the contract contains an arbitration or mediation clause in the event that a dispute arises over its terms. In *Foley v Classique Coaches* [1934] 2 K.B. 1, a contract provided that the price to be paid under the contract would be agreed from time to time. Despite this uncertainty, the contract was upheld on the grounds that the agreement itself provided that any dispute over the price was to be resolved by an arbitrator.

PAROL (ORAL) EVIDENCE

The introduction of evidence as to the orally expressed understanding between the parties may be of assistance in clarifying ambiguity where a term is capable of being interpreted in a number of ways. In *ESB v Newman* (1933) 67 I.L.T.R. 124, the defendant had agreed to indemnify a customer of the ESB in respect of her liability to pay for electricity. The customer in fact had a number of accounts with the ESB, in respect of a variety of premises, and it was unclear initially whether the defendant had agreed to indemnify the customer in respect of all the accounts or just one. Using oral evidence, however, the court concluded that the agreement related to only one premises.

TERMS MAY BE IMPLIED BY STATUTE

The provisions of legislation (e.g. consumer legislation) may rectify an apparent ambiguity by implying certain terms into a contract. This is discussed further below.

TERMS MAY BE IMPLIED BY REFERENCE TO PRINCIPLE OF REASONABLENESS

In some cases, the courts may imply terms into a contract by reference to the principle of reasonableness. In such cases, the courts look to what one might reasonably infer from the context in which the agreement was made and the conduct of the parties. Again, it is not for the court to make a bad bargain better for the parties. The question to be asked here is whether it is reasonable to assume that the parties actually intended this term to arise. The "officious bystander" test is often used to answer this: would an officious (albeit neutral) bystander, observing the behaviour and statements of the parties, have reasonably assumed such a term to have been included? Another way of stating this is as follows: if the officious bystander were to have asked the parties if they intended to include such a term, how would the parties have reacted? If they would have said "yes, of course", the term will most likely be included.

Terms that Give Business Efficacy to a Contract

In some cases, the courts will imply into a contract terms that are reasonably necessary to give the contract "business efficacy", in other words, to give effect to the commercial expectations of the parties. This is discussed further below; in particular, see the discussion of *The Moorcock* (1889) 14 P.D. 64, which is very pertinent in this regard.

Terms May Be Implied by a Previous Course of Dealing or by the Custom of a Trade

A term may be implied into a contract by reference to prior dealings, provided the prior dealings are sufficiently frequent and consistent to justify the inclusion of the term. For instance, in *Spurling v Bradshaw* [1956] 1 W.L.R. 461, an exclusion clause was deemed to be incorporated into a contract in circumstances where it had been expressly included in prior contracts between the parties. Although the clause was not expressly notified to the defendant until after the particular contract was concluded, the clause was deemed to have been incorporated, as it had consistently been included in previous dealings between the parties. Such implications may serve to clarify an otherwise uncertain contract.

The custom of a trade may also supply such clarity if both parties are familiar with such customs and provided the customs are sufficiently well established. In *Hillas v Arcos* (1932) 147 L.T. 503, for instance, the contracting parties were deemed to be bound by terms common to the timber business, of which both parties had considerable experience. A similar conclusion arose from *Lynch Roofing Systems (Ballaghaderreen) Ltd v Bennett and Son* [1999] 2 I.R. 450, where an arbitration clause was implied into a contract, such clauses being common in the building trade.

6 Consideration

Introduction

Even where there is a valid offer and unconditional acceptance thereof, as well as an intention to create legal relations, a contract will not be enforceable unless at least one of the following conditions is met:

(a) The contract has been made in a deed under seal that has been signed by both parties. A deed is a formal legal document affixed with a seal (this is usually done by placing a red sticker on the deed and drawing a circle enclosing the letters "L.S."). Where a contract is contained in a deed that has been "signed, sealed and delivered", no consideration is required. Deeds under seal are used most often in family or partnership matters. A deed must be drawn up for the purpose of conveying an estate or interest in land. In normal business practice, deeds under seal are not used.

(b) The contract is supported by consideration.

Consideration as a Concept

The English common law dictates that in order for a promise to be enforceable, it must be exchanged for something of tangible value. This may include, for example: money, a good or item of property, a service or a promise to deliver any of the above. In *Currie v Misa* (1875) L.R. 10 Ex. 153, Lush J. defined consideration as "some right, interest, profit or benefit accruing to one party, or some forbearance, detriment, loss or responsibility, given, suffered or undertaken by the other".

Consider the following example: if Ivan promises to give his motorbike to Alex, this promise alone, without more, is not enforceable and may be seen as the promise of a gift. However, if Ivan gives his motorbike to Alex and in exchange Alex promises to give Ivan €1,000, the promise is now supported by consideration sufficient to give rise to a contract.

Generally, it is the person *to whom the promise is made* (the promisee) that is the party that must act or forbear in exchange for the promise. Indeed, Sir Frederick Pollock describes consideration as "the price for which the promise of the other is bought" (*Principles of Contract*, 8th edn (London: Stevens & Sons, 1911)).

The act or forbearance must be something of value; something that the courts can put a price on. In *O'Keeffe v Ryanair Holdings plc* [2003] 1 I.L.R.M. 14, for example, the plaintiff was the one-millionth customer of a well-known airline and had been promised free flights for life in recognition of this event. In exchange, Ms O'Keeffe had participated in publicity, appearing in the media. The free flights were not a gift, the High Court ruled. Ms O'Keeffe had provided consideration that had value: she had surrendered her anonymity and privacy for the benefit of the airline and her active participation in the publicity that was created constituted conduct sufficient to support a contract.

CONSIDERATION MUST MOVE FROM THE PROMISEE

As discussed above, in order for the contract to be enforceable, the consideration must "move from the promisee". This means that a person to whom a promise is made may not enforce a contractual promise unless that person herself has personally provided consideration in exchange. It is not possible, thus, for a promisee to rely on consideration provided by a third party. *Tweddle v Atkinson* (1861) 1 B. & S. 393 provides a classic example of this rule. In that case, the plaintiff, Mr Tweddle, was happily engaged to a young lady. In anticipation of the couple's marriage, the plaintiff's father and future father-in-law had promised each other that they would both give money to the plaintiff once the couple had wed. However, before the money was paid, the plaintiff's father-in-law had died. The plaintiff sued for the promised money, but as the plaintiff himself had not provided any consideration for the promise, he was not entitled to stake his claim. In the Irish case of *McCoubray v Thompson* (1868) 2 I.R.C.L. 226, the owner of a farm had agreed to give the land to the defendant if he agreed to pay half the value of the farm to McCoubray, a third party. When the land was transferred to the defendant, he refused to pay the promised sum to McCoubray. McCoubray sued for the sum promised but, as consideration had not been provided by him personally, he was not permitted to rely on the contract as between the owner of the farm and the defendant.

CONSIDERATION NEED NOT MOVE TO THE PROMISOR

It is not necessary, however, that the person who made the promise (the promiser) receive any benefit from the consideration. In fact, it is perfectly feasible for a third party to receive the benefit arising, if any.

In the US case of *Hamer v Sidway* 124 N.Y. 538 (1891), an uncle offered to pay his nephew $5,000 if he rejected alcohol, smoking and gambling and thus lived a life of virtue while he was studying at university. The promise was deemed to be enforceable on the basis that the nephew had forgone these "vices", even though his uncle was not likely to get any tangible benefit from his forbearance. (It is worth considering whether there would have been good consideration if the nephew had no interest in these matters.) Similarly, in *Jones v Padavatton* [1969] 1 W.L.R. 328, at the request of her mother, a woman gave up her job in the US to study in England. Although the mother did not stand to benefit from this arrangement, the consideration was valid (though the contract failed on other grounds: the court held that there had been no intention to create legal relations).

Sometimes judges find valuable consideration even where it is arguable that the benefit derived from a contract is wholly one-sided. In *North Ocean Shipping v Hyundai* [1979] Q.B. 705, Hyundai were shipbuilders who had agreed to build an oil tanker for North Ocean Shipping. The price was payable in five instalments. Hyundai agreed to a reverse letter of credit for repayment of the instalments should they have to default on construction. After the first payment, the US dollar devalued by 10%. As a result, Hyundai asked for a 10% increase in the building price on the subsequent instalments. North Ocean Shipping reluctantly agreed to the increase. After the tanker was delivered, North Ocean Shipping tried to claim the return of the additional 10% paid on the final instalments. It argued that there had been no consideration given for this price increase. The court noted that when the price increased, the reverse letter of credit was also increased by Hyundai and this served as consideration for the increased payments under the contract.

Consideration Must Have Some Tangible Value

Consideration must consist of something that the law regards as having some objective or tangible value (though the value may be nominal—indeed, the term "peppercorn rent" is sometimes used to describe an item of nominal value given in return for a promise). In this way, while consideration need not be *adequate* (see Chapter 1 and the right to enter a bad or foolish bargain), it must be *sufficient*. The law does not, for instance, regard prayers, or a promise to say prayers, as good consideration. In the case of *O'Neill v Murphy* [1936] N.I. 16, for instance, the Northern Ireland Court of Appeal refused to enforce a contract under which a religious order of nuns promised to pray for the intentions of a builder who was to carry out repairs to their convent. Prayers were too intangible, the court reasoned, to amount to good consideration. Rather, they amounted to "a mere voluntary courtesy". Similarly, in *White v Bluett* (1853) 23 L.J. Ex. 36, a son's promise to stop complaining to his father was deemed unenforceable, such a promise having no objectively quantifiable value.

However, in *Thomas v Thomas* (1842) 2 Q.B. 851, a widow paid £1 a year in exchange for the occupation of a house, the market rental value of which being considerably more than this nominal sum. Nonetheless, the court concluded that even this very nominal sum constituted consideration notwithstanding the fact that considerably more could have been obtained on the open market.

In *Chappell and Co Ltd v Nestlé Ltd* [1960] A.C. 87, the purchasers of a chocolate bar made by Nestlé could buy a record of "Rockin' Shoes" by sending Nestlé one shilling and six pence together with three empty chocolate wrappers. Chappell and Co, who owned the copyright in this song, sued Nestlé for royalties arising from the promotion. In doing so, Chappell claimed that the monies made by Nestlé should include not only the monetary price collected for each record but also the cumulative value of the wrappers, which, they argued, formed part of the consideration for the agreement to post the record. The House of Lords concluded that although Nestlé considered them to be of no value, the wrappers did form part of consideration. In other words, however trifling it may have been, the wrappers had some tangible value, and this was enough to render them good consideration.

This may be contrasted with the case of *Lipkin Gorman v Karpnale* [1991] 3 W.L.R. 10, where the House of Lords rejected the argument that when a casino gave out gaming chips, this constituted valuable, or sufficient, consideration. The chips were never forgone, they remained at all times the property of the casino, and were a device for enabling gambling to be conducted.

It is worth noting, additionally, that although the *inadequacy* (as opposed to insufficiency) of consideration may not be relevant in the formation of a contract, it may provide cogent evidence of fraud or unconscionability. For instance, in *Noonan (A Ward of Court) v O'Connell* (unreported, High Court, 10 April 1987), the sale of land at a grossly inadequate price, 50p, was struck down as unconscionable on the basis that the plaintiff, a man suffering from senile dementia, had been the victim of an unconscionable bargain. Here there was a serious inequality in the position of the plaintiff and defendant. Had the transfer been negotiated as between parties of more equal standing, the fact that the land was to be sold at such a nominal price may not have been an impediment to the enforceability of the contract. To summarise then, a peppercorn rent may still constitute good consideration but may lead to unenforceability if it helps to prove fraud or unconscionability.

Insufficient Consideration

Past Consideration Is No Consideration

Consideration cannot be used to support a contract where the consideration was given or acquired in the past, before the promise was made. If a promise is made after some gratuitous act has been performed by the promisee, the subsequent promise cannot be said to be supported by consideration. In other words, one cannot rely on a benefit already given as consideration for a new promise.

Take the following example: last week, unbeknownst to her, Mark washed Laura's car out of the kindness of his heart. Laura subsequently promises to pay Mark €50 for having done so. Because the €50 was not given in the context of an original exchange of promises, no contract may result. Mark's original unsolicited act of goodwill cannot constitute good consideration for this subsequent promise.

The classic example of this rule is provided by *Roscorla v Thomas* (1842) 3 Q.B. 234. In this case, the defendant sold a horse to the plaintiff. After the sale, the defendant stated that the horse was "sound and free from vice". The horse in fact turned out to be quite vicious and the plaintiff sued upon this apparent warranty. However, because the warranty was given after the sale had been completed, the warranty was not supported by consideration and could therefore not be relied upon. In *Smyth v Morrison* 10 Ir. Law Rep. 213, a similar situation was distinguished from *Roscorla*. Here the sale of a horse took place at the same time as the warranty about its soundness was given. As such, the transaction did not fall foul of the rule against past consideration. In *Morgan v Rainsford* (1845) 8 Ir. E.R. 299, improvements to a property which had already been made before another contract was entered into were deemed insufficient consideration for this subsequent contract. In the Northern Irish case of *Provincial Bank of Ireland v O'Donnell* (1932) 67 I.L.T.R. 142, the court ruled that monies loaned by a bank in the past did not amount to consideration supporting a subsequent contract.

Exception

A promise made after the promisee has conferred a benefit on another person *may* be enforceable if the exception in *Lampleigh v Braithwait* (1615) Hob. 105 applies.

This case dictates that past consideration *may* be considered good consideration where:

- the past consideration was given at the *request* of the *promisor*; and
- compensation had been *anticipated* for the service given.

The important distinction is that in these sorts of cases, the parties are taken not to have meant for the past consideration (i.e. an act or forbearance) to be gratuitous. In *Lampleigh v Braithwait*, Braithwait had killed a man and asked Lampleigh to travel to London to obtain for him a royal pardon. Lampleigh was successful and upon return with the pardon, Braithwait promised to pay Lampleigh £100 for his trouble. While the consideration for this reward (obtaining the pardon) was technically past, the court found that the promise was nonetheless enforceable. The court held that although no promise of reward was forthcoming at the time of the promisor's original request to travel to London to obtain the pardon, there was an implied understanding and anticipation that a fee would be paid.

Lampleigh was applied in the Irish case of *Bradford v Roulston* (1858) 8 I.R.C.L. 468. Roulston was employed by Bradford to source a buyer for Bradford's boat. Eventually, a buyer was found but when the bill of sale was to be completed, the buyer did not have sufficient funds to complete the transaction. Bradford resolved to withdraw from the transaction but Roulston urged him to sign the bill of sale, providing credit to the purchaser. After he signed it, Roulston promised in writing that he would ensure payment the following day. The consideration here was technically past; however, Pigot C.B. held that "[w]here there is a past consideration, consisting of a previous act done at the request of the defendant, it will support a subsequent promise; the promise being treated as coupled with the previous request". Here, Bradford could argue that he was entitled to the sum promised by Roulston because he had signed the bill of sale at Roulston's behest and had anticipated the fee would be paid.

The conditions for the satisfaction of this exception were summarised by Lord Scarman in *Pao On v Lau Yiu Long* [1980] A.C. 614:

1. The act must have been carried out at the promisor's request.
2. There must have been an understanding that the promisee would be remunerated either by payment or the conferral of some benefit.
3. The promise to pay, had it been promised in advance, would have been enforceable.

A Promise to Do What One Is Already Obliged by Law or Contract to Do Is Not Good Consideration

Consideration will also be insufficient if it takes the form of an act or forbearance that one is already obliged to do. For example, an appearance in court on foot of a subpoena would not constitute good consideration, as this act is required under law. This was the case in *Collins v Godefroy* (1831) 1

B. & Ad. 950, where the plaintiff had been promised six guineas to testify in a case in respect of which he had already been subpoenaed to give evidence. It was held that the giving of evidence did not constitute good consideration for the promise.

In *Glasbrook Bros v Glamorgan County Council* [1925] A.C. 270, the appellants sought police protection and security of their coal mine during a mining strike. The police had offered to pay occasional visits to check up on the mine, but the mine owners had insisted on a permanent police presence and agreed to pay £2,200 for this extra service. The mine owners subsequently reneged on this promise, arguing that the police were already obliged to provide such protection. The House of Lords ruled that because the mine owners had been afforded a service over and above that which the police reasonably believed to be appropriate, sufficient consideration had been provided.

In *Leeds United Football Club v Chief Constable of West Yorkshire Police* [2013] EWCA Civ 115, the court underscored the importance of differentiating between policing services that are aimed at preventing crime and so-called "special police services". Policing football matches on private land, for example, would require the exercise of special police services. This scheduled service may be contrasted with a situation where the police are called to respond to violence that spontaneously breaks out at a football match or the policing of the "extended footprint" of the streets around the grounds of a football stadium, the latter two activities being examples of services provided in furtherance to a duty already owed to the public as opposed to "special services". (See also *Harris v Sheffield United Football Club* [1988] Q.B. 77.)

In *Stilk v Myrick* (1809) 2 Camp. 317, after two of their shipmates had deserted, the remaining sailors on a ship demanded and were promised extra pay to perform certain duties. However, under their contract the sailors had already agreed to do whatever was required of them to sail the ship. As the sailors were already obliged to perform these duties if called on to do so, the promise was not supported by consideration.

In contrast, in *Hartley v Ponsonby* (1857) 7 E. & B. 872, Ponsonby was the captain of a ship. The plaintiff was part of the crew. On a voyage, the majority of the crew deserted. The remaining crew was so small as to increase significantly the danger of sailing the ship. The captain, in order to persuade the remaining crew to stay onboard and man the vessel, promised extra wages. When the voyage was completed, he refused to pay what he promised and the plaintiff sued for breach of contract. Lord Campbell C.J. distinguished this case from *Stilk v Myrick*, holding that here, the number of crewmen deserting changed the nature of the remaining sailors' duties to the point that the original contract could be said to have been discharged. In this way, the offer by the captain to pay the remaining crew extra wages to complete the voyage and the acceptance of the crew of this promise could be considered an entirely new contract supported by fresh consideration.

In *Ward v Byham* [1956] 2 All E.R. 318, a father promised to pay the mother of his child £1 per week in exchange for her caring for that child. Although a person is already obliged, by law, to care for any child in her custody, the mother had agreed to do more than this: she had promised to make sure the daughter was happy and to allow the daughter to choose her preferred place of residence. These additional benefits persuaded the court that sufficient consideration was provided for the £1 per week.

However, in *Williams v Williams* [1957] 1 W.L.R. 148, a different approach was entertained by Denning L.J., albeit in obiter comment. Here, a husband promised to pay £1 10s to his wife every week if she maintained herself and lived apart from him. Notwithstanding the argument that the wife in her "desertion" of the husband was required to maintain herself, Denning L.J. held that "a promise to perform an existing duty is, I think, sufficient consideration to support a promise, so long as there is nothing in the transaction which is contrary to the public interest".

In *McHugh v Kildare County Council* [2006] 1 I.R. 100, the plaintiff agreed to transfer 20% of his lands to the council if it would rezone the remainder of his lands. The plaintiff subsequently sought to withdraw from the agreement, arguing that the council owed an existing legal duty to consider rezoning applications without reward. Gilligan J. rejected this and approved Denning L.J.'s approach in *Williams*.

Both approaches were considered in *North Ocean Shipping v Hyundai* [1978] 3 All E.R. 1170. Here, Morcatta J. seemed to suggest that if the duty owed arises under statute, then performance of it may be sufficient consideration for a promise. However, Morcatta J. held that if the duty owed is a contractual obligation, it cannot provide consideration for a subsequent promise.

In *Kenny v An Post* [1988] J.I.S.L.L. 187, O'Hanlon J. reiterated the traditional approach as laid down in *Stilk v Myrick*.

However, some flexibility was provided in *Williams v Roffey Bros & Nicholls (Contractors) Ltd* [1990] 1 All E.R. 512. Here, the defendant was a contractor who subcontracted with the plaintiff for the refurbishment of a roof and the interior of 27 flats. The original price for the works was £20,000, to be paid in instalments as work was completed. The plaintiff subsequently realised that the agreed sum would not cover his costs, and finding himself in financial difficulty, the plaintiff requested a further £10,000 to finish the construction. The defendant reluctantly agreed but relied in court on *Stilk v Myrick*; that because the plaintiff was only promising to do what he was already bound to do for the defendant, the promise to pay an additional amount was unenforceable for want of consideration. Notwithstanding the fact that the plaintiff had already agreed to complete the work under the initial contract, the English Court of Appeal concluded that fresh consideration had been given in exchange for the agreement to pay the additional money. The court took a practical approach, reasoning that although the plaintiff was already obliged to finish the work, there was a real risk in this case that (without the extra finance) the work would not in fact be finished. The court further reasoned that given the possibility that Roffey would incur penalty costs for late completion of the project, it was, in practice, receiving an additional benefit for payment of the money. Consideration was also said to arise from the fact that an ad hoc system of payment was replaced with a more structured payment system. Glidewell L.J. stated that the law supported the following:

"(i) if A has entered into a contract with B to do work for, or to supply goods or services to B in return for payment by B and
(ii) at some stage before A has completely performed his obligations under the contract B has reason to doubt whether A will, or will be able to, complete his side of the bargain and
(iii) B thereupon promises A an additional payment in return for A's promise to perform his contractual obligations on time and
(iv) as a result of giving his promise B obtains in practice a benefit, or obviates a disbenefit, and
(v) B's promise is not given as a result of economic duress or fraud on the part of A, then;
(vi) the benefit to B is capable of being consideration for B's promise, so that the promise will be legally binding."

Clark in his text *Contract Law in Ireland*, 9th edn (Dublin: Round Hall, 2022) at para.2-22 has noted that *Williams v Roffey* has been held to apply only in cases where the promise by A involves providing services to B in return for B's promise of additional payment.

Performance of a duty owed to someone other than the promisor may support a subsequent promise. For instance: Chris owes Mary €4,000 for her car. Chris then promises Joel that he will pay Mary €4,000, if Joel pays the insurance on the car. Although Chris is already obliged to pay Mary the €4,000, he has nonetheless provided good consideration for Joel's agreement to pay the insurance. This is because Joel now has a right to sue Chris should Chris fail to pay Mary, a right he did not have previously (remember that although consideration must flow from the promisee, it need not necessarily flow *to* the promisor, in this case Joel).

In *Shadwell v Shadwell* (1860) 9 C.B. (N.S.) 159, the plaintiff, a budding barrister, had been engaged to marry a young woman. In recognition, his uncle offered him £150 a year until he was earning 600 guineas a year, provided that he married his betrothed. At that time, a promise to marry was enforceable at law, and the plaintiff was already obliged to marry his wife-to-be. Nonetheless, as he had taken on an obligation to a person other than his bride, the uncle's promise was deemed to be enforceable. (See also *Scotson v Pegg* (1861) 6 H. & N. 295.)

Part Payment of a Debt

Where a person owes money, a promise by the creditor to take a lesser sum in full satisfaction of the larger debt will not bind the creditor. The creditor would still be able to sue for the full amount. This is also known as the rule in *Pinnel's Case* (1602) 5 Co. Rep. 117a. In this case, a Mr Cole owed Pinnel £8 10s, due on 11 November. On 1 October, Pinnel had accepted £5 2s 6d in full settlement. The court set down the general rule, being that "payment of a lesser sum on the day in satisfaction of a greater cannot be any satisfaction for the whole". However, the court also recognised that in in this case, something extra was provided by Mr Cole suffice to constitute fresh consideration: the fact that the payment had been made before the deadline. The court stated:

> "[A] change in time or mode of payment, or the addition by the debtor of a tomtit or canary or the like will suffice to constitute [fresh] consideration".

In other words, by paying some money early, Mr Cole had provided Pinnel with a further benefit rather than just repaying part of the money he already owed. This further benefit constituted consideration for the promise to take a lesser sum in full satisfaction of the larger debt.

In *Foakes v Beer* (1884) 9 App. Cas. 605, as a result of a judgment against him, Dr Foakes owed Mrs Beer £2,090 plus interest. Beer gave Foakes a promise that if he paid £500 and the remainder in instalments (making no mention of the interest), she would not take any proceedings against him. Subsequently, Beer sought to recover the interest and was permitted to do so by the court. The promise to accept a lesser sum in full satisfaction of the larger debt was deemed not to be enforceable.

It should be noted that the decision in *Re Selectmove* [1995] 2 All E.R. 531 (followed by Keane J. in *Truck and Machinery Sales Ltd v Marubeni Komatsu Ltd* (unreported, High Court, 23 February 1996)) makes it clear that *Roffey Brothers* (discussed above) does not change the rule that payment of part of a debt will not constitute consideration for a promise to forgo the remainder of the debt.

There are certain exceptions to the rule that part payment does not constitute good consideration:

- Where the claim is disputed, the parties may decide that it is preferable to settle the matter rather than proceed to court. In such a case, the payment of a lesser sum, in settlement, will be supported by consideration.
- Where the amount of the claim is genuinely disputed or is uncertain, an agreement to part pay the debt may be valid.
- Where the amount paid is the result of a composition with creditors on liquidation or bankruptcy (i.e. a trader has a large number of creditors and faces bankruptcy. In the event of this happening, the creditors will run the risk of being paid little or nothing. It is therefore in the creditors' interests to receive payment of a lesser sum by agreement or composition).
- Where the payment is made by a third party. For example, in *Hirachand Punamchand v Temple* [1911] 2 K.B. 330, an army officer owed a moneylender a debt. The moneylender accepted payment of a lesser sum from the officer's father in full settlement of the whole debt, and this was said to be sufficient consideration.

Promissory Estoppel

INTRODUCTION

Where a person, A, makes a representation to B that they will not rely on their strict contractual rights, and B acts on this representation, B may legally prevent A from acting in contravention of the representation. This may occur even where no consideration exists for the new promise not to rely on one's strict contractual rights. This is called "promissory estoppel". It is an equitable remedy preventing a person from going back on their word where they have indicated that they will not rely on their strict rights under the contract. Although it is closely related to "estoppel by representation" at common law, equitable estoppel is in fact a much broader and more flexible concept. It is important to note that the estoppel does not arise simply on foot of a person's representation, without more. The estoppel is said to arise because the person to whom the representation is made has *relied* on the representation. It is the reliance that gives rise to the estoppel, not the representation.

THE *HIGH TREES* PRINCIPLE

The classic example of this principle is provided by Denning J. in *Central London Property Trust Ltd v High Trees House Ltd* [1947] K.B. 130. High Trees House was a London block of flats and was subject to a 99-year lease. The defendant company leased the flats from the plaintiff company. After the outbreak of World War II, it became very difficult for the defendant to find tenants to sublease the flats to, as many people had left the city to escape the risk of bombing. As a result, the defendant approached the plaintiff in January 1940 to request that rent be lowered. The plaintiff agreed to a reduction in writing. Notably, the duration was not specified for this reduction and no consideration was provided by the defendant; the plaintiff had agreed simply out of goodwill and solidarity, and not as a result of any new bargain. In 1945, the war having ended, the property returned to full occupancy. The plaintiff wrote to the defendant to request a return to the full rent and claiming arrears for the period since 1940. The plaintiff then brought a test action to recover part of the debt for the last half of 1945 (when the flats were in full occupancy). The Court of Appeal ruled that the plaintiff was entitled to the full rent from when the flats returned to full occupancy. Denning J. then hypothesised, in obiter, that if the plaintiff had tried to claim for the full rent from 1940 onwards, they would not have been allowed to do so. This would be because the plaintiff had *represented* that it would accept a reduction in the rent during this time and the defendant had *relied* upon that statement.

The plaintiff, in other words, would have been estopped from claiming for the full rent during the war, had they sought it. It is important to note that this estoppel lasted only for so long as the conditions that led to the representation being made—the ongoing war—subsisted. Once the war had ended, the plaintiff was entitled to rent at the full rate, i.e. once the conditions leading to the estoppel expired, the estoppel also expired. *Note:* This is not to say that estoppel acts only to suspend a legal right. This can be seen below, in particular in *Revenue Commissioners v Moroney* [1972] I.R. 372.

The test for promissory estoppel is as follows:

1. A person, X, makes a *representation* to another person, Y, to the effect that X will not rely on the strict terms of a contract previously made between the parties; and
2. Y *relies* on that statement.

In such circumstances, notwithstanding the absence of consideration for this promise not to rely on one's strict contractual rights, X will not be permitted to enforce the strict terms of the contract in contravention of the representation she has made.

In his decision, Denning J. relied on the older case of *Hughes v Metropolitan Railway Co* (1877) 2 App. Cas. 439. This case is known, retrospectively, as the first instance of promissory estoppel, but it did not receive this notoriety until Denning J. referred to it in *High Trees*. Here, the plaintiff owned property that he leased to the defendant railway company. Under the lease, the plaintiff was entitled to compel the defendant to repair the property by giving six months' notice. Notice was given in October 1874, meaning that the defendant had until April 1875 to complete any repair works. The defendant sent a letter asking that the plaintiff buy its leasehold interest. Negotiations began, but eventually broke down. At this point, the plaintiff reminded the defendant that the requested repairs had to be carried out by April 1875. The defendant argued that it should have a further six months to complete any necessary repairs from the date the negotiations broke down, and not from the date the original notice was given. The House of Lords ruled that by entering into negotiations, the plaintiff had impliedly represented that he would not enforce his strict legal rights regarding the time limit on the repairs and the defendant had relied upon this to its detriment. It was held that it would therefore be inequitable to hold the defendant to the original bargain. Lord Cairns stated that if a party to an agreement subsequently acts so as to lead the other party to believe that the strict rights arising from the contract will not be relied upon or will be suspended:

> "... the person who otherwise might have enforced those rights will not be allowed to enforce them where it would be inequitable, having regard to the dealings which have thus taken place between the parties".

In *Kenny v Kelly* [1988] I.R. 457, the applicant student sought, by way of judicial review, a declaration that she was entitled to a place at University College Dublin. The University had represented to her that she could defer her place at the University for one year. The prospective student acted on this by paying part of her fees upfront and by taking the deferral. Barron J. ruled that the University could not subsequently go back on its word: it was estopped from denying her entry. He stated: "the essence of promissory estoppel was said to be a promise intended to be binding, intended to be acted upon and in fact acted upon."

In *Revenue Commissioners v Moroney* [1972] I.R. 372, the defendant's father had assigned a certain leasehold premises to himself and his sons, the defendants. "Consideration" for this was the sum of £16,000. Although the deed of transfer indicated that the sons must pay their portion of this sum via a receipt clause, in fact, the father had indicated orally that payment would never be sought by him from them. On the father's death, the Revenue Commissioners claimed that the sons owed their father for the transfer. Kenny J. concluded that because the father had stated that his sons would not be liable to pay and the sons had acted on this reassurance by signing the transfer deed, the father's estate would be forever estopped from pursuing the debt.

CONDITIONS ATTACHED TO THE CREATION OF AN ESTOPPEL

There are two schools of thought as to what conditions or prerequisites must be present to give rise to estoppel. The *orthodox* perspective claims that equity should offer relief only where a number of strict conditions are met. The *liberal* approach takes a more flexible line. Much debate surrounds the applicability of these approaches, though according to Clark in his seminal text *Contract Law in Ireland*, 9th edn (Dublin: Round Hall, 2022), para.2-70: "[a]t the present time, Irish law remains rooted in a rather orthodox view of promissory estoppel." In the case of *The Barge Inn Ltd v Quinn Hospitality Ireland Operations 3 Ltd* [2013] IEHC 387, Laffoy J. espoused the following key ingredients of promissory estoppel, which take on a distinctly orthodox tenor:

(a) the pre-existing legal relationship between the parties;
(b) an unambiguous representation;
(c) reliance by the promisee (and possible detriment);
(d) some element of unfairness and unconscionability;
(e) that the estoppel is being used not as a cause of action but as a defence; and
(f) that the remedy is a matter for the court.

The decision in *The Barge Inn Ltd* has been cited with approval as regards the conditions for estoppel in the more recent Court of Appeal case of *Allied Irish Bank plc v Griffin* [2020] IECA 221.

Below, we shall discuss these essential ingredients.

PRE-EXISTING LEGAL RELATIONSHIP BETWEEN THE PARTIES

Promissory estoppel, in its orthodox form, estops a party from exercising their *existing* rights, either temporarily or indeed with more permanent effect. See *Revenue Commissioners v Moroney* [1972] I.R. 372 and *Healy v Ulster Bank Ireland Ltd* [2020] IECA 332 in the context of a contractual relationship. The doctrine does not create new rights. In particular, it is said that for promissory estoppel to arise, there must be a pre-existing legal relationship: estoppel cannot arise in a contractual vacuum. In this sense, promissory estoppel is sometimes said to be "a shield, not a sword". In other words, it provides a defence against the enforcement of existing contractual rights but it does not give rise to new actions where none existed before.

Take the following example: Ali promises to give Jack her contract law notes for an upcoming exam. Jack does not provide any consideration for this promise. As such, there is no contract in being. Ali is simply being altruistic. If Ali changes her mind and decides not to give Jack the notes, under the orthodox approach, Jack could not rely on the doctrine of estoppel to hold Ali to her "bargain" as there were no strict contractual rights to suspend. To hold otherwise would be to create a cause of action or "sword" for Jack to wield, as opposed to a defence to a cause of action.

In *Combe v Combe* [1951] 2 K.B. 215, a man promised his ex-wife £100 a year in financial support but reneged on this agreement. The wife had not provided consideration for this original promise. She later claimed that she was entitled to be paid on foot of the *High Trees* principle. The English Court of Appeal, however, denied her claim. As Denning L.J. observed:

> "The principle does not create new causes of action where none existed before. It only prevents a party from insisting on his strict legal rights, when it would be unjust to allow him to enforce them".

Likewise, in *Chartered Trust (Ireland) v Healy* (unreported, High Court, 10 December 1985), the plaintiff was prevented from relying upon a void contract for the sale of a car to ground estoppel. Because the contract was void, there were no strict contractual rights to suspend and Barron J. reiterated that a promissory estoppel could not give rise to a cause of action independently of a valid contract (a view confirmed in *Association of General Practitioners v Minister for Health* [1995] 2 I.L.R.M. 481).

While this orthodox approach appears to be the generally accepted view in Ireland, the Australian case of *Walton Stores v Maher* (1988) 76 A.L.R. 513 embraces the more liberal approach, suggesting that a pre-existing relationship is not required to rely on the doctrine of estoppel. In this case, the parties had commenced negotiations for the lease of a property. On foot of these negotiations (no completed contract was in being at the time), the lessors started to perform construction work on the site, in anticipation of the transaction. The prospective lessees were aware that this work was being performed, but when the work was 40 per cent complete, the lessees withdrew from negotiations. Even though there was no contract, the Australian High Court ruled that the lessees were estopped from withdrawing from the negotiations. In the circumstances, the court felt that it would be inequitable to allow such withdrawal.

THERE MUST BE AN UNAMBIGUOUS REPRESENTATION

The orthodox approach dictates that there must be a clear and unambiguous statement of fact or intention that a party will not rely on their strict contractual rights. In *Keegan and Roberts v Comhairle Chontae Átha Cliath* (unreported, High Court, 12 March 1981), certain assurances were deemed too ambiguous to give rise to an actionable estoppel. (See also *Woodhouse A.C. Israel Cocoa v Nigerian Produce Marketing* [1972] A.C. 741.) In *Folens v Minister for Education* [1984] I.L.R.M. 265, McWilliam J. held that in order to invoke the doctrine of estoppel, there needs to be a "definite commitment or representation".

In *CF v JDF* [2005] 4 I.R. 154, McGuinness J. provided the following synopsis as to the level of certainty required of a representation:

> "[I]n order to establish such an estoppel there must actually be a promise, or at least a reasonably clear direct representation or inducement of some kind. It is not sufficient to say that this or that was permitted to happen or that third parties looking at the situation thought that a particular outcome was likely."

Such a representation may be made by words or through conduct. However, a representation that has allegedly been made through conduct alone may be difficult to establish. An unsuccessful attempt at establishing same can be seen in the Canadian case of *Burrows v Subsurface Surveys Ltd* (1968) 68 D.L.R. (2d) 354. Here, the creditor of a loan was permitted to demand payment of an entire sum borrowed by the debtor if any repayment instalment was more than 10 days late. The debtor in this case was more than 10 days late repaying 11 out of 18 instalments. Despite the repeated tardiness, the creditor did not object nor demand full repayment of the sums owing. This, however, was held not to disentitle the creditor from demanding full repayment when the debtor was more than 10 days late repaying the nineteenth instalment. The court held that estoppel was only available if there was:

> "... some evidence that one of the parties entered into a course of negotiation which had the effect of leading the other to suppose that the strict rights under the contract would not be enforced, and I think that this implies that there must be evidence from which it can be inferred that the first party intended that the legal relations created by the contract would be altered as a result of the negotiations."

In this way, it was not enough to demonstrate that one party had "taken advantage of indulgences" given to him and that the other party had not formally objected to same. Something further (e.g. negotiation on this point) was required to prove that the conduct in question unambiguously constituted a representation that one party would not rely on their strict contractual rights.

In *National Asset Loan Management Ltd v McMahon* [2014] IEHC 71, Charleton J. stated that where estoppel is said to arise based on an assumption that exists between the parties that one party will not rely on his strict contractual rights, there must be:

> "... conduct which establishes an objective state of affairs whereby the party otherwise bound by the legal relations is placed in circumstances whereby it is understood that a new state of affairs governs the relations between the parties."

It is not enough to "jump to conclusions" without evidence that some altered state of obligation has arisen. He stated:

> "Estoppel is not based on bare assumption. Estoppel is based either on representations or on situations of behaviour that, reasonably construed, clearly withdraw or alter the strictures of legal obligations in such a way that it would be unfair to later enforce these."

The Northern Irish case of *Odyssey Pavilion LLP v Marcus Ward Ltd* [2011] NICh 10 concerned the Odyssey Millennium project, which was aimed at revitalising parts of Belfast City. The project included the building of the Odyssey Pavilion entertainment complex and was driven by Sheridan, a company headed by Peter Curistan. A company under the Sheridan Group, Marcus Ward Ltd, took up tenancy in one of the properties being let as part of the project. Curistan devised a policy whereby Sheridan would not charge or seek to recover rent from Marcus Ward Ltd until it was acquired by a third party. However, when the Odyssey Millennium project ran into trading difficulties, Sheridan assigned all of its rental arrears owing. The court held that Sheridan had made a promise or representation not to enforce its strict legal rights. This representation was ratified through conduct when the rent was neither offered nor requested, adding sufficient clarity. Girvan L.J. held that the focus is not on the subjective intention of the representor but on the conduct of that party and its effects on the position of the other party.

The main takeaway from the preceding examples is that it should be clear and unambiguous from the representation in question (whether made by words or conduct) that the promisor intends not to be bound by their strict contractual rights. The less clear and more ambiguous this representation, the more room there is for argument that no shift in obligations was intended to occur.

THERE MUST BE AN ACT OF RELIANCE BY THE PROMISEE (AND POSSIBLE DETRIMENT)

The orthodox view holds that the promisor's representation will not give rise to estoppel unless the promisee has relied upon that statement and altered their position as a result.

In *Daly v Minister for the Marine* [2001] 3 I.R. 513, for instance, the plaintiff had received a letter from the defendant stating in error that the plaintiff was eligible to claim under a departmental fisheries scheme. The Supreme Court ruled that although this representation was made, there was no evidence of reliance in this case and thus no estoppel could arise. Similarly, in *Ajayi v Briscoe* [1964] 1 W.L.R. 1326, the Privy Council refused to infer an estoppel from circumstances where there had been no reliance, as the promisee had not "altered his position" on foot of the representation. This is a fundamental point—it is not the *fact* of the representation but the *reliance* thereon that gives rise to the estoppel.

Until now, we have been discussing promissory estoppel. While detrimental reliance is an essential feature of *proprietary* estoppel (discussed briefly below), there is debate as to whether a promisee's reliance needs to be detrimental in order to give rise to *promissory* estoppel. In *W.J. Alan v El Nasr Export and Import Co* [1972] 2 Q.B. 189, Lord Denning suggested that there is no support for the proposition that reliance need be detrimental. Lord Denning reiterated this point in *Brikom Investments v Carr* [1979] Q.B. 467.

However, there are a number of cases that underline the importance of detrimental reliance as distinct from simple reliance as a prerequisite for a finding of promissory estoppel. In *McCambridge v Winters* (unreported, High Court, 28 August 1984), for example, Murphy J. cited with approval the judgment of Diplock J. in *Lowe v Lombank Ltd* [1960] 1 W.L.R. 196 where he held that for the doctrine of estoppel to be relied upon, the representation made must have been intended to be acted upon and had, in fact, been acted upon by the promisee to his detriment. In *North Down Hotels v Province Wide Filling Stations* [1993] N.I. 261, Carswell L.J. held that detrimental reliance was a prerequisite for the invocation of the doctrine of estoppel under the dicta in *Hughes v Metropolitan Railway Co*.

In *Daly v Minister for the Marine*, discussed above, the Supreme Court seemed to include as part of the test for promissory estoppel the need for detrimental reliance on a representation:

> "It is not unfair to characterise that as a daring submission, striking as it does, at the root of the concept of equitable estoppel ... It is the fact that it would be unconscionable for one party to be permitted to depart from a position, statement or representation, upon which the other party has acted to his detriment, that justifies the courts in intervening to restrain him from doing so."

It would therefore seem that detriment is a requirement for the successful invocation of the doctrine in this jurisdiction. In practice, the distinction between reliance and detrimental reliance is often semantic. McDermott and McDermott, in their text *Contract Law*, 2nd edn (Dublin: Bloomsbury Professional, 2017), para.3.139, note that estoppel may only be raised if it would be inequitable to allow the promisor to go back on their representation. The presence of some kind of inequity (which was discussed in *Hughes v Metropolitan Railway Co*) will often presuppose detriment. Indeed, Mee, "Lost in the Big House: Where Stands Irish Law on Equitable Estoppel?" (1998) 33 Ir. Jur. 187, argues:

> "If one interprets acting to one's 'detriment' to mean conduct which would make it unconscionable for the representor to withdraw the representation, then this difference seems to disappear."

Unfairness or Unconscionability Must Exist

As promissory estoppel is an equitable remedy, it is clear that an estoppel will only arise where unfairness or unconscionability would otherwise ensue. In other words, equity works to remedy an inequity: if no unfairness would result from the enforcement of strict legal rights, equity will not intervene. Equitable relief is, after all, discretionary and if no hardship would arise from the enforcement of the contract, an estoppel will not issue.

In *Traynor v Fegan* [1985] I.R. 586, the defendant's insurance company told the plaintiff that it had nominated solicitors to accept service of proceedings that the plaintiff wished to issue against it. However, the company had not nominated solicitors and, as such, the plaintiff was unable to serve proceedings. By the time the insurance company actually instructed solicitors, the plaintiff's claim was time-barred under the Statute of Limitations. The court held that there was clearly unfairness in allowing the defendant to subsequently rely on the defence that the proceedings were now time-barred against it. In *Williams v Stern* (1879) 5 Q.B.D. 409, a debtor owed money for the purchase of furniture on hire purchase. Although his creditor had promised not to pursue the debt until a specific date, he later reneged on this promise and seized the furniture upon learning that the debtor's landlord intended to seize the furniture in satisfaction of arrears of rent. The court ruled that no estoppel arose here, as the creditor was justified in acting as he did; if he hadn't acted, another of the debtor's creditors would have seized the furniture in question. As such, there was no inequity in acting to recover the furniture.

Similarly, in *D & C Builders Ltd v Rees* [1966] 2 Q.B. 617, Lord Denning suggested that promissory estoppel would not arise in favour of the defendants who had lied about their financial situation in order to extract a promise from the plaintiffs. In such circumstances, it would be inequitable to allow an estoppel to arise.

Estoppel Is Not a Cause of Action, but a Defence

As discussed above, estoppel must be used as a "shield" and not a "sword" under the orthodox approach. This analogy was first used in *Combe v Combe* (discussed above) and again in *Chartered Trust (Ireland) v Healy* (discussed above).

That the Remedy Is a Matter for the Court

It should be remembered that promissory estoppel is a discretionary remedy, meaning that the court has a broad discretion as to whether to recognise its application in a case.

Distinguishing Promissory Estoppel from Other Similar Concepts

Estoppel by Representation

At common law (as opposed to equity) a similar principle applies: estoppel by representation. For instance, in *McNeill v Miller* [1907] 2 I.R. 328, Mr McNeill, a car owner, left his car at the defendant's garage to be repaired. Although the defendant had reassured McNeill that the car would be insured while in its care, this turned out to be untrue. On the basis of this reassurance, McNeill omitted to obtain insurance for the car. The car having been destroyed in a fire, the garage owner was "estopped" from denying liability for damage to the car. Traditionally, at common law an estoppel would only operate where there was a statement relating to an existing fact and not where there was a statement of intention in relation to a future event. It is clear from *High Trees*, however, that this restriction does not apply in equity: the representation may be as to future conduct as well as existing fact.

Waiver

The doctrine of waiver is distinct from estoppel. Waiver includes an election between two or more courses of action and, upon election, not being permitted to change one's mind. In both *Hickman v Haynes* (1875) L.R. 10 C.P. 598 and *Charles Rickards Ltd v Oppenhaim* [1950] 1 K.B. 616, statements to the effect that goods would be accepted by customers later than originally promised served to "waive" the original deadlines. In other words, by agreeing to accept late delivery, the customers could no longer rely on the original deadlines.

Proprietary Estoppel

Proprietary estoppel concerns promises made *specifically* in respect of property. Where a person acts to their detriment on foot of a representation that they will acquire an interest in property, the person may be able to claim an interest in the property. For instance, in *Smith v Halpin* [1997] 3 I.L.R.M. 38, a father had told his son that the family home "is yours after your mother's day". In reliance on this statement, the son built an extension onto the house. Because of this reliance, the son could claim the house after his mother's death. Unlike promissory estoppel, proprietary estoppel does not require an existing contractual relationship between the parties. Proprietary estoppel may also give rise to a cause of action in its own right. In other words, it can be used as a "sword" rather than just a "shield".

Legitimate Expectation

The doctrine of promissory estoppel shares some features in common with the remedy of "legitimate expectation" (e.g. the making of a representation, the presence of unjustness should the promisor be allowed to resile from his words). However, it is important to note that legitimate expectation is an entirely separate relief that arises only where a person relies on the statement or past practices of a public body.

8 Privity of Contract

Introduction

Privity of contract states that a contract cannot be enforceable in favour of or against a third party, i.e. someone who is not a party to that contract.

Take the following example: Céile promises to sell her car to Aoife in exchange for €2,000. Céile is delighted and intends to use the money to go on holidays with her friend Deirdre. When Céile delivers the car, Aoife only gives her half of what was contracted for. Although it would be open to Céile to sue Aoife for breach of contract, Céile's friend Deirdre could not bring proceedings, despite the fact that this upset has affected her also. This is because Deirdre is not a party to the contract as between Céile and Aoife.

The following are important features of the doctrine of privity:

(a) A person cannot enforce rights under a contract if they are not a party to the contract.
(b) A person cannot have contractual obligations imposed on or enforced against them if they are not a party to the contract.
(c) A party to a contract cannot have their position detrimentally altered by means of a further agreement to which they are not a party.
(d) Remedies available under contract law (e.g. specific performance or damages) may not be sought or granted to third parties who are not privy to the contract in question.

Examples of the Privity Rule

In *Tweddle v Atkinson* (1861) 1 B. & S. 393, the plaintiff was engaged to marry G's daughter. In recognition of the impending marriage, G entered into an agreement with the plaintiff's father, each promising the other that he would pay the plaintiff (who was not a party to the contract) a sum of money on marriage. G subsequently died and the executors of his estate refused to pay the plaintiff. As the plaintiff was not a party to the contract between G and the plaintiff's father, his claim failed.

In the Irish case of *McCoubray v Thompson* (1868) 2 I.R.C.L. 226, the owner of a farm had agreed to give the land to the defendant if he agreed to pay half the value of the farm to McCoubray, a third party. When the land was transferred to the defendant, he refused to pay the promised sum to McCoubray. Although he was the intended beneficiary, McCoubray could not sue for the money, as he was not privy to the contract.

The principle was confirmed in *Dunlop v Selfridge* [1915] A.C. 847. Here, the plaintiff company had sold its tyres to a wholesaler under contract. The contract provided that these tyres could not then be sold on below the recommended retail price. The defendant was a retailer that had purchased the tyres from the wholesaler. It was held that as the retailer was not privy to the contract between the plaintiff and the wholesaler, it was not bound by the pricing clause therein.

In *Clitheroe v Simpson* (1879) 4 L.R. (Ir.) 59, a father and son agreed, as part of a property transfer to the son, that the latter would pay his sister a sum of money. The sister's estate was precluded from suing for this sum due to the doctrine of privity. Similarly, in *Beswick v Beswick* [1968] A.C. 59, a nephew had promised to support his uncle's wife after the uncle's death. As the widow was not a party to the agreement, she could not sue the nephew in respect of the promised allowance.

The privity rule often poses problems where a contractor (e.g. building contractor) subcontracts certain aspects of work to another party. In other words: Robert may have a contract with Elizabeth-Ann, who in turn subcontracts with Kevin. According to the doctrine of privity, Robert may sue Elizabeth-Ann and Elizabeth-Ann may sue Kevin, but in contract, Robert may not sue Kevin, as these two parties are not party to a common contract.

In *Murphy v Bower* (1868) I.R. 2 C.L. 506, Murphy had agreed to carry out construction work for a railway company (i.e. Murphy was a contractor of the railway company). The railway company had separately employed Bower as an engineer to check and certify that Murphy's work was up to standard. Without certification, Murphy would not be paid. When Bower failed to certify the work, Murphy sued him, but was unsuccessful. Murphy, not having been a party to the contract with Bower, could not sue him.

COMPARISON WITH CONSIDERATION

At first glance, the privity rule appears very similar to the requirement that consideration move from the promisee. You might recognise some of the cases cited as cases in which consideration issues also arose (e.g. *McCoubray v Thompson*, *Dunlop v Selfridge*). Nonetheless, these concepts are technically mutually exclusive.

Exceptions to the Privity Requirements

Instinctively, the results of the privity rule may seem harsh. Take *McCoubray v Thompson*: was it fair that Thompson should walk away with the money, despite his promise? Needless to say, several exceptions have developed in response to the apparent harshness of the rule.

Legislative Exceptions

In some specific cases, the Oireachtas has provided exceptions to the effects of the privity rule:

- Under s.11 of the Married Women's Property Act 1882, Parliament gave widows and children of a deceased man the right to sue upon a policy of life insurance despite not being privy to said contract themselves. Section 7 of the Married Women's Status Act 1957 expanded this to a right of action in the case of endowment policies (a type of life insurance contract) also. This right of action applies to policies that: (a) have been expressed to be for the benefit of the spouse and/or child of the policyholder, or (b) expressly state an intention to confer a benefit on the spouse and/or child.
- Section 8 of the Married Women's Status Act 1957 creates a cause of action in all contracts other than those covered by s.7 (discussed above) if the contract is expressed to be for the benefit of a husband, wife or child of one of the contracting parties or if the contract is to confer a benefit on said husband, wife or child. (See, for example, *O'Keeffe v Ryanair Holdings plc* [2003] 1 I.L.R.M. 14 where damages were awarded in favour of the plaintiff and her husband.)
- The Consumer Rights Act 2022 introduces a number of changes to the privity rule as it pertains to consumer contracts. Section 46 states that where a consumer gives goods to another consumer as a gift, that other consumer shall be entitled to exercise any rights and remedies under Part 2, as against the trader, in the same way the original consumer would.
- Section 47 of the Consumer Rights Act 2022 provides that where a consumer purchases a motor vehicle and where a lack of conformity would render a motor vehicle a danger to the public, including anyone travelling in the motor vehicle, any person who uses the vehicle with the consent of the consumer and suffers a loss because of this lack of conformity may initiate a claim against the trader in damages as if they were a consumer.

Equity's Exceptions

Equity has taken a flexible approach to the doctrine of privity and acts to imply a trust in favour of the named beneficiary, where appropriate.

In other words: if Gary and David made a contract for the benefit of Sarah, equity would say that Gary and David held the benefit *on trust* for Sarah. As the named beneficiary, Sarah could then sue the "trustees" (Gary and David) for the benefit in question.

The operation of this workaround may be seen in the Irish case of *Drimmie v Davies* [1899] 1 I.R. 176. A father and son established a dental practice together, as a partnership. The partnership deed obliged the son to support his mother and other family members and pay annuities to them in the event that the father predeceased the son. The deed was deemed to have created a trust in favour of the mother and other family members, given that the clause in question was devised for the benefit thereof. The mother and other family members were therefore able to sue as beneficiaries under the trust. The court held that "the party to whose use or for whose benefit the contract had been entered into has a remedy in equity against the person with whom it was expressed to be made". Likewise, in *Tomlinson v Gill* (1756) Amb. 330, Gill had agreed to pay off the creditors of a woman's late husband. Although Gill had made the agreement only with the widow, the creditors not being privy to the contract, the creditors were nonetheless entitled to sue as beneficiaries under a "trust" created by the contract. This was notwithstanding the fact that no express intention was communicated to create a trust, nor was a trust fund established.

While the *Drimmie v Davies* line of authority has not been directly challenged in the Irish courts to date, it should not be presumed that a trust will arise in *every* case where a third party is named as beneficiary. Judges have proved less and less willing to allow the use of the trust device as an artificial means of avoiding the privity rule. In practice, it is rarely invoked and granted.

Although in *O'Leary v Irish National Insurance Co Ltd* [1958] Ir. Jur. Rep. 1, the court left unanswered the question as to whether an intention to create a trust must be shown in order for the third party to claim as a beneficiary of same, in *Cadbury Ireland Ltd v Kerry Co-op Creameries Ltd* [1982] I.L.R.M. 77, it was held that such an intention must be present.

Agency

Another way of avoiding the privity rule is through an agency arrangement. An agent is a person who acts not on their own behalf but on behalf of another person (the "principal"). In a contractual context, the agent may be given authority to act in a way that binds the principal. The principal, moreover, is entitled to benefit from the contract as if they had made it themselves. A good example arises in the case of a trade union, which, in industrial negotiations, is deemed to act as agent for its worker members. An agent may be distinguished from an independent contractor who acts in their own interest. An agent may be "disclosed" (where the other party knows that the agent is acting for a principal) or "undisclosed" (where the relationship of agent and principal is not revealed). The "disclosed" option is more prevalent in practice.

An agent may act with:

- *express authority*: where the relationship of agency is *expressly* created by the parties, i.e. there is a clear agreement to this effect;
- *implied authority*: where the relationship of agency is implicit (i.e. not express in a contract); where the *conduct* of the parties indicates that one party is necessarily acting as an agent of another party;
- *apparent authority*: where there is no actual relationship of agency, but where there is nonetheless good reason to believe that a party has authority to act as agent for another person, e.g. in relation to a company, a director of the company might have apparent authority.

In order for the acts of an agent to bind the principal, according to *Sheppard v Murphy* (1867) 1 I.R. Eq. 490, there must be an intention to create the relationship of agency. In *Scruttons Ltd v Midland Silicones Ltd* [1962] A.C. 446, the question arose as to whether a firm of stevedores (people who contract to unload a ship's cargo) could rely on a limitation clause in a contract between the carrier and a client, despite the firm of stevedores being apparent third parties to the contract. The House of Lords ruled that the third party was not entitled to benefit from the limitation clause unless:

(a) the contract makes it clear that the stevedores are intended to be protected;
(b) the contract clearly provides that the carrier was acting as agent for the purposes of securing a benefit for the principal (the stevedores);
(c) the carrier has the authority to contract on the stevedores' behalf; and
(d) consideration flowed from the principal.

The test was not satisfied in *Scruttons* as there was no evidence of an intention to benefit the stevedores. In *New Zealand Shipping Co Ltd v A.M. Satterthwaite and Co Ltd (The "Eurymedon")* [1975] A.C. 154, the above conditions were satisfied such that a firm of stevedores was able to rely on a clause in a contract to which it was not a party. Here, a drilling machine was to be transported by ship from Liverpool to New Zealand. The consignors in England employed a carrier to ship the drilling machine.

Under this contract, the liability of the carriers, their employees, agents and independent contractors was limited and they could not be sued more than one year from the date on which any damage accrued. The carrier company was a subsidiary of a company that also owned a stevedore firm and this stevedore firm was employed to unload the drilling machine. Owing to the stevedores' negligence, the drill was damaged. The stevedores tried to rely on the limitation clause in the contract between the carrier and consignor. The Privy Council, having applied the four conditions laid out in *Scruttons*, concluded that a relationship of agency existed and thus the stevedores could rely on the clause. The court interpreted the clause as a promise of exemption made to the stevedores through the carrier as their agent.

An Irish example of this exception arose in *Hearn and Matchroom Boxing v Collins* (unreported, High Court, 3 February 1998). In this case, the first plaintiff—manager of boxer Stephen Collins—successfully relied on an agreement between the boxer and the second plaintiff, a management company. The agreement (as between the second plaintiff and the defendant) contained a clause that stated that if the defendant boxer won the WBO Middleweight title, he would extend the existing management agreement with the first plaintiff for a period of one year. The court concluded that the second plaintiff had contracted as agent for the first plaintiff and that the first plaintiff could thus rely on the contract. The contract was clearly intended to benefit the first plaintiff, the second plaintiff had clearly acted on his behalf and with his authority, and the first plaintiff had furnished consideration by agreeing to work as Collins' manager. As such, all four of the requirements set out in *Scruttons* were satisfied.

Exceptions Pertaining to Land

Certain covenants that "touch and concern" real property (land) may be enforced against and by persons who are not parties to the original transaction, e.g. successors in title.

Confidentiality Clauses

Where a person enters into a confidentiality clause, it is possible to invoke the clause against a person who receives information in breach of the clause. (See *Oblique Financial Services Ltd v The Promise Production Co Ltd* [1994] 1 I.L.R.M. 74.)

Implication of Collateral Contracts

In some cases, where A and B enter into a contract for the benefit of C, it may be feasible to imply a fresh contract (called a "collateral contract") between the third party and one of the contractors. In *Shanklin Pier Ltd v Detel Products Ltd* [1951] 2 K.B. 854, the plaintiff hired a contractor to repaint its pier. In turn, the contractor bought paints from the defendant. The contractor, however, bought the paint on the instructions of Shanklin Pier, who had received assurances from the defendant that its paints, once applied, would last for 7 to 10 years. In fact, the paint was of poor quality and faded within three months. The court ruled that although the contractor had bought the paint from the defendant, there was a collateral contract between Shanklin Pier and the defendant to the effect that the paint would last for 10 years.

Sale of Goods Contracts

There are a number of statutory exemptions to the privity doctrine, especially in the area of consumer law. Two of those—ss.46 and 47 of the Consumer Rights Act 2022—were considered above.

Law Reform Commission Proposals

The Law Reform Commission published a *Report on Privity of Contract and Third Party Rights* (LRC 88-2008) in 2008 which recommended a number of provisional changes to the law as it pertains to the doctrine of privity. This report is available at: *https://www.lawreform.ie/_fileupload/Reports/Report%20Privity.pdf*.

Capacity to Contract   9

Introduction

In order for a contract to be fully enforceable, all of the parties thereto must have the capacity to contract. In particular, a contract may be avoided where one of the parties lacked the capacity to contract, for example, because of mental incapacity, intoxication or other similar impediments. Contract law regards certain vulnerable categories of person as deserving of protection and thus in some cases, even where there appears to be full consent on the part of both contracting parties, the law may regard a party as being incapable of forming a valid contract or may otherwise limit such capacity. It may not be necessary to prove capacity in every case where a contract is made. The law generally assumes, unless the contrary is established, that adults entering into a contract have the full capacity to do so. In other words, the onus of proving absence of capacity is on the person who alleges such absence. This chapter shall discuss the categories of party that might fall foul of the doctrine of capacity depending on the circumstances.

Infancy: General

At common law, a person under the age of 21 was considered an infant. Following the enactment of the Age of Majority Act 1985, the age of majority was reduced to 18 (if unmarried). The definition of infant excluded persons under 18 who were married. It should be noted that as of January 2019, the legal age requirement for marriage is 18 years and it is no longer possible to obtain a Court Exemption Order allowing a marriage to proceed if one or both parties are under 18 years. In practice, therefore, infancy now describes those who have not attained the age of majority, being 18 years.

Contracts made with infants may be divided into three categories:

(a) contracts that are absolutely void under the Infants Relief Act 1874;
(b) contracts that are binding on an infant unless and until they repudiate the contracts;
(c) contracts that are binding on the infant.

Contracts Void under the Infants Relief Act 1874

Following the enactment of the Infants Relief Act 1874, certain contracts with minors were deemed to be absolutely void. This meant that they could not be enforced even at the instance of the infant.

The 1874 Act deems three types of contract to be void:

(a) contracts for the repayment of *money* lent or to be lent *to* an infant;
(b) contracts for *goods* supplied or to be supplied *to* an infant;
(c) all accounts stated with minors.

According to s.2 of the Act, such contracts are absolutely void and cannot, in general, be enforced by or against the infant in question. Further, it is not possible for the infant to ratify the contract after they reach the age of 18 (as would be possible with a voidable contract: see below). A key exception to this category is contracts for necessaries. It should be noted that the Act does not apply where *services* are being supplied to an infant. Further, the Act only applies where the money or goods in question are supplied *to* an infant and not *by an infant to an adult*. Such contracts are not considered to be void absolutely under the Act.

Sir Edward Coke, in one of his legal treatises *Commentary upon Littleton*, noted as follows:

> "An infant may bind himself to pay for his necessary eat, drink, apparel, necessary physic, and such other necessaries, and likewise for his good teaching or instruction, whereby he may profit himself afterwards, but if he bind himself in an obligation or other writing, with a penalty for the payment of any other, that obligation shall not bind him."

In other words, the 1874 Act does not apply to "necessaries" or "necessary goods" which are supplied to an infant. "Necessaries" is defined in s.2 of the Sale of Goods Act 1893 as:

> "… goods suitable to the condition of life of such infant or minor … and to his actual requirements at the time of the sale and delivery."

In other words, necessaries are the basic items that one requires in order to maintain a decent standard of living. As noted in Sir Edward Coke's quote above, examples may include food, drink, clothes, education and accommodation. The supplier of the goods bears the onus of proving that the item in question is a necessary, otherwise the contract may be found to be void under the 1874 Act: that the goods were generally suitable to the condition of life of a minor and *also* that they were suitable to his *actual* requirements at the time of the sale and delivery.

Clearly, an item that is *merely* for ornamentation or is purely an item of luxury would not be a necessary. In *Skrine v Gordon* (1875) I.R. 9 C.L. 479, a hunting horse was deemed not to be a "necessary" even for a gentleman of means. The judge noted that "luxuries or amusement are quite different from necessaries". Similarly, in *Ryder v Wombwell* (1868) L.R. 4 Ex. 32, jewelled cufflinks were deemed not to be a "necessary" even for a wealthy infant. In *First Charter Financial Corp Ltd v Musclow* 49 D.L.R. (3d) 138 (B.C. Sup. Ct, 1974), a Canadian case, the court found that while in the past a motor vehicle would be considered a luxury, in modern times it would be generally regarded as a necessary, especially where it is used for travel, work and/or general domestic reasons.

Again, in addition to proving a particular good is capable of being a necessary, the plaintiff must prove that, as a matter of fact, it is a necessary in the particular circumstances of the minor. For example, in *Chapple v Cooper* (1844) 13 M. & W. 252, the court held that "[a]rticles of *mere* luxury are always excluded though luxurious items of *utility* are in *some* cases included" (emphasis added). In *Scarborough v Sturzaker* (1905) 1 Tas. L.R. 117, an Australian case, it was held that a bicycle may be deemed a necessary if used to convey the infant to and from his place of work which was 11 miles away from his house. The Law Reform Commission's *Report on Minors' Contracts* (LRC 15-1985) provided the following example:

> "Two small computers, costing £500, are sold to two seventeen-year-old minors. The first minor is from a relatively disadvantaged social background but is an excellent student, studying computer science at the university. Arguably the computer is, for him, a necessary. The second minor is from a more advantaged social background but is virtually innumerate; he has bought the computer as no more than a plaything to amuse himself and impress his friends. Quite possibly, for him, the computer is not a necessary."

It is clear, therefore, that the individual circumstances of the infant in question will bear weight when ascertaining whether an otherwise luxurious item is a necessary. Clark in *Contract Law in Ireland*, 9th edn (Dublin: Round Hall, 2022) at para.16-07 provides another useful example of this:

> "[A] set of encyclopaedias sold to an infant television researcher, blogger or journalist may be a necessary but, in general, would not be if supplied to an infant with a mere thirst for knowledge."

In *Nash v Inman* [1908] 2 K.B. 1, an undergraduate at Oxford University (the age of majority at the time being 21) purchased 11 "fancy waistcoats" from a Savile Row tailor. The infant was not able to establish that he was adequately supplied with clothing. Therefore, the waistcoats in question were held to be surplus to his *actual* requirements at the time of contract and the contract was held to be void.

Older cases pertaining to this topic should be read with caution, given that what may constitute a necessary will change with time. This was noted in *First Charter Financial Corp Ltd* (discussed above): "[w]hat was not a necessary 10 years ago may very well be a necessary today."

Section 2 of the Sale of Goods Act 1893 makes clear that even if an item is deemed to be a necessary, the infant is only required to pay what a court would regard as a "reasonable price" for the item. The infant may not, therefore, be required to pay the full contract price by the court.

Further, even if a contract is for the supply of necessaries, it may not be enforceable if its terms are generally to the detriment of the minor. In *Fawcett v Smethurst* (1914) 84 L.J.K.B. 473, a motor car was considered to be a necessary. However, the contract, which concerned the hire of the motor vehicle, included several onerous terms, including an express term that placed responsibility for *any* loss or damage to the vehicle on the infant in *all* circumstances. This exclusion clause made it so that the contract, when viewed as a whole, was not advantageous to the infant. As such, it was deemed to be unenforceable.

The exception relating to necessaries applies only if the contract is executed (performed in full) and not executory (pending performance). In other words, the infant is only required to pay for necessaries where the goods in question have been delivered to them. If the goods have not yet been delivered, the infant is perfectly free to reject delivery, even of necessaries.

CONTRACTS THAT ARE VALID UNLESS REPUDIATED

A contract where an infant is capable of being subjected to a series of recurring obligations is voidable. In other words, the infant is bound unless they repudiate the contract either before *or* within a reasonable time of their attaining the age of majority. As such, these contracts are void*able*, i.e. enforceable unless successfully avoided. Once repudiated, the contract becomes "null and void ab initio" (see *Paget v Paget* (1882) 11 L.R. Ir. 26). There are five general types of contract that fall under this category of continuing contract:

1. Insurance contracts. (See *Stapleton v Prudential Insurance* (1928) 62 I.L.T.R. 56 which pertained to a contract for life insurance made by a

13-year-old girl. This was a continuing contract that required the payment of yearly premiums. It was held that the girl could repudiate the contract when she attained full age if she did so within a reasonable time thereof.)
2. Contracts to subscribe for the purchase of shares.
3. A contract to enter a partnership.
4. Marriage settlements.
5. Contracts for the lease or purchase of land with continuing obligations, e.g. rent payments.

As stated, if the infant wishes to repudiate such a contract, he must do so either before or within a reasonable time of attaining the age of majority (see, for example, *Dublin and Wicklow Railway Co v Black* (1852) 8 Exch. 181). What is "reasonable" will depend on the facts of the case. Where a contract with recurring obligations is repudiated:

(a) the infant need not perform any obligations that have not yet accrued;
(b) the infant must meet obligations that have already accrued;
(c) the infant cannot recover any monies already paid under the contract unless there has been a total failure of consideration (they have received no benefit whatsoever under the contract).

In *Stapleton v Prudential Insurance*, while the infant was permitted to repudiate upon attaining full age, it did not follow that the premiums paid before repudiation could be returned to her. The court held that if she had died between the date of the contract and the date that she repudiated it, the company would have been bound to pay out. Therefore, it could not be held that no benefit (consideration) had passed during those years. Similarly, an infant who has already paid instalments or rent will not be able to reclaim such monies unless there has been a *total* failure of consideration, i.e. no benefit has been received. Another good example that demonstrates this rule is *Blake v Concannon* (1870) I.R. 4 C.L. 323. Here, an infant leased lands from the plaintiff. He possessed and enjoyed the lands until he attained majority and repudiated the contract of tenancy. Because he had received a benefit (consideration) for his rental payments (he had possessed and enjoyed the lands), he was not permitted to recover rent already paid.

Contracts that Are Binding on the Infant

We have already seen that contracts for necessaries are binding as against an infant, as an exception to the Infants Relief Act 1874. Another type of contract that is taken to be "valid" or binding on the infant is a beneficial contract for services, i.e. one that is for the benefit of the infant. If it is not proved that the contract for services is for the benefit of the infant, the contract is a voidable contract, meaning it is open to the infant to repudiate the contract much in the same way as a continuing contract, discussed above.

The courts will look to a range of factors when attempting to establish whether the contract for services benefits the infant, including:

(a) whether a financial benefit is obtained by the minor on foot of the contract;
(b) the presence of any disadvantageous terms in the contract;
(c) whether the infant is receiving instruction, education or training on foot of the contract (however, it should be noted that this is not necessarily dispositive).

As regards (c), *Roberts v Gray* [1913] 1 K.B. 520 provides a good example of a contract for tuition that was deemed to be for the benefit of the infant. Here, an infant was contracted to tour with the plaintiff, a professional billiards player, in return for which he would receive tuition in this sport. The contract was overall to the benefit of the infant and thus enforceable. In contrast, in *De Francesco v Barnum* (1890) 45 Ch. D. 430, a 14-year-old girl was apprenticed as a stage dancer under very harsh terms. The girl was obliged to do her instructor's bidding, could not perform without his consent, could be sent abroad at his whim, and was prevented from marrying against his will. By contrast, the dance instructor had next to no obligations *towards* his apprentice. He did not have to employ her, and when he did, could pay her a pittance. He could, moreover, terminate the contract at any stage. This clearly one-sided contract was deemed to be voidable as overwhelmingly onerous. Therefore, notwithstanding elements of (c) above, the presence of (b) was impactful on the outcome.

Similarly, in *Shears v Mendeloff* (1914) 30 T.L.R. 342, a contract between a young boxer and a manager was deemed voidable: the contract was wholly sided in favour of the manager, who was entitled to a quarter of the infant's purse (the infant having to foot any expenses arising), even though the manager was not obliged to secure him any fights.

It should be noted that the Protection of Young Persons (Employment) Act 1996 provides for a number of protections from more onerous clauses, e.g. prohibition on the hours that may be worked.

In *Doyle v White City Stadium* [1935] 1 K.B. 110, a licence given to a minor, Jack Doyle, by the British Boxing Board of Control contained a clause that permitted the forfeiture of a fight purse if he was disqualified. The plaintiff was subsequently disqualified for hitting a blow below the belt and the defendant sought to withhold the fight purse. The court concluded that the plaintiff was bound by this contract as it was overall to his benefit, the clause being included ultimately with a view to protecting the welfare of boxers (both the plaintiff and his opponent) by incentivising the observance of certain rules. The contract was held to be incidental to the means whereby the infant earned his living.

In *Chaplin v Leslie Frewin Publishers (Ltd)* [1966] Ch. 71, the infant plaintiff was the son of the famous actor, Charlie Chaplin, who had become estranged from his father and had fallen on hard times. He entered into an agreement to sell his own autobiography which was ultimately ghost-written. There was significant publicity surrounding the book. However, prior to publication, the plaintiff attempted to repudiate the contract. The contract was nonetheless deemed overall to be to his benefit in that it would enable him to earn a living and support his family.

In *Keays v Great Southern Railway* [1941] I.R. 534, the plaintiff, a 12-year-old girl, bought a season ticket from the defendant railway company for the purposes of getting to and from school. The ticket contained a limitation clause excusing the railway company from liability should the infant be injured as a result of its negligence. The plaintiff was injured in a railway accident and sued the defendant. The court held that the contract was "very unfair to the infant because it deprives her of practically every common law right that she has against the railway company in respect of ... negligence."

In *Proform Sports Management Ltd v Proactive Sports Management Ltd* [2007] 1 All E.R. 542, the footballer Wayne Rooney entered a two-year representation contract with the plaintiff company when he was just 15 years old. At the time, Rooney was signed with Everton, which gave him instruction and training as well as playing opportunities. Rooney attempted to enter into a representation agreement with the defendant and the plaintiff company sued. The court held that the original representation contract was not a beneficial contract for service and therefore not binding on the minor. Of particular import to the court was that the contract was not analogous to a contract for education, apprenticeship or training, unlike Rooney's contract with Everton. Further, the management company could not be said to be undertaking matters that were essential to the minor's livelihood or the advancement of his career as a professional footballer. *Chaplin* and *Doyle* were distinguished in this regard. In those cases, it was held that the contracts in question allowed the minor to earn his living or start to do so.

Reform

The Law Reform Commission's *Report on Minors' Contracts* (LRC 15-1985) made 28 recommendations to address the deficiencies in the current law as it pertains to the contractual capacity of minors. The report can be found here: *https://www.lawreform.ie/_fileupload/Reports/rMinorsContracts.htm*.

"Mental Incapacity"

The common law position is that a person suffering from "mental incapacity" may be bound by a contract unless their incapacity was known by the other party (see *Imperial Loan Co v Stone* [1892] 1 Q.B. 599). Where knowledge is proven, the contract is voidable at the option of the person who lacked capacity. If knowledge is not proven, the validity of the contract will be judged as if the person suffering from the incapacity was fully capable of contracting, unless equity can intervene (in circumstances of unconscionability and unfairness). For a more thorough discussion, see *Hart v O'Connor* [1985] 1 A.C. 1000, *Hassard v Smith* (1872) I.R. 6 Eq. 429 and *Grealish v Murphy* [1946] I.R. 35.

The Assisted Decision-Making (Capacity) Act 2015 was fully commenced in April 2023. Section 3(1) and (2) thereof provide for the general presumption of capacity:

> "(1) Subject to subsections (2) to (6), for the purposes of this Act, a person's capacity shall be assessed on the basis of his or her ability to understand, at the time that a decision is to be made, the nature and consequences of the decision to be made by him or her in the context of the available choices at that time.
>
> (2) A person lacks the capacity to make a decision if he or she is unable—
>
> (a) to understand the information relevant to the decision,
> (b) to retain that information long enough to make a voluntary choice,
> (c) to use or weigh that information as part of the process of making the decision, or
> (d) to communicate his or her decision (whether by talking, writing, using sign language, assistive technology, or any other means) or, if the implementation of the decision requires the act of a third party, to communicate by any means with that third party."

Section 3(3) dictates that a person is not to be regarded as unable to understand the information relevant to a decision if they are able to understand an explanation of it given to them in a way that is appropriate to their circumstances. Further, the fact that a person is able to retain the information relevant to a decision for only a short period does not prevent them from being regarded as enjoying capacity, according to s.3(4). The fact that a person lacks capacity in respect of a decision on a particular matter at a particular time does not prevent them from being regarded as having capacity to make decisions relating to the same matter at a different time or in other matters (s.3(5) and (6)).

Section 137(1) of the 2015 Act states:

> "A person who lacks capacity to enter into a contract for the sale of goods or services shall pay the supplier a reasonable sum for goods or services supplied at his or her request only if the goods or services are suitable to the person's—
> (a) condition in life, and
> (b) actual requirements,
> at the time when the goods or services, as the case may be, are so supplied."

In other words, where a person lacks capacity under the 2015 Act to enter a contract and goods or services have been supplied thereto, a reasonable sum must be paid by the person lacking capacity where the goods or services were provided at their request, if the goods/services are suitable for the person's condition in life and their actual requirements at the time of supply. This section allows persons lacking in capacity to obtain necessary goods and services at a fair price. The concept mirrors the concept of necessaries vis-à-vis minors (discussed above).

McDermott and McDermott, in their text *Contract Law*, 2nd edn (Dublin: Bloomsbury Professional, 2017), para.18.66, note that where s.137 does not apply, it appears that the common law position still applies. Therefore, the person allegedly suffering from incapacity will be able to avoid a contract if they can prove their incapacity and that the other party was or ought to have been aware of same.

It should also be noted that the 2015 Act provides for a number of arrangements (e.g. assisted decision-making, co-decision-making) for assisting persons who lack capacity to make decisions, including decisions of a contractual nature. There is also provision thereunder for a decision-making representative to be appointed by the Circuit Court for substituted decision-making purposes.

INTOXICATION

An intoxicated person is liable under a contract made while intoxicated unless:

(a) the intoxication was such that the party did not know what they were doing; and
(b) the other contracting party was aware of the intoxication per se (although it is not essential to establish that the other party was aware of the *level* of drunkenness, or the fact that the intoxicated party did not know what they were doing).

Intoxication may arise from drunkenness or drug use. It is irrelevant whether the state of intoxication arose as a result of a voluntary or involuntary act. As with mental incapacity, the onus of proof is on the person alleging intoxication (see *White v McCooey* (unreported, High Court, 24 June 1976)). Even where the test above has been satisfied, however, a contract for necessaries may still be enforced against the incapacitated party. Section 2 of the Sale of Goods Act 1893 allows a contract for necessaries to be enforced against a person who was intoxicated at the time of the contract. If the degree of intoxication falls short of the above standard, the contract may still be held to be "unconscionable" under the doctrine of "improvident bargains" (see Chapter 18).

Convicts

Section 8 of the Forfeiture Act 1870 provided that a "convict" was incapable of contracting, either expressly or by implication. The 1870 Act was repealed by s.16 and Schedule 3 of the Criminal Law Act 1997 and it would appear, as a result, that a prisoner now has a right to enter into a contract. This freedom is only exercisable, however, subject to the Prison Rules 2007–2020.

Formalities of Contract

INTRODUCTION

In order for certain types of contract to be valid or enforceable in a court of law, certain formal procedures have to be followed. With the passing of time, however, formality has waned in importance and given way to more practical ways of doing business. Exceptions to this generalisation exist but are limited. There is a general rule, for example, that a contract does not have to be in writing in order to be enforceable. This can be seen in *Pernod Ricard v FII Fyffes plc* (unreported, High Court, 21 October 1988), in which an oral agreement for the multi-million pound sale of shares was held to be enforceable, notwithstanding the lack of a written contract. The parties had orally agreed all essential elements of the sale.

CONTRACTS THAT MUST BE EVIDENCED IN WRITING

While an oral contract will generally suffice, there exist several categories of contract that, unless executed in or evidenced in writing (via, for example, a memorandum or note), will not be enforceable in a court of law. The definition of "in writing" has evolved over the years and in tandem with business needs. For example, in s.2(2) of the Electronic Commerce Act 2000, "writing" includes electronic modes of representing or reproducing words in visible form. Writing requirements are necessitated by, in particular:

(a) the Statute of Frauds (Ireland) 1695;
(b) the Land and Conveyancing Law Reform Act 2009;
(c) the Arbitration Act 2010.

STATUTE OF FRAUDS (IRELAND) 1695

Section 2 of the Statute of Frauds (Ireland) 1695 provided as follows:

"[N]o action shall be brought ... whereby to charge the defendant upon any special promise to answer for the debt, default or miscarriage of another person, or to charge any person upon any agreement made upon consideration of marriage, or upon any contract or [sic] sale of lands, tenements or hereditaments or any interest in or concerning them, or upon any agreement that is not to be formed within the space of one year from the making thereof, unless the agreement upon which such action shall be brought, or some memorandum or note thereof, shall be in writing, and signed by the party to be charged therewith, or some other person thereunto by him lawfully authorised."

As can be seen, the Statute applies to:

(a) contracts to pay for the debt of another;
(b) contracts made in consideration of marriage;
(c) contracts not to be performed within one year;
(d) contracts for the sale of lands or an interest therein.

The Statute essentially requires that a contract to which it applies (e.g. the sale of lands) cannot be enforced unless there is written evidence of the contract's existence and its essential terms. The Land and Conveyancing Law Reform Act 2009 introduced sweeping changes in the areas of real estate and conveyancing and has changed the wording of s.2 of the Statute as it pertains to "any contract or sale of lands, tenements or hereditaments, or any interest in or concerning them". This will be discussed further below. The Consumer Rights Act 2022 has also introduced significant changes as concerns the evidencing of contracts for goods over the value of €12.

CONTRACTS TO PAY FOR THE DEBT OF ANOTHER

When a person issues a *guarantee*, they agree to pay the debt of a third party *only* if that person defaults on the debt. In such a case, liability is merely secondary: it arises *only* if the primary debtor fails to pay. In this way, there are three actors: the principal debtor, the secondary debtor (or "guarantor") and the creditor.

Consider the following example of a guarantee: Michael (secondary debtor) asks Aoife (creditor) to supply goods to Cillian (principal debtor). Michael states that *if* Cillian does not pay for the goods once supplied, Aoife can seek payment from Michael. Michael's promise is said to be a collateral promise, the consideration for it being Aoife's act of supplying goods to Cillian, the principal debtor.

By contrast, a person giving an *indemnity* agrees to take primary responsibility for the payment of the debt or contingent debt regardless of whether the original debtor defaults or not, thus relieving them of the obligation to pay.

An example of an indemnity might be as follows: Michael asks Aoife to supply goods to Cillian and promises that he (Michael) will pay for them. In this case, Michael alone is liable to pay for the goods. Essentially, Michael is standing in the shoes of Cillian as solely liable to pay the debt. The promise is said to be an original promise and not a collateral one.

The requirement of writing applies only to guarantees and not to indemnities. The distinction was discussed in *Commodity Broking Co Ltd v Meehan* [1985] I.R. 12. Here, the promise by an owner of a company to repay the company's debt to the bank was held to be an indemnity because "[t]here was never any hope that the company could pay its debt". In this way, repayment was not contingent on the principal debtor's (company's) default. Rather, the owner had agreed to pay in any event. The owner stepped into the shoes of the company.

It is clear that the 1695 Statute applies to the guaranteeing of debt or default but also extends to promises to answer for the "miscarriage" of another. This includes the tortious obligations of another. For example, in *Kirkham v Marter* (1819) 2 B. & Ald. 613, the plaintiff suffered when the defendant's son caused the death of his horse. The defendant promised, orally, to compensate the plaintiff for this loss. This promise was not enforceable as it did not comply with the Statute of Frauds—there was no written note of the oral agreement.

In *Actionstrength Ltd v International Glass Engineering SpA* [2003] 2 A.C. 541, International Glass Engineering SpA had been retained to construct a plate glass factory in East Yorkshire for St-Gobain. Actionstrength Ltd were engaged to provide labour to International Glass Engineering SpA for this purpose. Relations between International Glass Engineering SpA and Actionstrength Ltd became fraught when International Glass Engineering SpA was late paying Actionstrength Ltd for its services. An oral agreement was reached between Actionstrength Ltd and St-Gobain: that in consideration for Actionstrength Ltd not withdrawing its labour, St-Gobain would try to persuade International Glass Engineering SpA to meet its payments and, if that did not work, it would withhold monies from International Glass Engineering SpA for the purpose of compensating Actionstrength Ltd. When the situation did not improve, Actionstrength Ltd withdrew its services and tried to enforce the oral promise made by St-Gobain. St-Gobain argued that as its promise was a guarantee and did not comply with the Statute of Frauds (having never been written down), it was unenforceable. Lord Hoffmann agreed with this argument.

Using the words "guarantee" or "indemnity" in a contract is not necessarily dispositive. The test is: what were the true intentions of the parties? To ascertain this, Smith L.J. in *Pitts v Jones* [2008] Q.B. 706 stated that the court might ask: "what was the object of the contract or transaction"?

The writing requirement with respect to guarantees is subject to a number of discrete exceptions. For example, the 1695 Statute does not apply where liability arises on an implied promise or an account stated. Several of these arise in agency law.

Contracts the Consideration for which Is Marriage

Under the Statute of Frauds (Ireland) 1695, a *contract of marriage* does not have to be in writing. Traditionally, however, there needed to be written evidence of a contract where a person (for example, the parents of the bride or groom to-be) agreed to transfer property or money to the engaged couple, the *consideration for which* being the couple's agreement to marry. It is no longer possible to enforce an agreement to marry (see the Family Law Act 1981). Therefore, it is likely that this writing requirement will have very little relevance in modern contract law. Indeed, the English counterpart has been repealed.

Contract Not to Be Performed within One Year

Where obligations under a contract are likely to continue for more than one year, said contract must be evidenced in writing. In other words, unless the parties intend, at the time of entering the contract, to perform their contractual duties within a year, the Statute of Frauds will apply (see *Farrington v Donoghue* (1866) I.R. 1 C.L. 675). The rationale underpinning this seems to be that over time, memories may fade and if the agreement is not supported by evidence in writing, the court may have to rely on deficient oral testimony to decide any disagreements arising from said contract. In *Naughton v Limestone Land Co* [1952] Ir. Jur. Rep. 19, an oral agreement that bound the plaintiff to work for the defendant for four years following his studies was held to be unenforceable for lack of written evidence.

The test used to discern if the contract falls within this category is whether, at the time that the contract came into being, the parties intended or contemplated that it would take more than one year to perform. Even if the contract outlasts one year, if the parties originally intended that it be performed within a year, written evidence will not be required. Similarly, the fact that a party performs the contract within one year does not by itself bring the contract outside the Statute.

In *Farrington v Donohoe* (1866) I.R. 1 C.L. 675, there was an oral promise to maintain a five-year-old child until she was able to do so for herself. The child died within one year of the agreement. It was held that the agreement was not intended to be performed within just one year. It had been intended to have been of a much longer duration (until the child could maintain herself) and was therefore unenforceable without written evidence. In *Hynes v Hynes* (unreported, High Court, 21 December 1984), the High Court rejected a claim that a verbal contract for the transfer of a business from one brother to another was unenforceable in circumstances where there was no memo in writing of the agreement. It was held that at the time the agreement was entered into, the intention was that the agreement would be implemented immediately.

CONTRACTS FOR THE SALE OF LANDS OR AN INTEREST THEREIN

Section 51(1) of the Land and Conveyancing Law Reform Act 2009 repealed the words "or upon any contract or sale of lands, tenements or hereditaments, or any interest in or concerning them" used in s.2 of the 1695 Statute (as set out above) and replaced the words with the following formulation:

> "Subject to subsection (2), no action shall be brought to enforce any contract for the sale or other disposition of land unless the agreement on which such action is brought, or some memorandum or note of it, is in writing and signed by the person against whom the action is brought or that person's authorised agent."

In other words, any contract involving the sale of land must be in writing or evidenced in writing. Section 51(2) of the 2009 Act specifies that it does not affect the law relating to part performance or any other equitable doctrines which shall be discussed below.

Section 51(1) applies to contracts for "sale or other disposition of land". The rationale underpinning this rule stems from the significant cost of land and the fact that it is of limited supply. Interests over land may include freehold interests, leases, contracts of assignments, etc. but may also include the sale of things attached to the land (i.e. fixtures) in certain circumstances. The English courts have drawn a distinction between *fructus naturales* and *fructus industriales*. The former concerns those "fruits of nature" that occur naturally on a property and not by the efforts of humans (e.g. wild game, timber). The latter concerns those produced primarily as a result of the efforts of humans and must be severed from the land before sale. While a contract concerning the former (e.g. the right to hunt wild game on the land) might be considered one for the disposition of an interest over land, a contract involving the latter may constitute a sale of goods instead. In *Mackie v Wilde and Longin* [1998] 2 I.R. 578, for example, a contract concerning fishing rights (the right to draw fish from the water) over a river was held to fall within the Statute of Frauds, amounting to an interest over the lands. As such, some note or memorandum of the contract was required. By way of contrast, in *Scully v Corboy* [1950] I.R. 140, the letting of "meadowing" that was fit and ripe for cutting was considered to be a contract for the sale of goods as opposed to an interest over the land. As a consequence, part payment dispensed with the need for a memorandum. Had the case been decided otherwise, the instances of part payment would not have been enough to evidence the contract in lieu of a written memorandum of the deal. The decision in *Scully* may be explained by the fact that the meadowing in that case was fit and ripe for cutting and the contract envisaged its immediate removal.

Repealed: Contracts for the Sale of Goods in Excess of €12

Historically, s.13 of the 1695 Statute stipulated that any contract for the sale of goods worth more than €12 (formerly IR£10) could not be enforceable unless the buyer: accepts and receives part of the goods sold; *or* gives something in earnest to bind the bargain; *or* the buyer makes part payment. Unless one of these requirements was met, a memo was required of the contract. This section was substantially replaced by s.4 of the Sale of Goods Act 1893, which provided that a contract for the sale of goods worth more than €12 was *not* enforceable if there was no note or memo of the contract made and signed by the party to be charged or their agent in that behalf. Similar exceptions were provided by the 1893 Act, i.e. that if the buyer accepts part of the goods so sold; or gives up something in earnest to bind the contract; or makes part payment, then no note or memorandum in writing signed by the parties need exist. Section 4 of the 1893 Act has been entirely repealed by the Consumer Rights Act 2022.

Requirements of the 1695 Statute and Section 51 of the 2009 Act

The Memorandum: An Overview

It is not necessary that the parties intend, by their actions, to create a memorandum of the agreement. Letters written by solicitors, estate agents, etc. describing the terms of an oral agreement have been held to constitute a memorandum, regardless of intent.

In *Tradax (Ireland) Ltd v Irish Grain Board Ltd* [1984] I.R. 1, a letter from the defendant purporting to repudiate (reject) the relevant agreement contained a review of the material terms of the oral agreement. It was taken (in conjunction with an earlier telex) to be a sufficient note or memo of the contract.

The memorandum must have come into existence before the commencement of the action brought to enforce the contract. The note or memorandum of agreement need not be particularly formal, though it must be signed by the person against whom enforcement of the contract is sought.

For instance, in *Doherty v Gallagher* (unreported, High Court, 9 June 1975), the details of the sale of a property were appended to the bottom of a cheque, which was signed. This was held to be sufficient as a note of the contract.

The note or memo must also contain certain details. At the very least, it must identify the "parties, the property and the price" (as affirmed in *Godley v Power* (1961) 95 I.L.T.R. 135). If these three material terms are set out, then the contract will usually be enforceable unless it is clear that the parties intended *other terms* to be essential to the contract. Failure to add these essential terms will render the memorandum defective.

Signature

"Signature" has been interpreted generously: a rubber stamp, typed words, an illiterate's mark have all been taken as satisfying this requirement. In *Casey v Irish Intercontinental Bank* [1979] I.R. 364, a solicitor asked his secretary to type a letter setting out the material terms of a contract on headed notepaper. This headed notepaper was deemed to constitute a signature in the absence of a personal signature. In *Maloney v O'Connor* [2015] IEHC 678, the signature "Ger", being short for Geraldine, was accepted as being the nickname by which the signatory was generally known. The signature must authenticate the document (see *McQuaid v Lynam* [1965] I.R. 564) rather than be added as a point of information. In other words, it must be clear that the signatory is signing off on or approving the document.

Parties to the Contract

The memorandum must contain the names of all parties to the contract or at least describe them in such a way that they are sufficiently identifiable (see *Guardian Builders Ltd v Patrick Kelly & Park Avenue Ltd* (unreported, High Court, 31 March 1981)). The words may not be sufficient to identify one of the parties but if proof of identity from an external source is available, the memo may suffice. In *Bacon v Kavanagh* (1908) 42 I.L.T.R. 120, the words "you" and "your employment" in a contract of guarantee were deemed to be sufficiently clear to identify the party in question, after surrounding circumstances were referred to. In *Law v Roberts* [1964] I.R. 292, a court concluded that although a party's correct name had not been used in a note of a contract for the lease of a property, the identity of both parties was sufficiently clear from the correspondence and surrounding evidence.

Price

In *McQuaid v Lynam* [1965] I.R. 564, the failure to set out the amount of rent involved meant that the note of a contract was not valid. It is sufficient, however, if the note affords some method of identifying the price. In *Lynch v O'Meara* (unreported, High Court, 23 October 1973), it was held to be unnecessary to add into a memorandum the mode of payment, be it cash or cheque.

SUBJECT MATTER OF THE CONTRACT, I.E. WHAT IS BEING SOLD OR BOUGHT

In *Law v Roberts* (discussed above), the vendor complained that the note of a contract did not sufficiently identify the precise property interest that was being sold. The court nonetheless concluded that the subject matter of the contract was sufficiently clear, as the purchaser in this case had indicated a willingness to accept whatever interest the vendor possessed.

ESSENTIAL DETAILS OF THE AGREEMENT ACCURATELY STATED

If the parties have separately indicated the presence of *other* essential features of the contract, the memorandum must also make reference to these features. Otherwise the contract is unenforceable unless some other means of enforcement exists. Only terms thought to be material by the parties are essential (*Black v Kavanagh* (1973) 108 I.L.T.R. 91). The courts are prepared to hold that unless there is clear evidence to the contrary, it may not be essential for a memorandum to specify whether a deposit is payable, for example. Materiality is a question of fact. In *Guardian Builders Ltd v Patrick Kelly & Park Avenue Ltd* (unreported, High Court, 31 March 1981), notwithstanding the fact that the parties had discussed a variety of matters (e.g. the provision of roads), said terms were not deemed material. What was material here was the delivery of vacant possession of the site. The surrounding evidence showed this to be a crucial part of the case.

Remember that the agreement itself might separately be held to be void for uncertainty if there is failure to agree on terms as opposed to failure to record said terms. That being said, judicial intervention may rectify such failures. In *Kelly v Park Hall School* [1979] I.R. 340, for example, a failure to agree on a date for signing the contract was not fatal as the Supreme Court implied a term into the contract that this be done within a reasonable time.

JOINDER OF DOCUMENTS

A note or memorandum may be made up of more than one document which, though not sufficient alone to evidence a contract, may be read together as sufficient evidence of same. This is called the "joinder of documents". For instance, in *McQuaid v Lynam* [1965] I.R. 564, a receipt for a payment and an application for a loan were read together as constituting a memorandum of an agreement to rent premises.

In *Tradax (Ireland) Ltd v Irish Grain Board Ltd* [1984] I.R. 1, the plaintiff had orally agreed to purchase barley from the defendant. The court relied on a letter purporting to reject this oral agreement together with a telex containing the details of the contract as jointly constituting a memo for this purpose. The letter had referred to the terms of the contract and to the earlier telex.

This latter fact is of crucial importance: for two or more documents to be read together, there must be a sufficient acknowledgement in one document of the existence of the other document(s). In other words, there must be something connecting the documents together, such as a reference in one document to the other. In *Kelly v Ross & Ross* (unreported, High Court, 29 April 1980), for instance, a court refused to read nine documents together (particulars, conditions of sale, drawings, a solicitor's attendance docket, an estate agent's day book, correspondence) as constituting a memo of a contract, as none of the documents contained sufficient reference to any of the others.

As discussed above, in order for a party to be bound by a contract, the note or memorandum must be signed by that party (or an agent acting on their behalf), as evidence of the authenticity of the agreement. If only one document in a series for which joinder is requested is signed, difficulties will arise, because the signature must authenticate the entire memorandum. In other words: how can an earlier signed document refer to a later unsigned document if that document did not exist when the signature occurred? *McQuaid v Lynam* set out the following requirements where multiple documents are tendered as a note:

> "I think that the modern cases ... establish that a number of documents may together constitute a note or memorandum in writing if they have come into existence in connection with the same transaction or if they contain internal references which connect them with each other. But as the memorandum or note considered as a whole must be signed, it would seem to follow that the document which is signed must be the last of the documents in point of time, for it would be absurd to hold that a person who signed a document could be regarded as having signed another document which was not in existence when he signed the first."

In *Keena v Coughlan* [2019] IEHC 12, it was claimed that a contract to purchase the Ard Rí Hotel in Waterford was evidenced in writing by a receipt for a deposit of 10% of the purchase price paid later that day, coupled with certain emails that followed payment of the deposits. The court referred to the requirement that the signed document in a series must be the final document to come into existence and noted that it may be applied loosely where the documents came into being close in time. It acknowledged that if a vendor and purchaser respectively write out a receipt and cheque, it would be going too far to say that the vendor could not rely on same constituting a memorandum if the purchaser signed their cheque a few seconds before the vendor signed the receipt. Ultimately, in *Keena* the emails relied on were exchanged sufficiently contemporaneously to satisfy *McQuaid*.

"Subject to Contract"

As we have discussed in Chapter 4, the phrase "subject to contract" will usually be taken to mean that the parties have yet to reach an agreement. In England, case law indicates that the inclusion of this phrase on a document means that same cannot constitute a memorandum, as a memorandum must acknowledge that an oral contract exists. In Ireland, however, there is authority for the position that so long as the oral agreement does not contain the phrase "subject to contract", any inclusion of the term in a document will not prevent a court from finding that said document is capable of constituting a memorandum of a completed oral agreement. In *Kelly v Park Hall School* [1979] I.R. 340, the parties agreed, verbally, to the sale of land. The defendant's solicitor wrote to the plaintiff and stated in writing that "I confirm that we have agreed terms 'subject to contract'…". The Supreme Court found that this letter acknowledged that an oral contract had been completed. *Kelly* has been subsequently distinguished on its own facts in *Mulhall v Haren* [1981] I.R. 364. Subsequently, the traditional approach as espoused in England, that the memorandum *must* evidence a concluded contract, has been restated in several Irish decisions: *Carthy v O'Neill* [1981] I.L.R.M. 443 and *Kelly v Irish Landscape Nursery Ltd* [1981] I.L.R.M. 433. In *Boyle and Boyle v Lee and Goyns* [1992] I.L.R.M. 65, the Supreme Court again confined *Kelly* to its own facts and approved the court's approach in *Mulhall v Haren*. (See also the discussion of *JLT Financial Services Ltd v Gannon* [2017] IESC 70 set out in Chapter 4.)

Part Performance of a Contract—Equitable Means of Enforcing a Contract

The doctrine of part performance is an equitable doctrine that may lead to the enforcement of a contract for the sale of an interest in land that fails to satisfy the requirements of the 1695 Statute. The rationale for same is often said to be to prevent the Statute of Frauds itself being used as an instrument of fraud, as a means of justifying unconscionable conduct. Essentially, where an oral agreement for the sale of land has been performed in full or in part, the requirement of writing may be overlooked. In such a case, equity considers that the part performance provides evidence of the existence of the contract, and thus allows the contract to be enforced.

The classic example of part performance is where a person, on foot of an oral contract, is permitted to move onto the property the subject of the contract. For instance, in *Kingswood Estate v Anderson* [1963] 2 Q.B. 169, the plaintiff persuaded the defendant to move out of her existing accommodation and into new accommodation. The plaintiff promised that the defendant and her son could stay in the new accommodation for as long as they both lived. Although the contract was not evidenced in writing, it was deemed enforceable on the basis of part performance. In this case, the act of moving from the old house to the new house at the request of the plaintiff was sufficient. (See also *Kennedy v Kennedy* (unreported, High Court, 12 January 1984).)

Likewise, in *Rawlinson v Ames* [1925] Ch. 96, the parties orally agreed that the defendant would lease an apartment from Rawlinson. At Ames' request, Rawlinson made some modifications to the flat, which Ames inspected. The parties' acts were deemed to constitute part performance of the contract, relieving them of the obligation to provide written evidence of the contract.

The acts of part performance must have been carried out *by*, or *at the request of*, the party seeking to deny the enforceability of the contract. At the very least, the latter must have been aware of and must have acquiesced in the acts of part performance. The party seeking to enforce the contract must, moreover, provide unequivocal evidence of the contract's existence.

In *Silver Wraith v Siúicre Éireann* (unreported, High Court, 8 June 1989), Keane J. stated in obiter that the test to be applied is whether, as a matter of probability, the party relying on the acts of part performance can show that the acts of part performance can be held unequivocally referable to the type of contract alleged. This strict test seems to have been modified by *Mackie v Wilde* [1998] 2 I.R. 578. Here, Barron J. concluded:

> "What is required is that the acts relied upon as being acts of part performance be such that on examination of the contract which has been found to have been concluded and to which they are alleged to refer show an intention to perform that contract."

Barron J. held that the doctrine of part performance requires the following:

"(1) there was a concluded oral contract;
(2) that the plaintiff acted in such a way that showed an intention to perform that contract;

(3) that the defendant induced such acts or stood by while they were being performed; and
(4) it would be unconscionable and a breach of good faith to allow the defendant to rely upon the terms of the Statute of Frauds to prevent performance of the contract."

Finally, Barron J. held that it was permissible for the court to look at the alleged contract to see what was allegedly agreed before looking at the acts of part performance. Historically, the court first focused on the acts to see if they could be explained by the existence of a contract such as the one alleged. Barron J. rejected this approach.

Paying for the land (e.g. a deposit) will usually not be sufficient in itself to satisfy the part-performance requirement, though there are some exceptions to this view. In *Steadman v Steadman* [1976] A.C. 536, the parties were negotiating a settlement following the failure of their marriage. The husband was in arrears of maintenance to the sum of £194. It was agreed that the wife would surrender her interest in the family home in exchange for a lump sum and the arrears of maintenance be remitted save for £100. The husband paid the £100 and asked his solicitor to prepare a deed of transfer for his wife to sign. The wife refused to sign this deed of transfer. The House of Lords held that the husband's payment of £100 and the preparation of the deed of transfer were sufficient acts of part performance of the oral agreement. The House of Lords also stated that if the payment is referable to the contract for the disposition of an interest in land and if the payee accepts the money (for example, by lodging the cheque) then it may be inequitable to allow the payee to exploit the Statute.

In *Howlin v Power* (unreported, High Court, 5 May 1978), the defendant entered into an oral agreement to surrender a leasehold interest to the plaintiff. The plaintiff paid £220, constituting part of the purchase price. The defendant refused to complete the transaction and tendered repayment of the deposit. The plaintiff sought to rely on the doctrine of part performance. The court was prepared to follow the decision in *Steadman* that the payment of money could amount to an act of part performance in general. However, it noted:

> "[T]he doctrine of part performance is still confined to cases in which it would be fraudulent or inequitable for a defendant to rely on the statute because a plaintiff has prejudiced himself in some way by reason of the contract."

Here, there was no element of inequity or unconscionableness given the fact that the sum paid over was comparatively small and it was tendered in repayment to the plaintiff. As such, the doctrine failed.

In *Dakota Packaging Ltd v AHP Manufacturing BV t/a Wyeth Medica Ireland* [2005] 2 I.R. 54, Fennelly J. left unanswered the question of whether part performance applies only to contracts for the sale of land or whether it could be used in other cases.

11 Electronic Commerce

INTRODUCTION

Nowadays, more and more transactions are made using electronic methods. Although some specific issues arise regarding the application of contract law in this context, generally no distinction is made between a contract entered into online and a printed contract signed by the parties. While certain laws are specific to electronic commerce, a number of pieces of domestic legislation apply mutually to both online and offline contracts (e.g. the Consumer Rights Act 2022). The principles of contract law (e.g. the need for consideration, the intention to enter legal relations) are also generally applicable to contracts made online as they are to written or oral contracts. While it is outside the scope of this text to provide an exhaustive overview of electronic commerce in Ireland, this chapter aims to acquaint the reader with some key concepts.

FORMATION OF A CONTRACT

OFFER AND ACCEPTANCE

Section 19(1) of the Electronic Commerce Act 2000 provides that an electronic contract shall not be denied legal effect, validity or enforceability solely because it is wholly or partly in electronic form or has been concluded wholly or partly by electronic communication. Section 19(2) of the 2000 Act states that an offer, acceptance or any related communication (e.g. revocation) may, unless otherwise agreed by the parties, be made by way of electronic communication. As can be seen from the text of s.19, it is possible to have a contract consist wholly or partly (e.g. a mixture of paper documents and email correspondence) of electronic communication.

Much like offline advertisements, an internet advertisement will generally be treated as an invitation to treat. As such, the purchaser will usually be taken to make an offer by, for example, selecting and ordering the good or service from a website. The seller/supplier will then choose whether or not to accept this offer. McDermott and McDermott, in their text *Contract Law*, 2nd edn (Dublin: Bloomsbury Professional, 2017), para.6.20, note, however, that "[u]ltimately the test must be that of the intention of the retailer, objectively ascertained, and there is no reason why a web page could not amount to an offer in appropriate circumstances."

Electronic Signature

The use of e-signatures is provided for by both domestic and EU legislation. While the Electronic Commerce Act 2000 remains the principal Irish instrument governing e-signatures in Ireland, it should be noted that Regulation (EU) No. 910/2014 (the "eIDAS") provides a common EU-wide framework that requires mutual recognition of electronic signatures. The eIDAS has direct effect in Ireland and where there is a conflict between its terms and the terms of the 2000 Act, the Regulation will take precedence. However, where the Act and Regulation *differ* as oppose to *conflict* (i.e. impose separate rather than conflicting requirements), both must be complied with.

The eIDAS provides for three different types of e-signatures:

1. Simple Electronic Signature;
2. Advanced Electronic Signature;
3. Qualified Electronic Signature.

Simple Electronic Signature ("SES") is defined under art.3 of the eIDAS as "data in electronic form which is attached to or logically associated with other data in electronic form and which is used by the signatory to sign". It can take the form of a typed signature or initials written on an electronic device, or a scanned copy of a wet-signature (i.e. a .jpeg image of a signature), or a signature generated by software, e.g. DocuSign.

Advanced Electronic Signature ("AES") is defined in art.3 as "an electronic signature which meets the requirements set out in Article 26". Article 26 provides that said signatures are:

(a) uniquely linked to the signatory;
(b) capable of identifying the signatory;
(c) created using electronic signature creation data that the signatory can, with a high level of confidence, use under his sole control; and
(d) linked to the data signed therewith in such a way that any subsequent change in data is detectable.

Qualified Electronic Signature ("QES") is defined in art.3 as "an advanced electronic signature that is created by a qualified electronic signature creation device, and which is based on a qualified certificate for electronic signatures". Given the increased level of security offered by a QES, the eIDAS, under Recital 49 thereof, provides that said signatures have the equivalent legal effect of a handwritten signature.

The 2000 Act provides only for SES, AES, and Advanced Electronic Signature based on a Qualified Certificate (AESQC). While these categories seem similar to the types of signature provided for in the eIDAS at first glance, they are not direct equivalents thereto, having distinct requirements. For example, the AESQC under the 2000 Act goes beyond the definition of an AES under the 2000 Act but not quite as far as a QES under the eIDAS.

While most contracts can be concluded using e-signatures, others (e.g. wills, enduring powers of attorney, trusts) cannot be concluded in this way, under s.10 of the 2000 Act. Previously, contracts for interests in land were also excluded under s.10. The Electronic Commerce Act 2000 (Application of Sections 12 to 23 to Registered Land) Regulations 2022 apply the provisions of the 2000 Act to transactions that "create, acquire, dispose or register" an interest in registered land, i.e. property that is registered in the Land Registry. The full effect of this introduction is, at the time of writing, yet to be seen. Transactions involving unregistered title currently remain outside the scope of the Act.

Under the 2000 Act, signatories to a contract must consent to the use of e-signatures. This consent may be explicit or implicit (e.g. from contemporaneous emails). The 2000 Act also provides formalities for witnessing electronic signatures.

INCORPORATION OF TERMS

As will be discussed later in this text, where terms are not clear and unambiguous, they may not be incorporated into a contract. This principle applies also to electronic contracts.

In the Australian case of *eBay International AG v Creative Festival Entertainment Pty Ltd* (2006) 170 F.C.R. 450, the defendant was the organiser of an annual music festival, "Big Day Out" (BDO). It sold the tickets on a number of platforms including on Ticketmaster's website. In order to prevent ticket scalping, the defendant had cancelled a number of tickets that were sold on eBay's website at an inflated price. This was due to a condition of sale that was printed on the back of all tickets: that they may not be resold for profit (condition 6). This condition was set out on the BDO website. Ticketmaster's online terms and conditions of sale included a condition that all sales were subject to the promoter's conditions of sale. The defendant contended that the conditions were sufficiently brought to the attention of the customer on the Ticketmaster website, and in any case, the condition was set out on the back of the tickets themselves. As such, it contended that this condition had been incorporated into the contract of sale. The court noted that the sale of the tickets took place wholly online and no specific reference was made on the Ticketmaster website to condition 6. In circumstances where the tickets arrived some weeks after the point of contract, the fact that condition 6 was set out on the back of every ticket did not cure this. The court held that condition 6 did not form part of the respective contracts concluded on the Ticketmaster website. The implications of this case were that in order for terms and conditions to be legally binding, a service provider must have done all that was reasonably necessary to bring the terms to the customer's attention.

It is now customary for businesses, prior to the point of sale, to include a hyperlink to any pertinent terms and conditions that the business wishes to be binding, and to require customers to positively acknowledge that they have read and accepted said terms and conditions. The Irish Supreme Court in *Ryanair Ltd v Billigfluege.de GmbH/Ticket Point Reiseburo GmbH* [2015] IESC 1 acknowledged this by citing Laffoy J.'s decision in the High Court case of *Ryanair Ltd v On the Beach Ltd* [2013] IEHC 124, stating:

> "The conclusion of Laffoy J in the *On the Beach* decision was that the expression of assent to the terms and conditions of the websites of airlines and travel agencies through the clicking or ticking of a box is a practice generally and regularly followed in those commercial sectors. Moreover, she noted, in accordance with that practice, the terms and conditions of use of the website are available throughout such websites by way of hyperlink, with the objective of binding the user of the website to these terms."

CONSUMER RIGHTS ARISING FROM ELECTRONIC CONTRACTS

In circumstances where a contract is concluded as between businesses, obligations that might arise under legislation may be contracted out of depending on the circumstances. However, where consumers are involved, it is not permissible to contract out of one's statutory obligations. Consumer legislation, both domestic and EU, shall be discussed in more detail later in this text. However, it should be noted at this remove that consumer protection legislation applicable to offline contracts also applies to online contracts. Particular emphasis should be placed on the Consumer Rights Act 2022.

CONSUMER RIGHTS ACT 2022

There are a number of significant contractual rights that are implied into digital contracts as a result of the 2022 Act, including (but not limited to) the following:

- Section 106 of the 2022 Act provides that before a consumer is bound by a distance contract (the definition of which includes an online contract), the trader shall make available certain information (set out in Schedule 3 of the

2022 Act) which must be provided in "plain and intelligible language" and in a way appropriate to the means of distance communication. (See Chapter 15 for more details.)
- The 2022 Act provides a right to cancel within 14 days ("cooling off period") where goods are purchased by way of a distance contract.
- Part 3 of the 2022 Act also provides significant safeguards to ensure the conformity of digital content and digital services with digital content or service contracts (see ss.53–55 of the 2022 Act).
- If goods, services, digital content and digital services do not comply with the 2022 Act, consumers have recourse to a suite of remedies, e.g. termination, repair or replacement, proportionate reduction in price. (See Chapter 15 for more details.)

Express Terms

Introduction

In general, it is for the parties to a contract to determine its contents (e.g. subject matter, price, other terms). Courts are most reluctant to interfere in the creation of contractual terms. That being said, not every statement made by a party will form part of the contract, e.g. a statement made during early negotiations or statements that the parties do not intend to be contractual (e.g. advertising or trader's puff). Courts are often tasked with ascertaining whether statements made in the course of contractual negotiations form part of a contract, or whether they are external thereto. The incorporation of express terms in this way will be the subject of this chapter.

Can Oral Statements Form Part of a Contract?

In general (though with some notable exceptions—see Chapter 10), a contract may be made orally, in writing, or by a combination of both written and oral statements. In general, there is no legal difference between a contract made orally and a written contract: both are equally valid (though it will, of course, be easier to prove the content of a written contract).

Warranty or Representation?

Where a written contract is entered into and represents "the whole of the contract" between the parties, it is taken to exclusively set out the terms of the contract. However, where a contract is made orally, or by a combination of written and oral statements, determining the content of the contract may prove more elusive. In this regard, a distinction is made between two types of statement made in the course of contractual negotiations: a warranty and a mere representation.

- *Warranty*: The word "warranty" has different distinct meanings in contract law. It can be used to describe a term, the breach of which does not entitle the victim to rescind the contract but rather entitles them to sue for damages (described further at the end of this chapter). It can also refer to a retailer's or manufacturer's warranty to cover an item against malfunction for a period of time. When used as a comparison to a "mere representation", the term "warranty" means a statement that *has* contractual effect. If a warranty is breached, the appropriate remedy is provided by suing for breach of contract.

- *Mere representation*: While a representation may prove instrumental in inducing a person to enter into a contract, it does not form part of the contract. In other words, the content of the representation *has no* contractual effect. Where a representation turns out to be untrue, or is not fulfilled, the appropriate remedy lies in suing in tort for misrepresentation.

Whether a statement was intended by the parties to be a warranty of a contract, or qualifies as a mere representation, is a question of fact to be decided based on the circumstances of each case. However, a number of questions/tests may be instructive.

DOES THE PERSON MAKING THE STATEMENT HAVE A SPECIAL SKILL OR KNOWLEDGE?

Where a person purports to exercise a particular skill or knowledge, greater weight may be attached to a statement made by that person within their area of expertise. In *Dick Bentley Productions v Harold Smith Motors* [1965] 2 All E.R. 65, an experienced car dealer sold a car to a private individual, stating that the car had been driven 20,000 miles since its engine had been changed (the true figure was 100,000 miles). The dealer's statement was held to be a warranty, given his expertise on the matter. The dealer had *warranted* the mileage of the car. Likewise, in *Schawel v Reade* (1912) 46 I.L.T.R. 281, the seller of a horse assured the buyer that the horse was sound: "you need not look for anything; the horse is perfectly sound. If there was anything the matter with the horse I should tell you." It transpired after sale that the horse had an eye defect. Given the experience of the horse dealer in such matters, the court concluded that the statement as to the horse's health was a warranty of the contract as opposed to a mere representation. In *Oscar Chess Ltd v Williams* [1957] 1 W.L.R. 370, a private individual (relying on the car's registration book) innocently misstated the age of a car he was selling. He thought the car was a 1948 model, as evidenced by the registration book, but it transpired that it was a 1939 model. Given his lack of expertise in such matters, the statement was not deemed to amount to a warranty of the contract. The court held:

"The intention of the parties can only be deduced from the totality of the evidence. The question whether a warranty was intended depends on the conduct of the parties, on their words and behaviour, rather than their thoughts."

Here it was clear that the seller had no personal knowledge of the year when the car was made. He had become the owner after a great many number of changes. In such a case, it was unlikely that he intended to warrant the year of manufacture. The most he would have done was state his belief.

The case of *Hummingbird Motors v Hobbs* [1986] R.T.R. 276 is also instructive. Here, the defendant purchased a vehicle at auction, the odometer reading 34,900 miles. He then sold the car on to the plaintiff, signing the plaintiff's standard form which contained a declaration that the odometer reading was correct to the best of his knowledge and belief. In fact, the vehicle had done 80,000 miles. The English Court of Appeal held that the defendant had not intended to warrant the mileage, given his level of knowledge. The declaration amounted to a mere representation only. However, if the history of the vehicle *had* been known to the defendant as the only registered owner of the vehicle, a warranty might have been inferred in the circumstances.

Is the Statement One of Belief or One of Fact?

If, objectively speaking, the statement merely indicates the belief or opinion of the person making the statement and it is apparent that they do not take any responsibility for the accuracy of the statement, it is unlikely that the party intended the statement to be a warranty.

In *Anderson v Backlund* 159 Minn. 423 (1924), the vendor of land expressed his opinion that there would be plenty of water to sustain the land he was selling, as he had "yet to see the rains fail in Minnesota". This was held to be a statement of *opinion* rather a statement of *fact* (the situation might have been different if the vendor had been a meteorologist and tendering this statement as fact informed by his professional expertise). In *McGuinness v Hunter* (1853) 6 Ir. Jur. 103, the defendant, who owned a horse, told the plaintiff who was interested in buying the horse that the horse was "all right and I know nothing wrong about him". The plaintiff purchased the horse and soon afterwards it died. The court held that the second part of the statement amounted to a mere representation. However, the use of the words "is all right" amounted to a promissory statement. It was held to be a warranty, with contractual effect.

The courts will sometimes focus on whether the representee acted on faith of the truth of the statement rather than whether the representor intended the statement to be a warranty. In *Schawel v Reade*, discussed above, the seller of a horse assured the buyer that the horse was sound. On hearing this, the agent stopped his inspection of the horse and purchased it in good faith. He acted on the statement to his detriment, the horse having an undisclosed eye defect. The seller's comments were considered to be a warranty. In *Bank of Ireland v Smith* [1966] I.R. 646, the defendant auctioneers stated in an advertisement that land to be sold in a court sale was sown with barley and undersown with permanent pasture. This statement was incorrect but was made innocently and honestly. Notwithstanding this, Kenny J. noted the "injustice" that often follows where a person cannot recover damages for the innocently made statement. He cited *Oscar Chess Ltd v Williams* wherein Denning L.J. stated:

> "The question whether a warranty was intended depends on the *conduct* of the parties, on their words and behaviour rather than on their thoughts. If an *intelligent bystander would reasonably infer that a warranty was intended, that will suffice*" (emphasis added).

He also referred to *Dick Bentley Productions Ltd v Smith (Motors) Ltd* where the same judge indicated that:

> "… if a representation is made in the course of dealings for a contract for the *very purpose of inducing the other party to act on it, and it actually induces him* to act on it by entering the contract, that is *prima facie ground for inferring that the representation was intended as a warranty*" (emphasis added).

Denning L.J. went on to say:

> "[T]he maker of the representation can rebut this inference if he can show that it really was an innocent misrepresentation, in that he was in fact *innocent of fault* in making it, and that it would not be *reasonable* in the circumstances for him to be bound by it" (emphasis added).

In the case before him, Kenny J. noted that the statement in the advertisement was made with the intention of inducing a purchaser to act on it and the purchaser was in fact induced to enter the contract by it. The representation was honestly made and the maker was innocent of fault in making it. However, critically, it was held that it would be *unreasonable* that the defendant should not be bound by the statement made in the context of a court sale. The purchaser was therefore entitled to recover damages for breach of warranty.

In *Carey v Independent Newspapers* [2004] 3 I.R. 52, the plaintiff was headhunted from the *Ireland on Sunday* newspaper by the *Evening Herald*. She agreed to take up a position at the latter because of assurances she had been given in relation to her working hours: that she would not have to work the early morning shift at the office. Shortly after she started working at the newspaper, her editor was replaced and it became clear that the plaintiff was expected to work the early morning shift at the office. The plaintiff was unable to fulfil this obligation and her employment with the defendant came to an end. Gilligan J. held that it was clear that the assurances given were intended to induce the plaintiff to give up her job with *Ireland on Sunday* and join the *Evening Herald*, which the plaintiff relied upon in good faith. As such, the promises given were taken to be warranties.

HAVE THE PARTIES STIPULATED THAT THE STATEMENT FORMS PART OF THE CONTRACT?

A statement will be considered a warranty as opposed to a mere representation if the parties have expressly stipulated that it should be incorporated into the contract. If, on the other hand, the matter is not mentioned at the time the contract is concluded, it is less likely that incorporation has occurred. In this regard, timing is crucial. In *Routledge v McKay* [1954] 1 W.L.R. 615, a written contract for the sale of a bike made no mention of its age, though the matter had been discussed some four weeks earlier. The court concluded that the earlier statement (which had misrepresented the age of the bike) did not form part of the contract.

HOW CRUCIAL WAS THE STATEMENT IN THE CONCLUSION OF THE CONTRACT?

In *Bannerman v White* (1861) 10 C.B. (N.S.) 844, the purchaser of hops had asked if they had been treated with sulphur, adding that if they had been, he would not have been interested in their purchase. The plaintiff incorrectly stated that they had not been so treated. Given the importance attached to this matter by the defendant, the statement that the hops were untreated was deemed to be a warranty of the contract. Similarly, in *Couchman v Hill* [1947] 1 All E.R. 103, the buyer of a heifer stressed the importance he attached to the fact that the heifer had not been "served" by a bull. When the heifer turned out to be pregnant, the court concluded that a statement to the effect that the heifer had not been served was a warranty of the contract.

How Much Time Elapsed between the Making of the Statement and the Conclusion of the Contract?

If the statement was made directly before the contract was made, it is more than likely that the statement is a warranty. If it was made some weeks earlier (as in *Routledge v McKay*, above, where the statement as to the age of the bike was made four weeks before the contract was concluded), it is less likely to be a term. The time lag is relevant in determining whether the statement is a term of the contract, though it will not always be conclusive: in *Schawel v Reade* (see above), a four-week gap between the making of a statement as to the health of a horse and the conclusion of the contract did not preclude the earlier statement from forming part of the contract.

In all cases, however, a statement will not form part of the contract (and indeed will not be actionable as a misrepresentation) unless it is made *before* the contract is concluded. In *Roscorla v Thomas* (1842) 3 Q.B. 234, the defendant sold a horse to the plaintiff. *After* the sale, the defendant stated that the horse was "sound and free from vice". The horse in fact turned out to be quite vicious and the plaintiff sued upon this apparent warranty. However, because the warranty was given *after* the sale had been completed, the warranty was not supported by consideration and could therefore not be relied upon. In *Olley v Marlborough Court* [1949] 1 K.B. 532, a couple, after booking into a hotel and paying in advance for a week's stay, proceeded to their room. In the room they found a notice exempting the hotel from any liability in respect of lost or stolen goods. The hotel, however, could not rely on this exclusion clause (Mrs Olley's mink coats having been stolen) as it had been brought to the couple's attention *after* they had concluded their contract to stay at the hotel.

Emphasis in Statement

The more emphatic and certain a statement is, the more likely it is that it will form part of the contract. Correspondingly, the vaguer a statement is, the less likely it is that the statement will be incorporated. For instance, in *Schawel v Reade*, the seller of a horse assured its buyer in very strong terms that the horse was in good health. The emphasis in the statement convinced the buyer to stop his own inspection of the horse. The statement was thus deemed to be a warranty of the contract. By contrast, if the buyer is asked to check for themselves the truth of the statement, it is less likely that the statement will form part of the contract. In *Ecay v Godfrey* (1947) 80 Lloyd's Rep. 286, the seller of a boat stated that he believed the boat to be sound, but nonetheless recommended that the buyer should, prior to purchase, engage a professional to verify this. In such circumstances, the seller's statement was deemed not to form part of the contract.

If the Contract Was Put into Writing, Did the Parties Intend the Written Contract to Be Conclusive?

It may well be that, on the facts, the parties intended that the written contract would be conclusive, and that any oral statements would not form part of the contract. Determining whether this is the case is a question of fact, but obviously if the parties have expressly stated that a written document is intended conclusively to represent the entirety of a contract, then it is unlikely that statements external to that document will form part of the contract.

Where Written and Oral Terms Conflict: the "Parol Evidence" Rule

"Parol evidence" is any statement that is not contained within a written contract. This might include oral *or* written discussions between the parties, earlier drafts of the written contract, or correspondence exchanged between the parties. The "parol evidence" rule, or the "rule against parol evidence", states that where there is a conflict between parol evidence and the written terms of a contract, precedence is given to the latter. In other words, parol evidence will not be admissible for the purposes of varying or contradicting the terms of a written contract. As noted in *Bank of Australasia v Palmer* [1897] A.C. 540, parol evidence cannot be received to:

> "... contradict, vary, add to or subtract from the terms of a written contract or the terms in which the parties have deliberately agreed to record any part of their contract."

At first glance, the rule seems harsh, as it excludes all parol evidence that has not been included in a written account of the contract.

The classic example of the application of this rule arose in *Henderson v Arthur* [1907] 1 K.B. 10. A written lease stated that the rent on a property would be payable in advance. Oral evidence established, however, that the parties had, prior to the conclusion of the contract, orally agreed that the rent would be payable in arrears. The English Court of Appeal nonetheless concluded that the rent was payable in advance: the oral evidence could not be used to contradict the written terms of the contract.

The parol evidence rule was applied in Ireland in the case of *Macklin and McDonald v Greacen & Co* [1983] I.R. 61. Here, the first defendant company and the second defendant director agreed to sell to the first plaintiff a pub licence attached to the Royal Bar, Church Square in Monaghan. This agreement was reduced to writing. Subsequently, the licensed premises was demolished by a bomb explosion. The plaintiff sought specific performance of the contract. The defendants contended that the contract was now unenforceable given that a licence to sell intoxicating liquor is inalienable under law and must be attached to a premises. As the written contract was confined to the sale of the licence only, the court refused to allow parol evidence to be heard to contradict the terms of the written contract.

There are a number of exceptions to the parol evidence rule that permit the introduction of parol evidence, which are dealt with below. The number and scope of exceptions has been said to undermine the parol evidence rule and reduce its impact in practice.

RECTIFICATION

Where a written document:

- purports to be a written record of an agreement, and
- contains a mistake

a principle of equity permits parol evidence to be introduced if the remedy sought is rectification (an order of the court for the correction of a document). Effectively, equity permits the written document to be altered so as to reflect the true nature of the agreement. This applies, however, only where it can be established that the written document was intended to constitute a record of the prior agreement, and that the written document differs from the prior agreement. In this way, the parol evidence is not *adding* to the written document, it is merely *correcting* it.

In *Macklin and McDonald v Greacen & Co*, parol evidence was not permitted to be adduced in circumstances where the plaintiff's claim was not one for rectification (rectification as a remedy was not sought), but rather for specific performance of an agreement to sell a pub licence.

INTERPRETATION OF AMBIGUOUS TERMS

If the express written terms of a contract are unclear or ambiguous, parol evidence may be admitted to clarify their true meaning. Parol evidence may also be adduced to cast light on the broader context in which a contract was agreed. For instance, in *Revenue Commissioners v Moroney* [1972] I.R. 372, extrinsic evidence was admitted to show that a written contract that appeared to be for the sale of property was in fact a transfer by gift.

In *Chambers v Kelly* (1873) 7 I.R.C.L. 231, the plaintiff vendor and defendant purchaser contracted for the sale of oaks growing on certain lands "together with all other trees growing through the oak plantations and mixed with the said oak". The question in dispute was what trees besides oaks were included in this agreement, the words "all other trees" and "oak plantations" being ambiguous. Evidence of conversations between the parties in reference to the sale, prior to the agreement, was allowed to be adduced to identify the subject matter of the contract: what parts of the land in question were the "oak plantations" and which trees constituted "all other trees growing through such oak plantations, and mixed with said oak"?

In *Ulster Bank v Synnott* (1871) 5 I.R. Eq. 595, the defendant, who was indebted to his banker, deposited with him certificates of Railway Debenture Stock along with a letter stating that the stocks were being deposited "against acceptances made" on the defendant's account. This statement was ambiguous, as it might have meant that the security was being deposited against acceptances already made or against future acceptances yet to be made. Parol evidence was used to clarify this.

Parol evidence will most likely not be permitted where the contents of a written contract are clear and unambiguous. In *Kinlen v Ennis UDC* [1916] 2 I.R. 299, the defendant wished to build a series of artisans' dwellings and had put the building work out to tender. The plaintiff was selected to carry out the works. A dispute arose between the parties as to the extent of works to be completed by the plaintiff. The House of Lords refused to allow a tender to be admitted in evidence to prove the extent of the works to be completed. Although the said parol evidence was in conflict with the terms of the written contract itself, there was no ambiguity in the written contract that needed clarification.

Custom or Trade Usage

If the parties to a contract acknowledge that a particular trade custom exists, then parol evidence might be permitted to acquaint the court with this custom. For instance, in *Smith v Wilson* (1832) 3 B. & Ad. 728, the phrase "1,000 rabbits" actually meant "1,200" rabbits (much like a baker's dozen comprises 13 rather than 12) as a result of a local custom. Parol evidence was admitted of this custom to clarify matters.

Understandings common to a particular trade may also serve to clarify the terms of a written document, as in *Wilson Strain v Pinkerton* (1897) 3 I.L.T.R. 86. In that case, oral evidence established that on the retirement of a bread roundsman, who sold bread door-to-door on credit terms, it was common practice in the trade for his employer to take over any outstanding debts.

It should be noted, however, that just because a custom might exist does not automatically mean parol evidence that speaks to its existence will be permitted to be adduced. If the written contract provides for a rule that is at odds with the custom, it will be assumed that the parties intended that the custom not apply. In *Malcomson v Morton* (1847) 11 Ir. L.R. 230, a written agreement existed between the parties to sell Indian corn "as per sample". A custom existed in the corn trade that contradicted this term. It was held that parol evidence as to this custom was not admissible to vary or contradict the written contract, given that the words "as per sample" in the contract were unambiguous.

WHERE THE WRITTEN DOCUMENT "DOES NOT RECORD THE TOTALITY OF THE CONTRACT"

If a contract document is said to be the entire contract, then parol evidence is *not* admissible. However, if it can be shown that the parties intended that the agreement would consist of the written document read in light of other documents or oral statements, then the parol evidence rule does not apply. In this way, the "rule" really acts as a presumption that if the document looks like it constitutes the entirety of the contract, it will be presumed to be so. This presumption is rebuttable by evidence to the contrary. In *Couchman v Hill* [1947] 1 All E.R. 103, for instance, the plaintiff had received oral assurances that a heifer he was purchasing had not been "serviced" by a bull. In fact, the heifer was pregnant and subsequently died in childbirth. While the sale catalogue had also confirmed the heifer as being "unserved", the conditions printed in the catalogue stipulated that all "lots were sold with all faults, imperfections and errors of description", expressly envisaging, through its phrasing, other external terms or representations. The court concluded that the catalogue had to be read in the light of the oral assurances made to the plaintiff. Together, the catalogue and these assurances made up a "whole" contract. The plaintiff was thus entitled to sue for a breach of contract.

In *Clayton Love & Sons (Dublin) Ltd v The British and Irish Steam Packet Co Ltd* (1970) 104 I.L.T.R. 157, the plaintiff contracted with the defendant for the transport by sea of consignments of quick-frozen scampi in a refrigerated hold in the defendant's ship. Preliminary negotiations took place by telephone, between the agents of the parties, as to the temperature the cargo was required to be kept at for the duration of the crossing. The court held that the terms of the contract were split as between the contents of these telephone conversations and the defendant's standard conditions of carriage. The standard conditions of carriage were not taken to be the *whole* contract. Davitt P. allowed parol evidence of the terms of phone conversations and held that these conversations could be added to the written contract so as to form one contract. Although the Supreme Court reversed Davitt P.'s judgment on another issue, the President's judgment on the parol evidence point was affirmed. In *Howden v Ulster Bank* [1924] I.R. 117, the question before the court was whether title to a vessel vested with the defendant trustee in bankruptcy or the plaintiff bankrupt. A memorandum of agreement seemed to favour the defendant in this regard, but the court found for the plaintiff after hearing oral testimony. The court stated:

> "[P]arol evidence of a verbal transaction is not excluded by the fact that a writing was made concerning or relating to it unless such writing was in fact *the transaction itself* and not merely a *note or memorandum of it or a portion of the transaction*" (emphasis added).

We have seen that if parol evidence contradicts rather than adds to a written contract and the latter has been expressly drafted by one party and agreed to, the courts will be less inclined to enforce the parol statement. However, if the written terms take the form of a printed, boilerplate form, a contradictory parol statement may be given preference. In *Evans v Merzario* [1976] 1 W.L.R. 1078, the plaintiff imported machines from Italy to England and the defendant was its forwarding agent. The defendant gave the plaintiff an oral assurance that their machines would be shipped in containers carried below deck. One of the machines was packed on deck and was lost at sea. Notwithstanding the fact that the oral assurance contradicted the standard contract conditions, the English Court of Appeal held that it constituted an enforceable contractual promise.

Oral Statement Limiting or Qualifying Operation of Contract

Parol evidence may be admissible to show that there was no contract at all or that there were, in fact, two contracts. In *Pym v Campbell* (1856) 6 E. & B. 370, the plaintiff invented a "crushing, washing, and amalgamating machine". The defendant agreed in writing to purchase a share of the benefits of the invention. The court allowed the defendant to adduce oral terms of acknowledgement that the sale was subject to an inspection and approval by an engineer. This was a condition precedent (this will be discussed below), and if it did not transpire, the contract ceased to be. It was established that the engineer did not inspect or approve the invention and, as such, no contract was in being between the parties.

To Prove the Amount of Consideration

Parol evidence may be admitted to prove:
- (a) the amount of consideration to be paid if the contract omits this;
- (b) whether the price has in fact been paid;

(c) whether a memorandum or note of a contract, which apparently satisfies the Statute of Frauds (Ireland) 1695, is accurate.

In *Black v Grealy* (unreported, High Court, 10 December 1977), evidence was adduced to demonstrate that a memorandum (as opposed to a contract) which stated the consideration to be £40,000 was inaccurate. The true figure was £46,000.

COLLATERAL CONTRACTS

Where it can be shown that the parties intended to enter into *two* separate contracts, one written contract and another "collateral" contract consisting of written words and/or oral statements, both will be enforced separately. This is a good way of evading the strict effects of the parol evidence rule. In a number of the cases discussed above, the court found that a collateral contract existed in addition to the main contract. It often is said to occur when one party entered into a main contract because of a promise made by the other party to induce same. The promise/inducement might be enforceable as a collateral contract between the parties if it is found that "but for" the collateral contract, the main contract would not have been made. For example, in *City and Westminster Properties v Mudd* [1959] Ch. 129, while a written agreement stipulated that leased premises were to be used for business purposes only, the parties had orally agreed that the tenant could also reside therein. The oral statement gave rise, the courts concluded, to a collateral contract that could be enforced alongside the lease.

There must be consideration for a collateral contract to be enforced. For example: a landlord promises to repair the dishwasher *if* the promisee signs a lease. The lease subsequently is silent as to any obligation to repair. In signing the lease, the promisee provides consideration for his landlord's promise of repair, which itself is considered to constitute a collateral contract. In *Webster v Higgin* [1948] 2 All E.R. 127, a plaintiff bought a vehicle owned by the defendant. He was told by one of the defendant's employees that "if you buy the Hillman we will guarantee that it's in good condition and that you will have no trouble with it". An exclusion clause in the contract document attempted to undermine this promise by excluding all warranties. The court held that the promise by the employee as to the roadworthiness of the vehicle was a collateral promise that was not affected by the exclusion clause in the main contract. It was held that the plaintiff's entering the main contract of purchase was sufficient consideration for the collateral contract.

Should a contract for sale of land be unenforceable due to the memorandum of the agreement being defective, this may be remedied by finding a collateral contract. In *Godley v Power* (1961) 95 I.L.T.R. 135, during negotiations for the sale of a pub, the parties had agreed that any bottles stored on the premises at the time of sale ("the stock in trade") would be included in the sale. The stock in trade was not properly referenced in the written memorandum of the agreement to sell the pub. The Supreme Court held that the contract for the sale of the premises and the stock in trade were in fact two contracts, with the latter being a collateral contract. As such, the memorandum setting out the terms of the sale of the premises did not have to include the terms of the contract for the sale of the stock in trade.

It should be noted that a collateral contract also requires an intention to be legally bound by the promise made. In *Allied Irish Banks plc v Galvin Developments (Killarney) Ltd* [2011] IEHC 314, the court held that the defendant had established a collateral contract by which AIB had agreed, in pre-contract meetings, to limit its right of recourse to the defendants to 50% of the debt. This assurance was reduced to writing in the Heads of Terms but did not appear in the subsequent letters of sanction provided to the defendants. The court acknowledged that:

> "... not every statement or promise made in the course of negotiations for a contract may give rise to a finding that a collateral contract exists. To be so treated, a statement *must be intended to have contractual effect*" (emphasis added).

The court found that the Heads of Terms document was a commercial agreement that, while not being intended to constitute an unconditional binding agreement between the parties, was not devoid of contractual effect. Critically, it was noted that the assurances provided in the Heads of Terms were intended to induce the defendants to continue negotiations and obtain the facilities referred to therein. As such, it was held that the bank intended to be bound by this assurance. The Heads of Terms therefore constituted a collateral contract.

In contrast, in *Ulster Bank Ireland Ltd v Deane* [2012] IEHC 248, the court would not accept that generalised oral assertions said to have been made by bank officials in the course of negotiations could be relied on for the purpose of qualifying the terms of facility letters relating to a loan. The court distinguished the circumstances before it from the facts in *AIB v Galvin Developments (Killarney) Ltd*, stating:

> "The defendants have offered no evidence other than verbal discussions which they say altered the terms of facility letters, but such evidence is inadmissible, being in breach of the parol evidence rule".

However, the more recent case of *Allied Irish Bank plc v Cuddy* [2020] IECA 211 has rejected the supposed rule that oral assurances cannot give rise to a collateral contract. The court noted that nowhere in the *Galvin* judgment did the court make a finding that a collateral contract can only be made where supporting documentary material is available of an assurance. The court in *Cuddy* held that:

> "... as a matter of principle, a collateral contract can be set up, on the basis of oral representations or assurances, which may then affect the operation of a written contract."

This was so notwithstanding the parol evidence rule, which usually operates to disallow the admission of oral evidence that contradicts a written contract.

IMPACT OF THE PAROL EVIDENCE RULE

In practice, the parol evidence rule may be of very limited impact. Arguably, the exceptions are so wide and varied that the rule will only apply very rarely. Nonetheless, the parol evidence rule illustrates the dangers that may arise where oral statements are not reduced to writing.

CONDITIONS PRECEDENT/SUBSEQUENT

In some cases, a contract may be conditional on the occurrence of a particular event. Terms of this nature are generally divided into "conditions precedent" (which must be met *before* the contract becomes legally binding—see *Pym v Campbell* (1856) 6 E. & B. 370) and "conditions subsequent" (which must be met subsequent to the formation of the contract, if it is to remain enforceable). Whether there is a condition precedent or subsequent is ultimately a matter of construction. The traditional view was that terminology mattered. The modern approach is that the importance of distinguishing whether a term is a condition precedent or subsequent seems to be waning. It is the effect of the condition that matters—whether non-fulfilment prevents a binding contract from coming into existence (see *O'Connor v Coady* [2004] 3 I.R. 271).

The Relevant Importance of Contract Terms

What Is the Difference between a "Condition" and a "Warranty"?

A "condition" is a contractual term the breach of which allows the affected party to regard the contract as having been "repudiated" by the party in breach. In other words, the innocent party is free to walk away from the contract (as they are no longer bound by their obligations) and can sue for damages (though this right may be waived or lost: see Sale of Goods Act 1893 s.11). The option is open to affirm the contract also. We have spoken about warranties as compared to mere representations above. To complicate matters, the word "warranty" is also used to describe a term the breach of which will give rise to a remedy in damages only (one cannot repudiate). The innocent party is still bound by their obligations under the contract. They cannot just walk away.

Whether a term is a condition or a warranty generally depends on whether or not the term is deemed to be fundamental to the contract. Conditions generally go to the core of contractual liability; they are integral or crucial to the agreement entered into. In *Bunge Corp (New York) v Tradax Export SA (Panama)* [1981] 2 All E.R. 513, the defendant agreed to supply the plaintiff with 5,000 tons of soya bean meal. The cargo was due to be carried on a ship nominated by the plaintiff. The plaintiff was supposed to give the defendant at least 15 days' notice of the readiness of the ship for loading, but only gave four days. The defendant argued that this was a fundamental breach of the contract and attempted to terminate the agreement. The plaintiff sued for wrongful termination of the agreement, arguing that the breach was not sufficiently serious to warrant termination. The House of Lords held that in a written contract, a term that has to be performed by one party as a prerequisite to the other party's ability to perform their obligations ought to be considered a condition. In shipping contracts, timing is essential and clauses relating to time require strict compliance. Here, by not adhering to the notice requirement, the plaintiff compromised the defendant's ability to fulfil its contractual obligations.

If, on the other hand, the term is fairly minor or peripheral, it is more likely to be treated as a warranty.

It is always possible to indicate expressly in a contract that a term is to be treated as either a condition or a warranty. For example, although it may not be of great consequence to the average consumer, a car buyer who dearly wants to purchase a *red* car could stipulate that the contractual term as to the car's colour is a condition and not merely a warranty. While such an indication may not be conclusive, the presence of an explicit indication may provide evidence that the term is, in this context, intended as a condition.

In *L. Schuler A.G. v Wickman Machine Tool Sales Ltd* [1973] 2 All E.R. 39, the written contract expressly stated at Clause 7 that "it shall be a condition of this agreement" that the defendant would send one or other of two named representatives to visit the six largest UK car manufacturers "at least once in every week" in order to market the plaintiff's panel presses. The defendant did not conduct the visits as contracted. As a result, the plaintiff sought to walk away from the contract and the defendant sued. The House of Lords held that Schuler was not entitled to terminate the contract, notwithstanding the fact that the contract expressly provided that Clause 7 was a condition. Clause 7, it was held, created some unreasonable results. There was no provision in it to substitute the named representatives for others, even on the death or retirement of named representatives. It also made no provision for the possibility that one of the firms may not be willing or able to receive a representative during any particular week. The court held that the more unreasonable the result, the more unlikely it is that the parties could have intended it to be a condition and if they did intend said result, this should have been made abundantly clear. To construe Clause 7 as a condition would make any breach of it a material breach. It was held that this could not have been the intention of the parties.

As discussed above, it is possible (under s.11 of the Sale of Goods Act 1893) for a buyer of goods to waive a condition, or, in the alternative, to treat it as a warranty. The condition, moreover, may, under the aforementioned section, be downgraded to warranty status if the buyer of goods has accepted part or all of those goods (thus, only damages are available). It should be noted, however, that this section does not apply to a contract to which Pt 2 of the Consumer Rights Act 2022 applies, i.e. it only applies to non-consumer contracts for the sale of goods.

It is quite common for certain contractual terms implied by legislation to be deemed, by statute, to be either conditions or warranties. This happens often with consumer protection legislation.

INNOMINATE (OR INDETERMINATE) TERMS

There is a third category of term, known as "innominate" terms (literally "a term with no name"). This is a peculiar hybrid, the breach of which may result, depending on the circumstances, in *either* the right to repudiate and seek damages *or*, alternatively, the right only to seek damages. There is a modern trend that favours the classification of terms as innominate rather than as warranties or conditions, given the flexibility afforded to such a classification. When an innominate term is breached, the legal ramifications depend on whether the breach deprived the injured party of substantially all the benefit it was intended he would enjoy from the contract. In other words, if the effects of the breach are significant, the term is treated as if it were a condition, with the result that the contract will be deemed to have been repudiated by the breach. If the effects, on the other hand, are relatively minor, the term is treated as if it were a warranty and only damages will issue.

In *Hong Kong Fir Shipping Co v Kawasaki* [1962] 1 All E.R. 474, the defendants hired (chartered) a ship for two years. A term of the contract required that the ship be "in every way fitted for ordinary cargo service" (i.e. seaworthy). Due to various mechanical breakdowns, low staffing levels and inexperienced staff, the ship's first sailing was delayed by nearly five months. The defendants sought to repudiate the contract on this basis, claiming that the condition as to seaworthiness had been breached. The English Court of Appeal reasoned that the "seaworthiness" term was wide enough that it could be breached in ways that were either quite serious or trifling. The court rejected the contention that the parties intended that *any* breach of the seaworthiness term, no matter how technical, would give rise to a right to rescind. As such, it was not a *condition* of the contract and rather could be more correctly characterised as an *innominate* term, the effect of which depended on the effect of the breach. Here, neither the unseaworthiness by itself nor the delay were so great as to frustrate the commercial purpose of the contract. As such, the defendants were not permitted to rescind the contract.

In *Cehave NV v Bremer Handelsgesellschaft (The Hansa Nord)* [1975] 3 W.L.R. 447, a portion of a cargo of 12,000 tons of citrus pulp pellets had been damaged while in transit by ship. The contract under which they were being transported required that the cargo be delivered in "good condition". The English Court of Appeal concluded that this was an innominate term, given how wide it was. If the entirety of the cargo were destroyed en route, undoubtedly the breach would have been treated as a condition. In this case, however, the damage not being particularly extensive, the court concluded that the breach gave rise to damages only, and not a right to treat the contract as having been terminated. The Court of Appeal set out a series of questions that should be asked when dealing with innominate terms:

1. Does the contract *expressly* confer a right of termination for such a breach? If so, the courts must respect this and allow rescission even if loss resulting is minimal.
2. If not, does the contract *impliedly* give a right to rescission or only a right to damages? If so, the answer will again be conclusive.
3. Does a statute or case law point towards the obligation being a condition or warranty?
4. Has the breach gone to the root of the contract so as to deprive the injured party of that which they contracted for?

General Principles in Relation to the Interpretation of Terms

In order to interpret the terms of a contract, the courts will have regard to a number of tools, e.g. the *contra proferentem* rule (explored in Chapter 14). In *Investors Compensation Scheme v West Bromwich Building Society* [1998] 1 W.L.R. 896, Lord Hoffmann laid down five rules for the interpretation of terms, which shall be paraphrased below:

(a) It should be ascertained as to what meaning the document would convey to a reasonable person having all the background knowledge that would have reasonably been available to the parties at the time of contracting.

(b) The matrix of fact (background) includes anything that was reasonably available to the parties (with the exception of those matters set out in (c)) that would have affected the way in which the language of the document would have been understood by a reasonable man.

(c) The law excludes from the admissible background the previous negotiations of the parties and their declarations of subjective intent. These are admissible only in an action for rectification.

(d) The meaning which a document (or any other utterance) would convey to a reasonable man is not the same thing as the meaning of its words. The meaning of a word is a matter for dictionaries and grammar. The meaning of a document is what the parties using those words against the matrix of fact would reasonably have been understood to mean.

(e) Words should be given their "natural and ordinary meaning" subject to evidence to the contrary.

These rules have been cited with approval by the Irish Supreme Court (e.g. in *Analog Devices BV v Zurich Insurance Co Ltd* [2005] 1 I.R. 274 and *Law Society of Ireland v Motor Insurers' Bureau of Ireland* [2017] IESC 31).

Implied Terms

Introduction

As a general rule, it is assumed that if the parties to a contract want to include a particular term, they will do so expressly. As the Supreme Court pointed out in *Tradax (Ireland) Ltd v Irish Grain Board Ltd* [1984] I.R. 1, a court's function does not extend to writing the contract *for* the parties. It is for the parties alone to determine the content of their contract, and the courts will generally be slow to intervene.

Nonetheless, in some cases, even though the parties have not expressly included such terms, the courts may imply certain terms into contracts. In other cases, the legislature will require the implication of certain terms. There are a number of types of terms that may be implied into a contract:

- terms implied in fact;
- terms implied by reference to custom/trade usage;
- terms implied by common law;
- terms implied by legislation; and
- terms implied by the Constitution.

Terms Implied in Fact

In some cases, it is assumed that the parties intended to include certain terms, despite the fact that they were not expressly set out by the parties, because they are "implied in fact". The key point here is that it is said that the parties *intended* the inclusion of these terms but omitted them either because they were so obvious as not to warrant inclusion, or due to an error or oversight. There are two tests for the implication of terms in fact. Both tests are used by the Irish judiciary to imply terms that are either obvious or that have been omitted by mischance.

"Officious Bystander" Test

This test concerns terms that, although intended by both parties for inclusion in the contract, are so obvious they do not need to be expressly stated. For instance, in *Kavanagh v Gilbert* (1875) I.R. 9 C.L. 136, a term was implied into a contract to the effect that an auctioneer would use all due care in completing a sale on behalf of the plaintiff. The court used the officious bystander test to ascertain whether implication was appropriate. This test presupposes that at the time the contract is made, if a hypothetical disinterested bystander were to have asked the parties whether they intended to include a particular term, the parties would both have readily responded in the affirmative.

This was explained by McKinnon L.J. in *Shirlaw v Southern Foundries* [1939] 2 K.B. 206:

> "... that which in any contract is left to be implied and need not be expressed is something so obvious that it goes without saying; so that, if while the parties were making their bargain, an officious bystander were to suggest some express provision for it in the agreement, they would testily suppress him with a common 'Oh, of course!'".

The term must have been obvious to both parties (not just one of them) and must not, moreover, conflict with any express terms of the contract. Nor will a term be implied where it is unclear that it would have been accepted by one of the parties in negotiation. For instance, in *Carna Foods v Eagle Star Insurance* [1997] 2 I.L.R.M. 499, the Supreme Court declined to imply into a contract a term requiring the giving of reasons for failure to renew an insurance contract, as it was not likely that the defendant would have accepted it as an express term. (See also *Sweeney v Duggan* [1997] 2 I.L.R.M. 211.) Similarly, in *Spring v National Amalgamated Stevedores and Dockers Society* [1956] 1 W.L.R. 585, a court declined to imply a reference to an agreement between various trade unions into a contract between the defendant trade union and its members, as it was highly unlikely that the members had even heard of the relevant agreement.

BUSINESS EFFICACY TEST

The business efficacy test permits the courts to imply terms that are required to make a contract effective from a commercial point of view. Again, it should be noted that it is *not* for the court to *improve* the contract for the parties. Rather, the court may imply terms the omission of which may *defeat the purpose* of the contract. *The Moorcock* (1889) 14 P.D. 64 provides a good example of this mechanism in operation. The defendant contracted to permit the use of his wharf by the plaintiff, the owner of a boat called "The Moorcock". In the course of landing, the boat was damaged due to a shallow, uneven ridge of sea bed adjacent to the wharf. Although the contract was silent on this point, the court concluded that in order to give business efficacy to the contract, the parties had to have intended a term that the jetty was safe for the mooring of boats. Otherwise, it would make no commercial sense for the plaintiff to pay for landing rights: a commercially astute contractor would hardly agree to put his investment at risk in this manner. This term was therefore implied into the contract.

In a remarkably similar case, *Butler v McAlpine* [1904] 2 I.R. 445, the Irish Court of Appeal implied into a contract for the hire of a barge a condition that the defendants would use reasonable care in berthing the barge. The barge was damaged when it struck a concrete block lying on the riverbed near the wharf which the defendants had leased. The court concluded that there was an implied duty to ensure that the wharf was safe for this purpose.

The test requires that the term be obvious to both parties at the time of contracting. In *Carroll v An Post National Lottery Co* [1996] 1 I.R. 443, the plaintiff claimed that there was an implied term in his contract with the defendant that its agents would use reasonable skill and care in entering his play into the Lotto draw. In circumstances where the defendant clearly expressed that it would not be liable for the negligence of its Lotto agents, it was clear to the court that such a term would be contrary to the intentions of the defendant. As such, the court held that it could not imply such term into the contract.

In *Dakota Packaging Ltd v APH Manufacturing BV t/a Wyeth Medica Ireland* (unreported, High Court, 10 October 2003), the defendant purchased packaging from the plaintiff. No formal contract existed between the parties. A dispute arose as to how much notice the defendant had to give to transfer its business elsewhere. In the High Court, Peart J. determined that 12 months' notice of the defendant's intention to terminate the trading relationship was reasonable. The defendant appealed. The Supreme Court ([2005] 2 I.R. 54) declined to imply this term, having found that no agreement in contract existed between the parties. Fennelly J. stated that "it is important to bear in mind that the courts will not lightly infer terms".

In *Aga Khan v Firestone* [1992] I.L.R.M. 31, it was reiterated that the business efficacy test will not be used to augment an agreement that is enforceable without intervention. The decision in *The Moorcock* dictates that intervention should only occur to prevent the failure of a contract.

Terms Implied by Reference to Custom or Trade Usage

As we have seen in Chapters 5 and 12, in some cases terms may be implied by reference to a custom in a particular locality or a usage common in a particular trade. The onus of proving that a custom exists lies on the person seeking to rely on it; they must establish that the custom is well known and widely accepted. In *Ó Conaill v Gaelic Echo* (1958) 92 I.L.T.R. 156, for instance, a term entitling a journalist to holiday pay, though not expressly included in his contract, was nonetheless implied, as it was a practice common in that profession.

The test requires that the term be obvious to both parties at the time of contracting of trade, and known to both parties, even though the terms were not expressly included in the contract. In *Carroll v Dublin Bus* [2005] IEHC 278, the plaintiff returned to work as a bus driver. He was able to establish that there was a custom in Dublin Bus to facilitate drivers who had returned to work after illness with a lighter route, where possible. Clarke J. held that in circumstances where the plaintiff had not been given such a route, the defendant had breached an implied term of the contract of employment between the parties.

This may only happen, however, if it is established that the term is in fact common to the trade, and well known, and that both of the parties were aware of its use. Different considerations clearly would apply, for instance, if one of the parties was not familiar with practices in the trade in question.

TERMS IMPLIED BY COMMON LAW

In very specific contexts, the courts may, at common law, imply terms *whether the parties intended them or not*. This will only occur, however, where the term is deemed to be strictly necessary and where it does not conflict with the express intentions of the parties. Such cases, moreover, tend to arise in very specific and specialised contexts, most notably in relation to contracts of employment and leases of social housing.

For instance, in *Liverpool City Council v Irwin* [1977] A.C. 239, a local authority rented out accommodation in a high-rise block. In these circumstances, the council was held to be subject to an implied term that the tenants would have reasonable access to their properties and that the common areas in the block would be kept in good repair. Although the council was found not to have breached these terms, the House of Lords concluded that, by necessity, such terms were implied by law into the contract with each tenant. A similar conclusion arose in *Siney v Dublin Corporation* [1980] I.R. 400, where the Irish Supreme Court implied into a contract for the lease of council housing a term that the housing was fit for human habitation.

At the very least, according to the Supreme Court case of *Burke v Dublin Corporation* [1991] I.R. 341, such housing should not cause a risk to the health of its inhabitants. Here, the heating system was found to be inefficient and posed a risk to the health of the plaintiffs. *Byrne v Martina Investments Ltd* (unreported, High Court, 30 January 1984) is authority, moreover, for the proposition that a landlord generally has an obligation to keep a property in good repair. In the English case of *JN Hipwell & Son v Szurek* [2018] EWCA Civ 674, a tenant was able to rely upon an implied term of safety when the electrical wiring was found to be unsafe and went unrepaired by the landlord. These cases tend to arise most frequently where a local authority is involved (the local authority, after all, having certain statutory obligations to tenants). Indeed, it has proved more difficult to imply similar terms into contracts between private purchasers and vendors. For example, in *Curling v Walsh* (unreported, High Court, 23 October 1987), Hamilton P. rejected the view that upon the sale of a house, the seller impliedly warranted that the premises was free from structural defects.

Contracts between employers and employees have also been deemed to attract certain terms implied by law, for instance:

- That employers will make best efforts to protect the health and safety of workers has been implied in many personal injury actions (see *McCann v Brinks Allied Ltd* [1997] 1 I.L.R.M. 461).
- That employers will give reasonable notice of the termination of employment (*Carvill v Irish Industrial Bank* [1968] I.R. 325; *Royal Trust Co of Canada v Kelly* (unreported, High Court, 27 February 1989); *Sheehy v Ryan* [2008] IESC 14);
- That employers and employees owe each other a duty not to breach the trust or confidence placed in each by the other. Thus, employees will not endeavour to undermine their employer's business (by, for instance, simultaneously working for a rival). Likewise, employers will not engage in dishonest activities that may stigmatise their employees or bring them into disrepute (*Malik v Bank of Credit and Commerce International SA* [1997] 3 W.L.R. 95).
- That employees who resign will receive an accurate reference completed with reasonable care (*Spring v Guardian Assurance plc* [1994] 3 W.L.R. 354).

Cases in which terms are implied without reference to the parties' supposed intention are in fact quite rare and tend to be confined to specific categories of contract requiring special scrutiny. In fact, in many of these cases, legislation has overtaken the common law; the obligations on landlords and tenants, as well as employers and employees, being quite comprehensively covered by legislation.

TERMS IMPLIED BY LEGISLATION

Several common law obligations have since been codified into legislation, where they are described as implied terms of contract. Consumer legislation (see Chapter 15) is a good example of this.

TERMS IMPLIED BY THE CONSTITUTION

In some cases, terms may be implied into a contract (particularly those involving public bodies) by reference to the Constitution of Ireland 1937. For instance, in *Glover v B.L.N.* [1973] I.R. 388, a contract allowing an employer to dismiss employees for serious misconduct had to be read in the light of an implied term that the employee was entitled to the application of fair procedures. This term was implied by reference to the constitutional principle of natural justice, which dictates that decisions that impact seriously on a person should be made only after that person has had the right to hear and challenge the case against them before an impartial body of persons.

Articles 40.6.1°iii and 40.6.2° have been taken as permitting citizens to form associations and unions as well as the freedom not to join same (the right of "disassociation"). In *Meskell v CIÉ* [1972] I.R. 121, the plaintiff was a bus conductor. The defendant offered the plaintiff a new contract of employment which obliged him to join a trade union. Failure to do so would lead to his termination. The court held that the right of disassociation must be respected by an employer.

Exclusion Clauses

Introduction

A person who has assumed a contractual obligation may be excused from liability in case of breach by an appropriately worded "exclusion" or "exemption" clause. In the alternative, liability may be limited to a specified sum by means of a "limitation clause". Such clauses may serve, moreover, to exclude or limit liability not only in contract but also in tort, that is, for civil wrongs. Notably, an exclusion clause may be made orally, though it is more common to find it in writing.

Exclusion and limitation clauses effectively serve to assign to one or other party the risk of a particular eventuality occurring. Where two parties with equal bargaining power freely agree the allocation of a risk, such agreements arguably should be enforced. However, exclusion clauses have generally attracted a fair degree of judicial and legislative scrutiny, especially where consumers are involved. Particular concerns arise where exclusion and limitation clauses appear in "standard form contracts" or "contracts of adhesion", commonly found where businesses deal with consumers. A standard form contract is a pre-formulated contract drafted by one of the parties alone (usually a business) and presented to the other party (usually a consumer) on a "take it or leave it" basis. The consumer is afforded no option for the negotiation of specific terms. They must either accept the terms dictated by the business or walk away from the agreement. There are clearly some benefits in this approach. Contracts of adhesion have the advantage of convenience, greatly increasing the ease with which consumers may purchase products. It would certainly be tedious if every consumer had to negotiate individual terms every time she wanted to buy a product. Nonetheless, as businesses generally exercise a monopoly on the drafting of consumer contracts, the risk arises that the business will use its position unfairly to prejudice consumers. Thus, while exclusion clauses are quite common, they are nonetheless controversial, as evidenced by the reticence of judges in enforcing such clauses. In particular, the judiciary has adopted a series of principles regarding:

   (a) the incorporation of such clauses (whether or not they form part of a contract);
   (b) the interpretation thereof; and
   (c) the enforceability of such clauses.

Each of these matters will be dealt with in turn below.

INCORPORATION OF EXCLUSION CLAUSES

"Incorporation" is the process by which a statement (in this case, an exclusion or limitation clause) becomes part of a contract. In common with all other terms of a contract, incorporation may occur by one or more of the following three methods:

- incorporation by signature;
- incorporation by reasonable notice;
- incorporation by reference to past dealings.

INCORPORATION BY SIGNATURE

Where a person signs a contractual document, they are deemed to be bound by everything in that document, including any exclusion clauses therein. The person signing is also bound by any other document to which that contract makes reference. For instance, if a person signs a document stating that they have read and accepted certain terms and conditions external to that document, they are bound by those terms and conditions (whether or not they have read them). It is important to note that in cases where a signature is appended to a contract containing an exclusion clause, it is no defence to establish that the signer was not aware of the existence of the clause. In fact, a failure to read or to understand the contract does not relieve the person who has signed the document. In particular, a person who is unable to read, or does not speak the language in which the contract is written, will nonetheless be bound by the contract once their signature has been added to the document. The case of *L'Estrange v Graucob* [1934] 2 K.B. 394 illustrates this point. Here, a woman signed an agreement to purchase slot machines in apparent ignorance of a clause in the agreement excluding liability for express or implied warranties. Although the terms of the contract were written on brown paper and in "regrettably small print", the court concluded that because she had signed the document, the purchaser was bound by everything therein, whether or not she had read it.

This principle only applies if the document can reasonably be expected to contain contractual terms. In *Grogan v Robin Meredith Plant Hire* (1996) 15 Tr. L.R. 371, for example, the plaintiff had signed an employment contract with the defendant. The plaintiff was then asked to sign a timesheet, upon which the defendant had printed additional terms that were intended to incorporate terms by reference. The court held that a timesheet was an administrative document and an ordinary reasonable person would not expect there to be any conditions of a contractual nature therein. Additionally, the doctrine of *non est factum* (see Chapter 17 for more information) is available where a person is tricked into signing a document under a fundamental mistake as to the nature of the document. In *Thoroughgood's case* (1584) 2 Co. Rep. 9a, it was established that an illiterate person who signs a document may not be liable if its contents have been *misrepresented* to her. A similar principle might apply to a person with a visual impairment. A modern manifestation of this principle arose in *Curtis v Chemical Cleaning Co* [1951] 1 K.B. 805. Here, the plaintiff engaged the defendant to professionally clean her wedding dress. The defendant asked the plaintiff to sign a form and the plaintiff inquired as to what the consequences of signing it would be. The defendant explained that the form merely included an exclusion of liability clause for damage caused during the cleaning process to any beading or sequins on the dress. In fact, the exclusion clause pertained to all possible damage that might be caused to the dress during the cleaning process. When the dress was damaged, the plaintiff brought a claim against the defendant who referred to the exclusion clause in its defence. The English Court of Appeal held that although a party is usually bound by all the contents of a signed written contract, even where they had not properly read the contract, a clause ought not to be deemed enforceable where the drafting party misrepresents the effect of the clause to the other party.

Although the general rule pertaining to the incorporation of an exclusion clause by signature has not been expressly overruled, the Irish case of *AGM Londis plc v Gorman's Supermarket Ltd and Kerrigan* [2014] IEHC 95 is notable. In this case, although neither of the defendants were consumers, there was a "considerable imbalance in the relative commercial sophistication" between the plaintiff on the one part and, in particular, the second defendant. The court acknowledged that "circumstances can arise in which a less than rigorous application of the 'signature rule' is merited." This approach would not allow the signatory to resile from the consequences of his signature, but rather:

> "... it can be argued that a signature cannot be treated, ipso facto in all instances and every circumstance, and without further consideration, to bind a significantly weaker party to every detail of contractual dealings which he genuinely purports not to understand and which the stronger counterparty admits were complicated by its own actions."

This might mark a possible softening of the Irish court's approach to the rule.

Incorporation by Reasonable Notice

This is the second way in which an exclusion clause may be incorporated into a contract. Where a contract is not physically signed, a person may be bound by an exclusion clause where the person is given reasonable prior notice of the clause. Thus, although a party may not be aware of an exclusion clause and may not have signed a document to the effect that the clause was binding on them, they may nonetheless be bound if reasonable steps were taken to bring the clause to their attention.

The classic test was set out in the first of the so-called "ticket cases" that we shall be examining: *Parker v South Eastern Railway Co* (1877) 2 C.P.D. 416. Here, a passenger left his bag for safekeeping in a railway cloakroom. At the time of deposit, the passenger was issued with a ticket, on the back of which was a clause limiting the railway company's liability in case of damage or loss to £10. The front of the ticket referred the passenger to the back of the ticket and thus to this clause. The bag was subsequently lost and the passenger claimed compensation. The English Court of Appeal held that he was bound by the limitation clause as all reasonable steps had been taken to bring the clause to his attention, even if he had not seen it. The judgment in this case records a number of questions that the court should ask in order to ascertain whether a party (Party B) is bound by an exclusion clause drafted by Party A. These are paraphrased as follows:

1. Was Party B aware of the conditions? If so, they are so bound.
2. Was notice given by Party A to Party B of the existence of the conditions? If not, Party B is not bound.
3. If notice *was* given but Party B did not know the notice contained writing, they will not necessarily be bound.
4. If Party B knew the ticket contained writing, then the court must ask whether reasonable notice of the conditions was given. If Party B knew that the ticket contained not merely writing but conditions, they will be bound even if they are unaware of the precise terms.

This test was applied in *Richardson Spence & Co v Rowntree* [1894] A.C. 297. Here, the plaintiff was a passenger on a boat travelling to Philadelphia. The plaintiff was given a folded ticket with no writing visible in its folded form. When the ticket was unfolded, it had a number of conditions, including one that limited liability for personal injury or loss of baggage to $100. The plaintiff did not read the conditions on the ticket but was subsequently injured on the voyage. The court found that while the plaintiff was aware that there was writing on the ticket, the plaintiff did not know that the writing pertained to the contract of carriage and the defendant did not do all that was reasonable in order to give the plaintiff notice of the liability-limiting conditions. As such, it was held that the limitation clause was not available to the defendant.

A document may incorporate terms that are set out in some other document, provided reasonable notice of that other document is given. In *Ryan v Great Southern & Western Railway* (1898) 32 I.L.T.R. 108, the plaintiff had been a train passenger with the defendant. On the face of his ticket, in small font, there was a reference to conditions that were binding on passengers, available for inspection elsewhere upon special inquiry. These standard conditions included a limitation clause. The court found that the plaintiff was unaware that the ticket had contained limiting conditions by incorporation and also that insufficient notice had been given of the term. In contrast, in *Early v Great Southern Railway* [1940] I.R. 414, the plaintiff purchased a ticket for a special train. In the station there was a poster that stated that said special tickets were issued subject to the notices and conditions set out in the company's timetables. The front of the ticket referred the passenger to the back, where the following notice was printed: "Issued subject to the conditions and regulations in the company's timetables, books, bills and notices." One of those conditions was that the holder of such a ticket did not have a right of action against the company for personal injuries. No copy of the timetable or other document containing this condition was available for inspection by passengers at the stop where the plaintiff boarded. Notwithstanding this, the plaintiff made no inquiry. The plaintiff was injured and the defendant sought to rely on this exclusion clause. The court held that the defendants had taken reasonable steps to bring the conditions to the attention of the plaintiff.

Treitel in his book *The Law of Contract*, 15th edn (London: Sweet & Maxwell, 2020) provides a list of examples of instances in which exemption or limitation clauses may not be incorporated:

> "... if there are no words on the face of the document drawing attention to it, or if, though there are such words, the back of the document is blank (only the front having been transmitted by fax), or if the words are made illegible by a date stamp, or if the exemption clause is buried in a mass of advertisements."

In *Shea v Great Southern Railway* [1944] Ir. Jur. Rep. 26, the plaintiff took a bicycle onto a crowded bus. The conductor gave him a ticket for his bicycle which stated: "Receipt for Cycle or Pram accompanied by passenger – At Owner's Risk – Issued subject to the Company's Rules and Regulations." A notice was also erected at the entrance to the bus which excluded liability for loss or damage to luggage or parcels. The conductor did not draw the passenger's attention to either of these. The plaintiff's bicycle was damaged.

Davitt J. identified the public policy rationale for the test as applied in the "ticket cases", being convenience. It would be far too complex to ensure that every condition was specifically brought to the passenger's attention. The reasonable notice test therefore had purpose. Here, the court stated:

> "It is plain to be seen from [the] notice that the ticket is issued subject to certain conditions and in normal circumstances any passenger can see that. If, for any reason, including the reason that he does not know of what the conditions are and cannot immediately find out, the passenger is not prepared to accept the conditions he is at liberty to get off the bus or remove his bicycle. I cannot accept the suggestion that the plaintiff had not a reasonable opportunity of reading what was on the face of his ticket."

While the basic test has not changed over the years, a heightened concern for the welfare of consumers has arguably led to a more rigorous assessment of what is or is not a reasonable step. Indeed, in *Hollingworth v Southern Ferries Ltd* [1977] 2 Lloyd's Rep. 70, the court opined:

> "I do not consider that mere reference to conditions of carriage in a brochure ... is sufficient to bring home fairly to an intending passenger that his common law and statutory rights to compensation for death or bodily injury ... are going to be removed from him."

A number of factors are of relevance in this context.

Timing of the Notice

Notice of an exemption clause will only be effective where it occurs before the contract is entered into. If it is given after the contract has concluded, it will not bind the other party.

In *Olley v Marlborough Court* [1949] 1 K.B. 532, a couple, after booking into a hotel and paying in advance for a week's stay, proceeded to their room. In the room they found a notice exempting the hotel from any liability in respect of lost or stolen goods. The hotel, however, could not rely on this exclusion clause (Mrs Olley's mink coats having been stolen) as it had been brought to the couple's attention after they had concluded their contract to stay at the hotel.

In *Thornton v Shoe Lane Parking* [1971] 1 All E.R. 686, on entering a multi-storey car park, an automated barrier machine issued the plaintiff with a ticket which referred to conditions displayed inside the car park. A notice inside the car park purported to exempt the car park owner from liability in respect of damage or personal injury however so caused. This was, however, deemed to be ineffective as the clause was only brought to the notice of the car owner *after* the contract to park his car was concluded. Denning M.R. held that the offer of parking was made via the terms stated on the outside of the multi-storey car park, which were accepted by approaching the barrier and taking a ticket. The contract was therefore formed before the exemption clause was brought to the plaintiff's attention. In any event, the court held that the car park had not given sufficient notice, and stated that the term:

> "... is so wide and so destructive of rights that the court should not hold any man bound by it unless it is drawn to his attention in the most explicit way ... In order to give sufficient notice, it would need to be printed in red ink with a red hand pointing to it – or something equally startling."

Form of the Notice

It must also be established that the notice is one that would reasonably be expected to contain conditions such as an exclusion clause. For instance, in *Chapleton v Barry UDC* [1940] 1 All E.R. 356, an exclusion clause was contained on the back of a ticket issued to customers who hired deckchairs for use on a beach. The English Court of Appeal concluded that the exclusion clause was not binding, firstly because of the timing of the notice but also because it was contained in a document that would not normally be expected to contain such terms. The court reasoned that the ticket was simply a receipt of payment, and that the ordinary reasonable person would not have expected it to contain conditions.

Prominence of the Notice

Size and visibility are clearly important factors in this context. The bigger the notice and the more prominent its location, the more likely it is that reasonable steps will have been taken (see Lord Denning's "red hand" rule discussed above). In *Sugar v LMS Railway* [1941] 1 All E.R. 172, the conditions on a railway ticket were deemed not to be binding, as they were obscured by a date stamp.

Onerous Nature of the Term

Additionally, the more onerous and unusual the term in question, the greater the efforts required to bring it to the customer's attention (again, see Lord Denning's "red hand" rule). The case of *Interfoto Picture Library Ltd v Stiletto Visual Programmes Ltd* [1988] 1 All E.R. 348, while not strictly concerned with exclusion clauses, is instructive. Here, the defendant had obtained permission to use photographs belonging to a photographic library. On delivery of the photos, the defendant received a delivery note the very bottom of which contained a statement that if the photos were not returned within 14 days, a fine of £5 *per photo per day* would apply. Having returned the photos a month after receipt, the defendant was presented with a bill for £3,783.50. The term, however, was not binding: the English Court of Appeal reasoned that given the very onerous and unusual nature of the term, the plaintiff had not done enough to bring it to the attention of the defendant. The court instead substituted an award of £3.50 per photo per week, holding that this was a more reasonable fine. The nub of this case is that the more serious the consequences of the clause, the more unusual and onerous its terms, the greater the efforts required to constitute reasonable steps. In this case, the plaintiff was obliged to bring the clause to the explicit attention of the defendant: a written notice in a delivery note was not sufficient for incorporation.

In *Goodlife Foods Ltd v Hall Fire Protection Ltd* [2018] EWCA Civ 1371, the English Court of Appeal held that an exemption clause must be viewed in the context of the entire contract and not in isolation. The market for the goods or services in question will also be instructive: if the terms used are typical of the industry, they may not be considered onerous by the court.

In *James Elliott Construction Ltd v Irish Asphalt Ltd* [2014] IESC 74, the Supreme Court noted that the limitation clause in question was particularly onerous. It was not printed on the delivery notices provided and it was not brought to the attention of anyone in the plaintiff company. While the term was included on the defendant's credit notes, these were only read by personnel in the accounts department of the plaintiff company who were not at managerial level. As such, it was held that not enough was done to bring the clause to the plaintiff's attention.

Reference to Conditions that May Be Obtained Elsewhere

Where a notice refers to conditions that may be consulted elsewhere, these conditions may be incorporated if the reader is reasonably able to access those conditions prior to conclusion of the contract. Whether this condition is met (for example, in cases where a bus ticket refers to the "rules and regulations" of the carrier) will thus depend on whether the bearer can easily access those rules and regulations. Nonetheless, in *Early v Great Southern Railway*, as we have seen, a railway passenger was deemed to be bound by conditions referred to (but not listed) on a railway ticket, even though a copy of those conditions was not available at the office where the ticket was purchased.

Past Dealings

An exclusion clause may be incorporated by reference to past dealings. For instance, in *Spurling v Bradshaw* [1956] 2 All E.R. 121, the defendant had stored eight barrels of orange juice at a warehouse run by the plaintiff. He had dealt with the plaintiff regularly in the past. On collection, the defendant discovered that the previously full barrels were now mysteriously empty. A document received by the defendant *after* the contract was made contained a clause excluding the plaintiff from liability in case of "loss or damage occasioned by negligence or wrongful act or default". As this document was received after the contract was entered into, the defendant argued that the clause did not apply. Nonetheless, as the parties had a long history of similar dealings, in which a similar clause had always been included, the plaintiff was not liable for the loss. Similarly, in *Miley v McKechnie* (1949) 84 I.L.T.R. 89, having deposited clothes at the defendant laundry, the plaintiff was given a receipt, marked "important", which excluded the defendant from liability for any damage to the clothes. The Circuit Court concluded that although this receipt was issued after the contract was entered into, the plaintiff and defendant had a history of past dealings, on each of which occasions the plaintiff had invariably been presented with a similar receipt. The laundry was thus not liable for damage to the plaintiff's clothes.

In order to give rise to incorporation, past dealings must be:

(a) sufficiently frequent; and
(b) sufficiently consistent.

One or two isolated transactions do not constitute a course of dealing unless both parties are of a similar bargaining strength and operate on terms that are understood to be common within their industry.

In *McCutcheon v MacBrayne* [1964] 1 W.L.R. 125, a Scottish car ferry sank resulting in the loss of the plaintiff's car. The ferry owner had not, on this occasion, required the car owner to sign a risk note (excusing the ferry owner from any liability for loss or damage). On some previous occasions (though not others), the plaintiff *had* signed such a note. In this case, however, the course of dealing was deemed too inconsistent to incorporate the risk note. Likewise, in *Hollier v Rambler Motors* [1972] 2 Q.B. 71, the plaintiff consumer had taken his car to a repair shop on three or four occasions over the course of five years. This was deemed insufficient to create a "course of dealing".

In *Lynch Roofing Systems Ltd v Christopher Bennett & Son (Construction) Ltd* [1999] 2 I.R. 450, the plaintiff subcontractor sought to issue proceedings against the defendant. The defendant sought to rely on an arbitration clause that would have the effect of staying proceedings. The defendant claimed that it had notified the plaintiff, prior to agreement, of its intent to use an industry standard contract document which contained the arbitration clause. The plaintiff claimed that it had not agreed to this nor had it examined the contract prior to the commencement of works. The court held that because both parties were carrying on the same business and were of equal bargaining power, standard conditions that were typically used in the industry could be incorporated into the contract.

INTERPRETING EXCLUSION AND LIMITATION CLAUSES

THE CONTRA PROFERENTUM RULE

The manner in which judges interpret or read exclusion clauses may also serve to limit their application. Exclusion clauses will invariably be read restrictively. In particular, the *contra proferentum* rule requires that any ambiguity in an exclusion clause must be read in the manner least advantageous to the person who is attempting to rely upon the clause (the *proferens*). In other words, in cases of uncertainty, the benefit of the doubt is given to the person against whom the exclusion clause is being invoked. This is an important rule from the perspective of a consumer, because it is usually the seller who attempts to rely on an exemption clause.

In *Andrews v Singer* [1934] 1 K.B. 17, a car with 500 miles on its clock was advertised as "new". A contractual clause excluding "any warranty or condition implied by common law, statute or otherwise" was deemed not to apply in this case, as the statement that the car was new was an *express* contractual term; the exclusion clause only referred to *implied* terms.

In *White v John Warrick & Co Ltd* [1953] 2 All E.R. 1021, the plaintiff hired a tricycle from the defendant and sustained personal injuries. The defendant sought to rely on a clause in their written contract which provided that "nothing in this agreement shall render the owners liable for any personal injury". It was held that this clause only limited the strict liability of the defendant in contract but not in tort.

In *Houghton v Trafalgar Insurance* [1954] 1 Q.B. 247, an exclusion clause exempted an insurance company from liability where an insured car was carrying an excessive "load". The term "load" was interpreted restrictively so that the clause did not apply to an accident involving a car carrying more people than it was designed for. "Excessive load" was deemed to mean an excess of goods, and not an excess of passengers. (See also *Sproule v Triumph Cycle* [1927] N.I. 83.)

In general, however, clauses that *limit* liability to a set amount (as opposed to those that exclude all liability) are not read as restrictively, as evidenced by *Ailsa Craig Fishing Co v Malvern Fishing and Securicor* [1983] 1 All E.R. 101. In this case, a ship docked at Aberdeen Harbour sank as a result of the negligence of the defendants. A clause limiting the liability of Securicor to £1,000 was deemed enforceable, the House of Lords concluding that the *contra proferentum* rule did not apply with the same rigour to limitation clauses. The courts indeed tend to regard such clauses as reasonable, as they set out the amount of damages that will be awarded in cases of breach, and thus create certain efficiencies, in particular by avoiding litigation on the amount of damages owed in cases of breach.

The Risk Covered

Another way the court restricts exclusion clauses is to hold that the words thereof are inapplicable to certain extreme eventualities. In *Ronan v Midland Railway Co* (1883) 14 L.R. (Ir.) 157, a clause stipulating that cattle travelling on the defendant's ship would travel at "the owner's risk" was deemed not to cover a situation where the cattle had been injured due to the deliberate and malicious actions of the ship's employees.

In *Pearson v Dublin Corporation* [1907] A.C. 351, the defendant provided the plaintiff with plans for the construction of a sewage system. The information in the plans was incorrect and caused the plaintiff to incur expense. The contract between the parties included a limitation clause which stated that the representation in the plans must not be relied on and the plaintiff must determine the facts for themselves. The House of Lords held that a limiting clause cannot be allowed to exclude liability for fraudulent misrepresentation made by the defendant.

It is unusual for the courts to permit a *proferens* to exclude liability for their own negligence or the negligence of their servants or agents. However, if the clause is explicit enough, it may be permitted.

The Main Purpose Rule

Sometimes if an exclusion clause is read literally, it produces undesirable consequences. The courts will generally look to the purpose for which the clause was created in order to avoid this. In *Glynn v Margotson* [1893] A.C. 351, a contract for the transport of oranges by ship from Malaga to Liverpool allowed the ship to stop en route at various ports in the Mediterranean, Black Sea or the Adriatic. An exclusion clause in the contract excluded liability for damage to the cargo as a result of delay in proceeding directly from Malaga to Liverpool. The House of Lords nonetheless concluded that the contract required delivery as soon as possible and unnecessary delays could not be excused. The main purpose of the clause was to facilitate safe passage, not to allow the captain to circumnavigate the Mediterranean at his leisure.

THE "CORE OBLIGATION" AND EXCLUSION CLAUSES

There is some debate regarding the effect of clauses that purport to exclude liability for breach of the "core obligation of the contract". In *L'Estrange v Graucob* [1934] 2 K.B. 394, the plaintiff contracted to purchase a cigarette vending machine from the defendant. An exclusion clause therein protected the seller if the machine was not delivered. This went to the very heart of the contract. Ultimately, however, the plaintiff was unsuccessful as it had signed the contract and was therefore bound by its contents.

The leading Irish case on the point is *Clayton Love & Sons (Dublin) Ltd v The British and Irish Steam Packet Co Ltd* (1970) 104 I.L.T.R. 157. Here, the defendant agreed to transport deep-frozen scampi from Dublin to Liverpool, the parties having resolved that the goods would remain frozen while in transit. The scampi were nonetheless stored at room temperature on board the ship, and thus destroyed. The defendant sought to rely on an exclusion clause that appeared to be broad enough to exclude liability in this case. The Supreme Court, however, concluded that as a rule of law, the clause could not be invoked to excuse a "fundamental breach", that is, a breach of the core obligation of the contract: to transport the scampi in good condition to Liverpool. Thus, exclusion clauses have been held not to apply to situations where, for instance, a purchased car simply did not run at all (*Karsales (Harrow) v Wallis* [1956] 1 W.L.R. 936) or in the case of a tipping truck that did not tip (*Astley Industrial Trust v Grimley* [1963] 2 All E.R. 33).

Clark in his text *Contract Law in Ireland*, 9th edn (Dublin: Round Hall 2022) at para.7-48 considers the criticism of this rule of law:

> "[I]t treats all exemption clauses and all parties as if they were alike; in fact there are cases where it may be reasonable to permit a limiting clause to operate so as to 'shrink' the core obligation, thereby reallocating risk."

Indeed, the UK courts consider the doctrine of fundamental breach to be less like a rule of law and more like a rule of interpretation. In *Photo Production Ltd v Securicor* [1980] 2 W.L.R. 283, the defendant contracted to provide security for the plaintiff's factory. A term in the contract exempted liability for any injurious act or default of the defendant's employees. As a result of the reckless conduct of one of the defendant's employees, the factory was burnt down. Despite this very obvious breach (the object of the contract being to *protect* the factory, not to *destroy* it!), the House of Lords ruled that the exclusion clause was enforceable, the plaintiff having freely contracted to accept the risk of such damage, with full knowledge of the risk. In so ruling, the Lords concluded that the doctrine of fundamental breach, while valid, was merely a rule of interpretation. Thus, if an exclusion clause is sufficiently clear and wide enough to cover the loss, and the parties have freely agreed to allocate risk in this manner, the exclusion clause will be enforced. It may be argued that if two businesses of equal bargaining power freely agree (with full knowledge) to allocate risk in such a way as to exempt one party from liability, such an agreement should be enforced. Indeed, although *Clayton Love* remains good law in Ireland, some judges have tentatively suggested a preference for the approach in *Photo Production*. For instance, in *Western Meats v National Ice and Cold Storage* [1982] I.L.R.M. 101, Barrington J. suggested that judges should respect the intentions of parties who freely agree to allocate full risk. This approach was also taken by the Irish courts in *Tokn Grass Products v Sexton & Co Ltd* (unreported, High Court, 13 October 1983).

OTHER LIMITATIONS ON EXCLUSION CLAUSES

A person generally may not rely on exclusion and limiting clauses in a contract to which they are not a party. An exclusion clause may be restricted if its terms have been orally misrepresented (see *Curtis v Chemical Cleaning & Dyeing Co Ltd* [1951] 1 K.B. 805), or if there is an overriding oral promise negating the exclusion clause (e.g. *Mendelssohn v Normand* [1970] 1 Q.B. 177, where a driver was orally assured that his car would be safe if left unlocked in a car park. This superseded the exclusion clause).

15 Consumer Rights under Contract

INTRODUCTION

In theory, the parties to a contract are free to agree the terms of their bargain. Historically, judges and lawmakers proved reluctant to interfere even when a contract seemed lopsided or unfair, preferring the view that the parties to the contract should be held to their bargain. The view was taken that the parties should look out for their own interests—the term *caveat emptor* (let the buyer beware) sums up this older perspective.

Nonetheless, in more recent decades the view has prevailed that certain terms in contracts should not be permitted, most notably where the contract is entered into between a consumer and a trader. The disparity in bargaining power and expertise justified, the legislature considered, laws that offered greater protection to consumers against sharp practices. Consumers generally do not have the time or inclination to negotiate the terms by which they are bound. As such, the task of drafting consumer contracts usually falls to the businesses with whom consumers contract. These businesses often hold the upperhand in that they may present contractual terms on a "take it or leave it" basis. To this end, legislation has been enacted that implies certain mandatory terms into all contracts between a consumer and a trader.

The Consumer Rights Act 2022 introduced sweeping changes in the area of consumer law. The Act provides for a range of rights and remedies for consumers that are party to sales contracts (Part 2), digital content and digital service contracts (Part 3), and service contracts (Part 4). It also deals with consumer information, cancellation and other rights (Part 5) and unfair terms in consumer contracts (Part 6). It is beyond the scope of this text to provide an exhaustive analysis of all 176 sections (and six schedules!) of the 2022 Act. Instead, the below will provide a whistle-stop tour of the major changes brought in by the Act and the key provisions of note. Before addressing the 2022 Act, however, it is important to refer to the Sale of Goods Act 1893 and the Sale of Goods and Supply of Services Act 1980, which until recently represented the governing legislation in the area of consumer law and protection.

Sale of Goods Act 1893, Sale of Goods and Supply of Services Act 1980, and the History of Consumer Law in Ireland

The Sale of Goods Act 1893 introduced certain standard terms that would be implied into all contracts for the sale of goods. Under s.14(3) of the 1893 Act, for example, goods sold were to be of "merchantable quality", meaning that:

> "... they are as fit for the purpose or purposes for which goods of that kind are commonly bought and as durable as it is reasonable to expect having regard to any description applied to them, the price (if relevant) and all the other relevant circumstances".

It should be noted that this provision no longer applies to a contract to which Part 2 of the Consumer Rights Act 2022 applies.

The Sale of Goods and Supply of Services Act 1980 amended the 1893 Act, introducing enhanced protections for consumers and new implied terms and increasing the number of remedies available to include replacement and repair of goods. The 1980 Act also extended the remit of the 1893 Act to cover contracts for the supply of services.

Under s.13 of the 1893 Act, as amended by the 1980 Act, goods were required to correspond with any description given of them. As we have seen above, s.14 required that goods supplied under contract be of "merchantable quality". It also required that goods be fit for their purpose, e.g. crabs bought for consumption for dinner must not cause food poisoning (see *Wallis v Russell* [1902] 2 I.R. 585). Section 15 required that goods conform to any sample provided.

Directive 1999/44/EC of the European Parliament and of the Council on certain aspects of the sale of consumer goods and associated guarantees (the "Consumer Sales and Guarantees Directive") introduced a new concept: "conformity with the contract". Under art.2(1) of the Directive, a trader must "deliver goods to the consumer which are in conformity with the contract of sale". Article 2(2) states that consumer goods were presumed to be in conformity with the contract if they complied with the description given by the trader, were fit for purpose, and met certain standards relating to the quality of goods. The Consumer Sales and Guarantees Directive was a minimum harmonisation directive, meaning that it set a minimum threshold that national legislation must meet, but permitted Member States to exceed its terms. As such, the 1893 Act, as amended, existed alongside the Consumer Sales and Guarantees Directive for many years and consumers could choose which of the two to rely upon. In practice, the 1893 Act was preferred.

Twenty years later, Directive (EU) 2019/771 of the European Parliament and of the Council on certain aspects concerning contracts for the sale of goods (the "Sale of Goods Directive") was introduced. Being a maximum harmonisation directive, it precluded Member States from deviating from its standards. In its wake, it was clear that the law as it pertained to consumers in Ireland was set to change from the long-standing status quo provided for by the 1893 Act, as amended.

Consumer Rights Act 2022

The Consumer Rights Act 2022 transposes the Sale of Goods Directive. It also gives effect to the following:

- Directive (EU) 2019/770 (the "Digital Content Directive");
- Directive (EU) 2019/2161 (the "Omnibus Directive"), which Directive itself amends:
    - Directive 93/13/EEC (the "Unfair Contract Terms Directive");
    - Directive 2005/29/EC (the "Unfair Commercial Practices Directive");
    - Directive 2011/83/EU (the "Consumer Rights Directive"); and
    - Directive 98/6/EC (the "Price Indication Directive").

As stated, the Consumer Rights Act 2022 overhauled consumer law in Ireland when enacted. While commercial sales and private transactions continue to be covered by the Sale of Goods Act 1893, as amended, consumer sales (contracts between a trader and a consumer entered on or after 29 November 2022) are now governed by the 2022 Act. As such, terminology such as "merchantable quality" no longer applies to these consumer contracts. The 2022 Act instead uses decidedly more European language (e.g. "conformity with sales contract") and espouses different remedies to those formerly applicable under the 1893 Act (e.g. "short term" right to terminate and "final right" to terminate). The below discussion will focus in the main on Part 2 of the Act, but shall also examine Parts 3–6.

Part 2 of the Act: Sales Contracts

Scope of Part 2

This Part of the 2022 Act pertains to contracts for goods. A sales contract for goods is defined in s.11(1) of the 2022 Act as a contract under which a trader "transfers, or undertakes to transfer, the ownership of goods to a consumer" and the consumer, in return, pays or promises to pay the price of the goods.

The definition is also extended to "trade-ins", where a consumer transfers or undertakes to transfer the ownership of goods to the trader in full or part payment of the price.

The application of Part 2 also extends to contracts for goods "with digital elements". In order to be considered a good "with a digital element", the digital good or digital service in question must be of a kind that is incorporated or interconnected with the good in such a way that the absence of the digital element would prevent the good from performing its functions. For example, a smartphone (a good) might be sold with a camera application (a digital element) under contract. That camera application might be such that its absence would prevent the smartphone from taking pictures using its hardware (front and back-facing cameras). Compare this to a smartphone that is sold with a game application that is *not* required for the phone to function. In the former case, Part 2 would apply to both the good (smartphone) and the digital element (camera application). However, in the latter instance, Part 2 would apply only to the smartphone. Supply of the game application would fall under Part 3 of the Act, which governs digital content or digital services.

Right to terminate where trader has no right to sell

Section 14 of the 2022 Act states that the trader must ensure that they have the right to sell the goods at the time when ownership is to be transferred. Where the trader does not have the right to sell the goods, the consumer shall have the right to terminate the sales contract in accordance with s.28 and the trader must comply with their obligations under s.30 (discussed below). Section 14 is implied into every contract for the sale of goods by virtue of s.20 of the Act.

Conformity with contract

Section 15(1) of the 2022 Act stipulates that where a sales contract is concluded between a trader and a consumer, the trader "shall deliver goods to the consumer that are in conformity with the sales contract at the relevant time". In order to be considered to be "in conformity with the sales contract", goods must comply with the requirements set out in ss.16–19 of the Act, namely:

- that the goods be free from charge and other encumbrance other than a charge or encumbrance that was disclosed to the consumer before entering the contract (s.16);
- that the goods comply with the subjective requirements for conformity (s.17);
- that the goods comply with the objective requirements for conformity (s.18);
- that the goods do not lack conformity as a result of incorrect installation (s.19).

Where goods are not in conformity with the sales contract, the consumer shall have the right to the remedies outlined in Chapter 3 of Part 2 (discussed below). Sections 16–19 are implied into every sales contract for goods.

The "subjective" requirements for conformity, as outlined in s.17, include:

- that goods be of the description, type, quantity and quality, and possess the functionality, compatibility, interoperability and other features, specified in the sales contract;
- that the goods be fit for any particular purpose for which the consumer requires them, providing that the consumer made this use known to the trader at the time of or before the conclusion of the contract and the trader has accepted this;
- that the goods be supplied with all the accessories and instructions, including on installation of the goods, specified in the contract;
- that the goods be updated as specified in the sales contract.

Section 17 also states that the information that the trader is required to provide the consumer in a distance or off-premises contract under ss.103, 104 and 106 (discussed below in *Part 5: Information*) shall form part of the sales contract. Such goods must comply with any term of the distance or off-premises contract deriving from this information in order to be in conformity. Therefore, not only is a failure to comply with the information requirements set out in Part 5 of the 2022 Act an offence under that Part, but any failure to provide that information means that the goods sold on foot of the distance or off-premises contract are not considered to be in conformity with the sales contract under Part 2. Section 17 also provides that spare parts and after-sales service shall be made available by the trader to the extent that is provided in any offer, description or advertisement published by the trader on behalf of the producer or on the trader's own behalf. It should be noted that the "subjective requirements for conformity" discussed above are dependent on the contract of sale itself (hence "subjective"). This can be contrasted with the "objective requirements for conformity" provided for by s.18 which take on a distinctively more general feel. They include:

- that the goods must be fit for all of the purposes for which goods of the same type would normally be used (taking into account, for example, applicable technical standards or sector-specific industry codes of conduct);
- that the goods must be of the quality and correspond to any description of a sample or model that the trader made available to the consumer before the conclusion of the sales contract;
- that the goods must be delivered with any accessories, including packaging, installation instructions or other instructions that the consumer may reasonably expect to receive; and

- that the goods must be of the quantity and possess the qualities and other features (including in relation to durability, functionality, compatibility and security) normal for goods of the same type that the consumer may reasonably expect, given the nature of the goods and taking into account any public statement in relation to the goods made by, or on behalf of, the trader or any other person constituting a previous link in the chain of transactions relating to the sales contract, including the producer, particularly in advertising or on labelling.

As regards the last point, the reference to "durability" means:

> "... the ability of the goods to maintain their functions and performance through normal use and to possess the ability to do so which is normal for goods of the same type and which the consumer can reasonably expect"

having regard to certain factors such as: the specific nature of the goods; the possible need for reasonable maintenance of the goods; any public statement on the durability of the goods made by or on behalf of any person constituting a link in the chain of transactions; and all other relevant circumstances (e.g. price of the goods, intensity or frequency of use).

As seen above, "public statements" made regarding goods are important when ascertaining what is reasonable to expect from the goods in terms of durability, functionality, compatibility and security. Part 2 therefore acknowledges, implicitly, that consumers are often influenced by claims or representations made about a product by or on behalf of a trader or another person associated with the sales contract, e.g. someone involved in the advertisement of a product. Section 18(3) states that a trader shall not be bound by such a public statement if they were not and could not reasonably have been aware of the statement, *or* if by the time the contract was concluded the statement had been corrected in the same way or a comparable way to which it had been made, *or* the decision of the consumer could not have been influenced by the public statement.

In relation to contracts for the sale of goods with digital elements, the trader is obliged under s.18 to inform the consumer of the existence of and provide updates, including security updates, necessary for the goods to be in conformity with the sales contract. Section 18(7) however, provides that where a consumer fails to install the update within a reasonable time, the trader will not be liable for any lack of conformity resulting solely from the failure to install the update if:

(a) the trader informed them of the need to install it (including the consequences for failing to do so); and

(b) the failure of the consumer to install the update or any incorrect installation of the consumer thereof was not due to shortcomings in the installation instructions provided.

Significantly, s.18(8) provides that there will be no lack of conformity with a sales contract if, at the time of the conclusion of the contract, the consumer was specifically informed that a particular characteristic of the goods "deviated from the requirements" and the consumer "expressly and separately accepted that deviation". For example, if a consumer was specifically informed that a coat had a broken zip and they expressly and separately accepted this, the consumer would not be entitled a remedy under Chapter 3 of Part 2 of the 2022 Act for lack of conformity.

Remedies under Part 2

If goods are not in conformity with the sales contract, the consumer shall have the right to remedies provided in Chapter 3 of Part 2 of the 2022 Act. These include:

- a "short-term" right to terminate the contract (s.24);
- a right to have the goods brought into conformity through repair or replacement (s.25);
- proportionate reduction in price (s.26);
- a "final-right" to terminate (s.26);
- a general right to withhold payment (s.32).

Section 24(2) of the Act states that the "short-term" right to terminate a contract lasts for 30 days from: the date the consumer or a person nominated thereby takes physical possession of the goods, or when the goods are delivered to a carrier who was commissioned by the consumer to deliver the goods, or when the contract requires the trader to install the goods, the date that that installation is completed. Sometimes, this 30-day period may be too long, e.g. where the goods in question are perishable. In such circumstances, the short-term right to terminate will last for a shorter period per s.24(4). In order to exercise the right to terminate under s.24, the consumer must comply with their obligations under s.28 of the Act and the trader must comply with its obligations under s.30.

Under s.23(2), the consumer may choose between the remedies of repair and replacement of the goods unless the remedy chosen would be impossible for the trader to carry out or compared to the alternative remedy, would impose disproportionate costs on the trader taking all circumstances into account, including: the value of the goods if there was no lack of conformity, the significance of the lack of conformity, and whether the alternative remedy could be provided without significant inconvenience to the consumer. If both repair and replacement are impossible to carry out or compared to the alternative remedy they would impose disproportionate costs on the trader, the trader may, under s.23(3), refuse to carry out either remedy. In this situation, the consumer has a right to a proportionate reduction in price or a "final right" to terminate the sales contract.

Section 25 of the Act sets out the way in which a repair or replacement is to be completed. It states that the trader must ensure that the repair or replacement is completed free of charge to the consumer, within a reasonable time (having regard to the nature and complexity of the goods, the nature and severity of the lack of conformity, and the effort required to complete the repair or replacement), and without significant inconvenience to the consumer. The trader must take back the goods for repair or replacement at its expense and not the consumer's.

Section 26 provides for the remedies of a "final right" to terminate and a proportionate price reduction. The remedies apply where:

(a) the consumer has exercised their right to request a repair or replacement and the trader has refused to bring the goods into conformity or where the trader has not completed the repair or replacement in accordance with s.25 or at all; or
(b) the same or a different instance of lack of conformity becomes apparent despite the trader's attempts to bring the goods into conformity; or
(c) the lack of conformity is of such a serious nature as to justify immediate reduction in price or the termination of the sales contract; or
(d) the trader has declared, or it is clear from the circumstances, that the trader will not bring the goods into conformity within a reasonable time or without significant inconvenience to the customer.

Where (b) applies, it shall be objectively determined, taking all circumstances into account, whether the customer shall be entitled to terminate or a proportionate reduction in price or if they shall be required to accept a further attempt(s) by the trader to bring the goods into conformity. In order to make this determination, the following may be taken into consideration: the type and value of the goods, the nature and significance of the lack of conformity, and whether the consumer can reasonably be expected to maintain confidence in the ability of the trader to bring the goods into conformity especially where the same issue keeps occurring.

Where (c) applies, it shall be objectively determined, having regard to the nature and severity of the lack of conformity, whether same is of such a serious nature as to justify recourse to either a final right to terminate or a proportionate price reduction. In order to make this determination, it might be asked whether the lack of conformity is such that the consumer cannot maintain confidence in the ability of the trader to bring the goods into conformity or the consumer's ability to make normal use of the goods is severely affected and the consumer cannot be reasonably expected to trust that this would be remedied by repair or replacement by the trader.

The consumer may not exercise a final right to terminate if the lack of conformity is minor, according to s.26(3). If it is minor, the appropriate remedy would be a proportionate reduction in price.

While a right to terminate the contract may be self-explanatory, s.27 sets out what is meant by a "proportionate reduction in the price" of goods: a consumer may require the trader to reduce the price of the goods that the consumer is to pay in a way that is proportionate to the decrease in the value of the goods due to the lack of conformity. Alternatively, the consumer may receive reimbursement from the trader of the price paid in excess of the amount of the proportionate reduction, without undue delay and in any event not later than 14 days after the trader received the goods back or evidence has been received of the goods having been returned. Any reimbursement must be made using the same means of payment as the consumer used to pay for the goods, unless the consumer expressly agrees otherwise and they do not incur any fees as a result of this change.

Section 28 applies, as stated above, where a consumer exercises a right to terminate the contract (e.g. under s.14 or a "short term" right to terminate the contract or a "final right" to terminate the contract). It sets out the obligations required of the consumer: that the right to terminate should be exercised by the consumer by means of a statement to the trader expressing the decision to terminate. The goods must be returned to the trader at the trader's expense. If the consumer fails to adhere to this section, they may be liable in damages for any loss or damage suffered by the trader as a result of their non-adherence. Section 29 sets out the remedies for non-conformity where the contract also provides for supply of digital content.

Section 30 sets out the trader's obligations where the sales contract is terminated. They must, upon receipt of the goods (or if the trader chooses, on receipt of evidence provided of the goods having been returned), reimburse the consumer for the goods and any costs incurred in returning the goods. This reimbursement should take place "without undue delay" and in any case not later than 14 days upon receipt of the goods or the aforementioned evidence of return. The same payment method used by the consumer to pay for the goods should be used to reimburse the consumer, unless they expressly agree otherwise. There should be no fee imposed on the customer in respect of the reimbursement. The trader may be liable in damages for any loss or damage suffered by the consumer as a result of a failure to comply with these requirements.

Section 32 acknowledges a general right of the consumer to withhold payment of any outstanding portion of the price where the trader has failed to deliver goods that are in conformity with the contract, until such time as the trader has fulfilled this obligation. Section 32(2) states that the portion withheld should be proportionate to the decrease in value of the goods received compared with the value of the goods had they been in conformity. In order to exercise the right to withhold payment until after the trader has fulfilled its obligation to deliver goods that are in conformity, the consumer must provide a statement to the trader expressing this decision.

Delivery and risk

Section 35 of the Act establishes that the goods remain at the trader's risk until the consumer comes into physical possession of them or a person nominated by the consumer acquires possession. This is unless the consumer commissions their own carrier to deliver the goods and this was not proposed by the trader. In such circumstances, the consumer assumes the risk.

According to s.36, unless the trader and consumer agree otherwise, the trader should deliver the goods "without undue delay" and in any event no later than 30 days after the conclusion of the contract. If the trader does not deliver the goods within this or another agreed time period, the consumer can "call upon" the trader to do so within an additional appropriate period of time. Section 36(4) states that the trader is not entitled to this additional time where they have refused to deliver the goods or where delivery within the initial period was essential. If the trader has refused to deliver the goods, fails to deliver the goods within this additional time period, or fails to deliver the goods within the period agreed with the customer where delivery within this time is essential, the consumer has the right to terminate the contract. Where the consumer wishes to terminate the sales contract, they have to exercise this right in accordance with s.28 (discussed above). The trader must comply with its obligations under s.30 (also discussed above).

Exclusion of liability

Section 39 prohibits the contracting out of the trader's obligations (e.g. subjective and objective requirements for conformity).

Changes to privity rule

Section 46 states that where a consumer gives goods to another consumer as a gift, that other consumer shall be entitled to exercise any rights and remedies under Part 2, as against the trader, in the same way the original consumer would.

Section 47 provides that where a consumer purchases a motor vehicle and where a lack of conformity would render that motor vehicle a danger to the public, including anyone travelling in the motor vehicle, any person who uses the vehicle with the consent of the consumer and suffers a loss because of this lack of conformity may initiate a claim against the trader in damages as if they were a consumer. The section seems to envisage that e-vehicles, such as electric bikes and scooters, come under its remit, in an expansion of the old version of the provision under the Sale of Goods Act 1893.

PART 3 OF THE ACT: DIGITAL CONTENT CONTRACTS AND DIGITAL SERVICE CONTRACTS

Part 3 of the Act transposes the Digital Content Directive (discussed above). It governs any contract under which a trader supplies digital content or a digital service to the consumer. A number of safeguards are introduced by this Part, including (but not limited to):

- A "right to supply" obligation, provided at s.50, which is similar to the obligation discussed above under s.14 as it pertains to goods. A consumer has a right to terminate the digital content or digital service contract where the trader does not have the right to supply. This must be exercised in accordance with s.66 (which sets out the consumer's obligations in such circumstances) and s.67 (which sets out the trader's obligations).
- An obligation that the trader supply digital content or a digital service that is in conformity with the contract (provided at s.51) and explicit subjective and objective requirements for conformity (see ss.52–55). It should be noted that ss.50 and 53–55 are implied into every digital content contract or digital service contract.
- Chapter 3 of Part 3 provides a suite of redress options available to consumers. As with Part 2 of the 2022 Act, these include:
    - a "short term" right to terminate the contract;
    - a right to have the digital content or service brought into conformity with the contract;
    - a right to a proportionate reduction in price or a "final right" to terminate the contract;
    - a general right to withhold payment.

Similar to Part 2, Part 3 provides for certain obligations that the consumer (s.66) and trader (s.67) must follow in the event of termination of a digital content or digital service contract.

Per s.71, a trader cannot contract out of its obligations under Part 3.

Part 4 of the Act: Service Contracts

This Part amends Part IV of the Sale of Goods and Supply of Services Act 1980 and governs non-digital services in respect of consumers. It does not cover contracts for rental of accommodation for residential purposes and goods supplied under hire-purchase agreements. If a contract for supply of a service relates to the supply of a service and the sale of goods or the supply of digital content or services, this Part only applies insofar as it relates to the supply of the service. Section 78 of the Act provides that a trader must supply a service in accordance with the contract. Performance of this service must be in conformity with the service contract. Again, this Part closely resembles the protections and obligations set out in Part 2 of the 2022 Act:

- The Part provides for both subjective requirements (s.80) and objective requirements (s.81) for conformity.
- These requirements are implied into every service contract and shall have effect as if they were terms of the contract (s.82).
- Section 94 prevents the contracting out of a trader's obligations under the contract.
- Chapter 3 of Part 4 provides remedies for failure to supply a service in conformity with the service contract:
  - a "short term" right to terminate the contract;
  - a right to have the service brought into conformity with the service contract;
  - a right to a proportionate reduction in price or a "final right" to terminate the contract;
  - a general right to withhold payment.

Section 83 provides that where, in respect of a service contract, the consumer has not paid the price or other consideration for the service, the contract does not specify the price or consideration, and the price is not fixed in another named way, the price shall be a *reasonable price* and no more.

There are certain obligations placed on the consumer (see s.88) and trader (s.89) in the event of termination of the contract.

Part 5 of the Act: Consumer Information, Cancellation and Other Rights

This Part replaces the Consumer (Information and Cancellation Rights) Regulations 2013 (S.I. No. 484 of 2013) and implements a number of updates from the Omnibus Directive (discussed above). This Part deals with, amongst other things, the information a consumer is entitled to before they buy goods, services, digital content or digital services.

The Act distinguishes between an "on-premises" contract, an "off-premises" contract and a "distance" contract in this regard.

An *on-premises contract* is "any contract between a trader and a consumer other than a distance contract or an off-premises contract".

An *off-premises contract* means any one of the following contracts between a trader and consumer:

(a) a contract that is concluded in the simultaneous physical presence of a trader and the consumer in a place that is *not* the business premises of the trader; or
(b) a contract for which an offer was made by the consumer in the simultaneous physical presence of the trader and consumer in a place that is *not* the business premises of the trader; or
(c) a contract that was concluded on the business premises of the trader or through any means of distance communication immediately after the consumer was personally and individually addressed in a place that is *not* the business premises of the trader in the simultaneous physical presence of the trader and the consumer;
(d) a contract that was concluded during an excursion organised by the trader with the aim or effect of promoting and selling the goods or services to the consumer.

In this way, doorstep sales and trade fair sales (being "off" the trader's premises) are two popular examples of off-premises contracts.

It should be noted that s.98 restricts the applicability of Part 5 in the case of off-premises contracts. This means that the information requirements outlined in this Part, for example, do not apply to off-premises contracts under which the payment to be made is €50 or under. Where two or more off-premises contracts with related subjects are concluded at the same time, the total payments to be made shall be taken into account in applying this monetary threshold.

A *distance contract* is defined in the Act as a:

"... contract concluded between a trader and a consumer under an organised distance sales or service-provision scheme without the simultaneous physical presence of the trader and the consumer, and with the exclusive use of one or more means of distance communication up to and including the time at which the contract is concluded".

In this way, internet sales, mail-order sales and telephone sales are examples of distance contracts.

According to s.101, the information that must be provided to consumers before they are bound by an *on-premises* contract is that which is set out in Schedule 2 of the Act, paraphrased below:

(a) the main characteristics of the goods, digital content, digital service, or service;
(b) the identity of the trader (including their trading name and legal identity);
(c) the geographical address and phone number of the trader;
(d) the total price including taxes or if the price cannot be reasonably calculated in advance, the manner in which the price is to be calculated;
(e) where applicable, all freight, delivery or postal charges additional to the price or if the charges cannot be reasonably calculated in advance, the fact that such additional charges may be payable;
(f) where applicable, the arrangements for payment, delivery, performance and the time by which the trader undertakes to deliver;
(g) where applicable, the trader's complaint-handling policy;
(h) the existence of a legal obligation on the trader to ensure whatever is being contracted for is in conformity with the contract;
(i) where applicable, the existence and conditions of any after-sales service or commercial guarantee;
(j) the duration of the contract or if the contract is of indeterminate duration or to be extended automatically, the conditions for terminating it;
(k) where applicable, the functionality, including applicable technical protection measures, of goods with digital elements, digital content or digital services;
(l) where applicable, any relevant compatibility and interoperability of goods with digital elements, digital content and digital services of which the trader is aware, or can reasonably be expected to have been aware;
(m) such information as may be specified in subsequent regulations.

This information must be provided in a clear and comprehensible manner, if that information is not already apparent from the context. This information does not have to be provided in the case of a contract that involves a day-to-day transaction and is performed immediately on conclusion of the contract. It is an offence for a trader not to provide the above information.

In the case of both *off-premises* and *distance* contracts, the information specified in Schedule 3 of the Act is provided to be given to consumers before they are bound by a contract (see ss.103 and 104). This information is paraphrased below:

(a) the main characteristics of the goods, digital content, digital service, or service;

(b) the identity of the trader (including the trader's trading name and legal identity);

(c) if the trader is acting on behalf of another trader, the identity and geographical address of that other trader;

(d) the geographical address of the trader, their telephone number, email address and details of any other means of online communications provided by the trader;

(e) the geographical address of the place of business of the trader if different from (d) above and where the trader acts on behalf of another trader, the place of business of that other trader if different from (c);

(f) the total price inclusive of taxes, or if it cannot be reasonably calculated in advance, the manner in which the price is to be calculated;

(g) where applicable, all freight, delivery, postal or additional charges, or if such cannot be reasonably calculated in advance, the fact that they may be payable;

(h) in the case of a contract of indeterminate duration or subscription: the total costs per billing period, the total monthly costs if fixed, or the manner in which the price is to be calculated if it cannot be reasonably calculated in advance;

(i) where applicable, that the price of that contracted for was personalised on the basis of automated decision-making;

(j) the cost of using the means of distance communication used;

(k) the arrangement for payment, delivery, performance and the time limit for same;

(l) where applicable, the trader's complaint-handling policy;

(m) where a right to cancel exists, the conditions, time limit and procedures for exercising this right in accordance with s.112;

(n) where applicable, that the consumer will have to bear the costs of returning the goods in case of cancellation of the contract, and in the case of a distance contract, if the goods cannot be returned by post by their nature, the cost of returning the goods;
(o) where the customer exercises their right to cancel after having made a request in accordance with s.119, that the customer is liable to pay the trader reasonable costs;
(p) where a right to cancel does not apply under s.111, the information that the consumer will not benefit from the right to cancel or the circumstances where the consumer loses that right;
(q) the existence of a legal obligation on the trader to supply whatever is contracted for in conformity with the contract;
(r) where applicable, the existence and conditions of any after-sales customer assistance, after-sales service or commercial guarantee;
(s) the existence of any relevant codes of practice and how they can be obtained;
(t) the duration of the contract or the conditions for termination if the contract is of indeterminate duration or is to be extended automatically;
(u) where applicable, the minimum duration of the consumer's obligations under the contract;
(v) where applicable, the existence and conditions of deposits or other financial guarantees to be paid;
(w) where applicable, the functionality, including applicable technical protection measures, of goods with digital elements, digital content or digital services;
(x) where applicable, any relevant compatibility and interoperability of goods with digital elements, digital content or digital services of which the trader is aware, or can reasonably be expected to have been aware;
(y) where applicable, the possibility of having recourse to an out-of-court complaint and redress scheme and the methods of accessing this.

It is an offence for a trader not to provide the above information. The information must be provided in a clear and comprehensible manner if the information is not already apparent from the context of an off-premises contract (s.103) and in "plain and intelligible language" in a way appropriate to the means of distance communication used in a distance contract context (s.106). Other requirements specific to the manner in which the above information should be provided are outlined in ss.103–105 (off-premises contracts) and ss.106–109 (distance contracts). Information requirements for off-premises contracts for repairs or maintenance are set out in s.104. Additional information requirements for distance contracts concluded on online marketplaces are set out in s.107 and by electronic means in s.108. The information provision requirements outlined above cannot be waived via contract, as per s.99.

Chapter 5 of Part 5 provides for a change of mind and cancellation in the case of distance or off-premises contracts (except those set out in s.111). A consumer may cancel a distance or off-premises contract before the expiry of the cancellation period (in accordance with s.115) without giving a reason. According to s.113, the length of this cancellation period or "cooling-off" period is usually 14 days; however, in the case of doorstep sales, the consumer has 30 days from when the contract was entered into to cancel. If a trader does not provide a consumer with the information on the right to cancel as set out in Schedule 3, the cancellation period expires after 12 months beginning on the day on which it would otherwise have expired under s.113. If the trader provides the consumer with the information on the right to cancel set out in Schedule 3 within 12 months of the day on which the cancellation period would have expired, the cancellation period shall instead expire on the period of 14 days beginning on the day on which the consumer receives that information (or 30 days beginning on the day on which the consumer receives that information in the case of doorstep sales). The rules pertaining to the exercise of a right to cancel are set out in s.115. The obligations of the trader in the event of cancellation are set out in s.117. The return of goods and obligations of the consumer in the event of cancellation are set out in s.118.

Chapter 6 of Part 5 deals with miscellaneous matters including the application of additional payments by the trader (s.123), charges for communications by telephone (s.124) and inertia selling (s.125) where goods are supplied by a trader without any request by or on behalf of the consumer.

Part 6 of the Act: Unfair Terms in Consumer Contracts

This Part replaces the European Communities (Unfair Terms in Consumer Contracts) Regulations 1995 (S.I. No. 27 of 1995). It provides for strengthened requirements regarding transparency and consumer contracts. Section 129 states that an "unfair term" in a consumer contract is not binding on the consumer. A term is unfair if, contrary to the requirement of good faith, it constitutes a "significant imbalance in the parties' rights and obligations under the contract to the detriment of the consumer". The Act provides for a "grey list" of consumer contract terms that are presumed to be unfair (s.133) and introduces a "black list" of terms that are always unfair (s.132). Examples of "grey list" terms include:

- a term that has the object or effect of inappropriately excluding or limiting the legal rights of the consumer in relation to a trader in the event of total or partial non-performance or inadequate performance of any contractual obligations;
- a term that has the object or effect of enabling the trader to alter the terms of the contract unilaterally without a valid reason;
- a term that has the object or effect of obliging the consumer to fulfil all of their obligations where the trader does not perform its obligations.

Examples of "black list" terms include:

- terms that exclude or limit the liability of a trader arising out of an act or omission on their part causing the death of or personal injury to a consumer;
- terms that allow the trader an exclusive right to determine whether what is being contracted for is in conformity;
- terms that grant the trader the exclusive right to interpret any term of the contract.

OTHER CONSUMER PROTECTIONS OF RECENT NOTE

Consumers are also protected against unfair, misleading or aggressive commercial practices under the Consumer Protection Act 2007, as amended.

Regulation (EU) 2022/2065 (the "Digital Services Act") came into force in November 2022 and was directly applicable to all EU Member States from 17 February 2024. Despite its direct application, domestic legislation was required to implement those provisions of the Regulation that provide for supervision and enforcement of rights. Ireland enacted the Digital Services Act 2024 in February 2024 to comply with this obligation. One of the aims of the Regulation is to protect consumers of digital services, provided by "intermediary services", by promoting transparency and accountability.

Consumers can now take collective legal action through a qualified entity through the Representative Actions for the Protection of the Collective Interests of Consumers Act 2023.

16 Misrepresentation

Introduction

We have already discussed above how a pre-contractual statement may be deemed to be a term of a contract. The consequences of breaching such a term will depend on whether it is a condition, warranty or innominate term. This chapter, however, will focus on representations that have *induced* a party to contract but which do not constitute part of the contract itself. If such a representation is *not true*, it is called a misrepresentation. Where a misrepresentation induces the other party to enter the contract, the innocent party may be able to recover damages or repudiate the contract. Available remedies lie in contract, tort and statute, as will be discussed below.

When Does Misrepresentation Arise?

The rule in *Colthurst v La Touche Colthurst* [2000] IEHC 14 provides that a misrepresentation has four elements:

(a) there must be a representation of fact;
(b) the representation must be made by or on behalf of one party to another party;
(c) the representation must be untrue; and
(d) the innocent party must have been induced to enter the contract because of the representation.

Statement of Fact vs. Statement of Opinion

Generally, the statement must be one of past or present fact. For example, if a vendor tells a potential purchaser that the book they are selling is a first-edition copy and it is not, this is a representation of fact.

This can be contrasted with statements of *opinion*. These do not usually amount to misrepresentations unless the party issuing the opinion has knowingly misstated their own opinion or had the opportunity to check its accuracy (particularly if the innocent party was unable to check the information for themselves). For example, if I state that in my opinion the ice-cream that I am selling is safe to eat, but I know that it is tainted with listeria bacteria, I have misstated my true opinion and this constitutes a misrepresentation of fact. Liability seems to attach where reliance on a statement was reasonable and to be expected.

For instance, in *Bissett v Wilkinson* [1927] A.C. 177, a vendor innocently stated that a property could hold 2,000 sheep. Though inaccurate, this statement was not held to be a misrepresentation. The vendor was merely stating an honest opinion. The land, moreover, had never held sheep and the vendor was thus not in a position to give an accurate estimation. In *Doheny v Bank of Ireland* (*Irish Times*, 12 December 1997), a bank supplied a reference stating that a customer was "respectable and trustworthy". In fact, as the bank well knew, the customer had a track-record of dishonest dealings. This was therefore held to be a misrepresentation. Likewise, in *Smith v Land and House Property Corp* (1884) 28 Ch. D. 7, the vendor of a hotel represented the then current occupant to be "a most desirable tenant". In truth, the plaintiff had experienced considerable difficulties with the tenant, in particular in extracting rent. The misstatement thus amounted to a misrepresentation.

Similar principles apply where the person expresses what purports to be an "expert opinion" or speaks with the benefit of specialised knowledge. In *Esso Petroleum Co Ltd v Mardon* [1976] Q.B. 801, a representative of an oil company with 40 years of experience in the trade overestimated the likely sales output of a petrol station. Although stated as an opinion, the estimate was deemed to amount to a misrepresentation, given that the opinion was based on considerable expertise.

Statement of Fact vs. "Trader's Puff"

As discussed above, a certain amount of hyperbole (or "trader's puff") is permitted in the course of advertising wares for sale. In *Dimmock v Hallett* (1866) 2 Ch. App. 21, a description of land as "fertile and improvable" was characterised as "sales talk", and thus not actionable as a misrepresentation. Exaggerated claims made on behalf of products will not generally amount to misrepresentation if, judged from an objective standpoint, they were not intended to be taken seriously. That said, the simple fact that a trader did not *intend* to be bound in law is not a sufficient defence if, on the facts, a serious promise is made to the consumer (see *Carlill v Carbolic Smokeball Co* [1893] 1 Q.B. 256).

Statement of Fact vs. Statement of Intention

Generally speaking, a misrepresentation arises only in relation to a statement of past or present fact and not in relation to statements of future intention. A statement of intention is just that: an aspiration or hope that may or may not be realised. In *Mulcahy v Mulcahy* [2011] IEHC 186, a statement by a brother to his siblings that he wanted the family property in order to make it a home for both his family and his mother was held to be the "selling point" for getting the agreement from the siblings to release their interest in the home. It was not deemed to be an actionable misrepresentation. However, this case might have had a different outcome if it emerged in evidence that the brother *never* had the stated intention. As with statements of opinion, a declaration that knowingly misrepresents a person's current state of mind may constitute a misrepresentation. For instance, in *Edgington v Fitzmaurice* (1855) 29 Ch. D. 459, a company prospectus soliciting potential investors deliberately misrepresented the purpose for which the company intended to use the money. Having lied as to their true state of mind, the promoters were deemed to have been guilty of fraudulent misrepresentation, Bowen L.J. observing that "the state of a man's mind is as much a statement of fact as his digestion".

Must Be a Statement of Fact, Not of Law

Generally, a misrepresentation may arise out of a statement of fact, not law. This principle was derived from the rule as it relates to recovery on foot of mistakes and law (discussed in the next chapter). However, a misrepresentation as to a private right (e.g. the existence of an easement over property) may give rise to a claim (see *Doolan v Murray* (unreported, High Court, 21 December 1993)). As with mistakes as to law, where there exists a difference in bargaining power between the parties, it may be that any misrepresentation as to law would be actionable.

The Statement Must Have Induced a Party to Enter into the Contract

The misrepresentation must have caused the innocent party to enter into the contract. This party must show that they relied, at least in part, on the misstatement, though it is not necessary to prove that the party who made the statement was aware of such reliance. The misrepresentation need not, however, be the *sole* or even the main impetus to contract, as long as it provides *a* reason why the contract was entered into. For instance, in *Edgington v Fitzmaurice*, the prospectors' misrepresentation only partly induced the plaintiff to enter into the contract, the plaintiff's own mistaken belief that he would gain rights over the property of the company also being instrumental. Nonetheless, as the prospectors' statement partly influenced his decision, the misrepresentation was actionable.

It is not possible, however, to avoid a contract where the party complaining of the misrepresentation was either not aware of the statement, knew it was false, or did not rely on it (see *Smith v Chadwick* (1884) 9 App. Cas. 187). For instance, in *Attwood v Small* (1838) 7 E.R. 684, the vendors of a mine misrepresented its prospects. The buyer, however, had not relied on this misstatement, preferring instead to conduct his own investigation. There having been no reliance on the misrepresentation, the contract remained valid. Likewise, in *Smith v Lynn* (1954) 85 I.L.T.R. 57, both the plaintiff and defendant were interested in purchasing the same property, which had been advertised as being in "excellent structural condition and decorative repair". In actuality, it was riddled with woodworm. The plaintiff bought the property and six weeks later put it back on the market. The plaintiff used the same advertisement and claimed to be selling for personal reasons. The defendant purchased the house but was found not to have relied on the advertisement—on the facts, he had wanted to buy the property long before it was offered for sale by the plaintiff. He had, moreover, examined the property himself and was not relying on claims made by the plaintiff. Similarly, in *Intrum Justitia BV v Legal and Trade Financial Services Ltd* [2005] IEHC 190, the plaintiff agreed to buy an Irish subsidiary company of the defendant. The defendant assured the plaintiff that there were "no skeletons in the cupboard" in relation to the subsidiary. The plaintiff engaged in a due diligence investigation process. Later, however, it was revealed that there were admissions of embezzlement on behalf of the company. The court found that there was no reliance here as the plaintiff relied on the due diligence process and not the misrepresentation.

It is not enough to claim that the misrepresentation could have been discovered if a search *had* been done or that the complaining party was invited to verify the representation but did not do so. In *Redgrave v Hurd* (1881) 20 Ch. D. 1, the vendors of a law practice represented that it was worth £300 per annum, when in fact it was unlikely to yield more than £200 per annum. The buyer was invited to check for himself, but did not do so. If he had done so, he would have discovered that the statement was likely untrue, but the court nonetheless concluded that he was entitled to plead misrepresentation. (See also *Phelps v White* (1881) 5 L.R. Ir. 318 and *Gahan v Boland* (unreported, Supreme Court, 20 January 1984).)

According to *Smith v Chadwick*, the misrepresentation must have been such that it would have induced a *reasonable* person to enter into the contract. This was an objective rather than a subjective approach taken by the courts. However, more recently, in *McCaughey v Irish Bank Resolution Corp* [2013] IESC 17, a hybrid approach seems to have been adopted. Here, the plaintiff, who had invested in a property fund, claimed he was misled (either actively or by concealment) as to the Certificate of Occupancy of the buildings (whether the hotels were considered transient or residential) in the defendant's promotional brochure. The plaintiff, on appeal, claimed that the trial judge placed too much emphasis on what a "reasonable person" or "prudent investor" would have done and argued that he, personally, would not have invested if he had known the truth. The Supreme Court held that the investor would not, given the surrounding circumstances, have chosen a different course of action even if the facts in question had been disclosed. In this way, the court referred to the subjective state of mind of the plaintiff in making its decision. It is clear, then, that an *element* of subjectivity is entertained in the court's determination of whether inducement in fact occurred.

CAN SILENCE AMOUNT TO MISREPRESENTATION?

As a general rule, misrepresentation arises as a result of an express statement, be it oral or in writing. By contrast, *failure to disclose* a material fact does not generally amount to misrepresentation in law.

For instance: if Alex advertises an old and broken-down car as being "new and in prime condition", this would amount to a misrepresentation. If, however, Alex advertises making no mention of the car's age or condition, no misrepresentation would arise.

In *Fletcher v Krell* (1873) 42 L.J.Q.B. 55, for instance, an applicant for a job as a governess failed to disclose that she had previously been married, a fact that, though irrelevant today, was quite material in Victorian times. As she had remained silent on the point, no misrepresentation arose: had she expressly stated that she had never been married, the situation would have been different. Yet, despite this general rule, a duty to disclose arises in a number of specific cases.

CONDUCT OF THE PARTIES

Silence may constitute a misrepresentation where one of the parties has, by their *conduct*, indicated that a particular state of affairs exists. In this regard, one must distinguish gestures and other forms of non-verbal communication from silence properly so-called. For instance, if the vendor of a cow, when asked if it was in good condition, nodded, grunted affirmatively or otherwise gestured in agreement, this may constitute a misrepresentation if the cow turns out to be in bad condition.

In *Spice Girls Ltd v Aprilia World Services* [2002] E.M.L.R. 478, a company approached Spice Girls Ltd with a view to securing a year-long sponsorship deal with the girl band. Although the band's management knew that one member intended to leave within the sponsorship period, the plaintiff agreed to the sponsorship deal and participated in a commercial photo shoot on foot of said contract. This amounted to misrepresentation, the management having indicated by its conduct that the band would continue to comprise five members, when in fact they knew that the number would shortly, and sadly, reduce to four. (See also *Green Park Properties v Dorku* [2001] H.K.L.R.D.

139, where it was held that a vendor's conduct in bringing a purchaser into a yard adjacent to a flat was a representation that the yard would also form part of the sale.)

Half-Truths

If a person makes a representation that is partly but not wholly true, silence as regards the full truth may amount to a misrepresentation. For instance, in *Curtis v Chemical Cleaning and Dyeing Co Ltd* [1951] 1 K.B. 805, an exclusion clause in a contract made with a laundry was orally represented to exclude liability *only* for loss of sequins and beads. In fact, the exclusion clause was much more extensive—silence as regards the full extent of the clause was deemed to limit the effect of the clause to loss of sequins and beads only. Similarly, in *Dimmock v Hallett* (1866) 2 Ch. App. 21, a potential buyer of a freehold estate in several farms was informed that the farms were let (which was true), but not that the tenants were scheduled to leave. This amounted to misrepresentation.

Subsequent Falsity

Silence regarding a change in represented circumstances may amount to a misrepresentation. In other words, where a statement that is true when made is subsequently rendered false, there is a duty to disclose the fact of the change in circumstances. In *With v O'Flanagan* [1936] 1 All E.R. 727, a doctor had originally stated that his practice was worth £200 a year. While this was true when the statement was made, the practice subsequently declined due to the illness of the doctor, with the result that by the time the practice was sold, it was worth virtually nothing. Having made the initial representation, the doctor was under a duty to disclose this material change in circumstances.

Property Contracts

It is generally considered that there is a positive duty to reveal the existence of covenants in leases, as well as unusual defects in title generally. This rule applies to the sale of leasehold interests only (see *Power v Barrett* (1887) 19 L.R. (Ir.) 450).

Unusual Defects

Where a defect is particularly unusual (especially where farm animals are concerned), there may be a duty to reveal its presence. For instance, in *Gill v McDowell* [1903] 2 I.R. 463, a misrepresentation arose where a cattle seller failed to reveal that an animal offered for sale possessed both male and female sex organs. The purchaser thought he was buying either a cow or a bull as he had bought the animal at a market where cows or bulls were sold. The court reasoned that this unusual fact should have been brought to the attention of the buyer. Likewise, in *Kennedy v Hennessy* (1906) 40 I.L.T.R. 84, a failure to reveal that a young heifer (an "unserved" cow) was in fact pregnant was deemed to amount to misrepresentation.

IF THE CONTRACT ITSELF MAKES DISCLOSURE MANDATORY

Clearly, if the contract itself requires disclosure of certain facts, a failure to disclose will be actionable. See *Munster Base Metals v Bula Ltd* (unreported, High Court, 27 July 1983) and *Geryani v O'Callaghan* (unreported, High Court, 25 January 1995). In *Geryani*, while the general law did not make disclosure of certain defects in a contract for the purchase of property mandatory, the conditions of contract made it necessary.

FIDUCIARY RELATIONSHIP

Where a relationship is "fiduciary" in nature, there is a duty to act in utmost good faith, and in particular to disclose all relevant facts to the other party. A fiduciary relationship presupposes that particular trust or confidence is reposed by one person in the integrity and fidelity of another. A key characteristic of such a relationship is that the fiduciary must act for the client's benefit rather than in their own personal interest. Examples of fiduciary relationships include those between a solicitor and client, a trustee and the beneficiaries of a trust, a parent and child, and a principal and agent.

INSURANCE CONTRACTS

Traditionally, the doctrine of *uberrima fides* (utmost good faith) applied to all insurance contracts. The doctrine supposes that a person seeking insurance ("proposer") is in the best place to know the circumstances relevant to their application, e.g. age, health, etc. The proposer therefore has a duty to disclose "every material circumstance which is known" to them (see s.18(1) of the Marine Insurance Act 1906). A material circumstance or fact is taken to be one that "would influence the judgment of a prudent insurer in fixing the premium, or determining whether he will take the risk" (see s.18(2) of the Marine Insurance Act 1906). The 1906 Act was enacted to cover marine insurance. However, in *Chariot Inns Ltd v Assicurazioni Generali SpA* [1981] I.L.R.M. 173, the Irish courts accepted the test of materiality therein as applicable to all forms of insurance against risks when property of any kind is involved. In the case of *Aro Road and Land Vehicles Ltd v Insurance Corporation of Ireland Ltd* [1986] I.R. 403, the court held that under the doctrine of *uberrima fides*:

"Not alone must that person answer to the best of his knowledge any question put to him in a proposal form, but, even when there is no proposal form, he is bound to divulge all matters within his knowledge which a reasonable and prudent insurer would consider material in deciding whether to underwrite the risk or to underwrite it on special terms."

The test is not whether there was any *intention* to deceive or defraud but whether the misrepresentation related, in fact, to a material circumstance. As per *Chariot Inns*, this is an objective test: the question is not what the proposer thinks is material nor is it what the insurer thinks is material. Materiality relates to a circumstance/matter that would reasonably influence the judgment of a prudent insurer in deciding whether they would take on the risk and on what terms. In *Aro*, Henchy J. noted that this rule has exceptions, in particular, that more relaxed criteria may apply to "over-the-counter" insurance agreements, where full disclosure may not be feasible. Further, in *Kelleher v Irish Life Assurance* (unreported, High Court, 16 December 1988), it was held that where the right to full disclosure is waived, the doctrine need not be adhered to. It was also held in *Kelleher* that there is no duty to disclose that of which the proposer is unaware (e.g. an undiagnosed medical issue). (See also *Coleman v New Ireland Assurance plc* [2009] IEHC 173.)

While parties to non-consumer insurance contracts are still subject to the doctrine of *uberrima fides*, the Consumer Insurance Contracts Act 2019 has fundamentally changed the law on the duty of disclosure as it applies to consumer contracts. Since September 2021, the proposer, where they are a consumer, is limited in the duty they owe to the insurer. Under s.8(7)(a) of the 2019 Act, they have a duty to provide responses to specific questions asked by the insurer "honestly and with reasonable care".

This is a significantly lower standard than that envisaged by the doctrine of *uberrima fides*. The test of reasonable care is by reference to that of the average consumer (see s.8(7)(a) of the 2019 Act). The following factors (see s.8(7)(b) of the 2019 Act) will be taken into consideration when determining whether the consumer has complied with this duty:

(a) the type of insurance contract and its target market;
(b) any relevant explanatory material or publicity produced or authorised by the insurer;
(c) whether the insurer's questions are clear and specific;
(d) whether the consumer is represented by an agent and the circumstances surrounding that representation;
(e) that some consumers can be expected to be in possession of more information than others.

Under the 2019 Act, the proposer is under no duty to volunteer any information over and above what is required by the questions asked by the insurer (see s.8(2) of the 2019 Act).

The 2019 Act applies to both life and non-life insurance contracts between the insurer and consumer (see s.2(1) of the 2019 Act). However, contracts of reinsurance and contracts of insurance for special purpose vehicles do not fall within the protection of the 2019 Act (see s.2(2) of the 2019 Act). The Act does not apply to contracts entered into before the Act's commencement (see s.2(1) of the 2019 Act). As such, the old law on the duty of disclosure (*uberrima fides*) remains relevant where the 2019 Act does not apply.

In contracts where the doctrine of *uberrima fides* applies (e.g. non-consumer insurance contracts), the remedy for non-disclosure or misrepresentation from the point of view of an insurance company is the avoidance of the policy (see s.18(1) of the Marine Insurance Act 1906). Section 9 of the 2019 Act introduces new, proportionate remedies that seek to ameliorate the harshness of this traditional outcome for consumers. The remedies look at the effects that the misrepresentation had on the interests of the insurer and the consumer by reference to whether the misrepresentation was innocent, negligent or fraudulent. The insurer is only entitled to rely on said remedies if it can establish that the non-disclosure of material information was an effective cause of the insurer entering into the contract and the terms therein (see s.8(6) of the 2019 Act).

For example, under s.9(5) the insurer is permitted to avoid a contract of insurance where an answer provided by a consumer includes a fraudulent misrepresentation or where the conduct of the consumer involves fraud. Fraudulent misrepresentation is defined in s.1 of the 2019 Act as:

> "a misrepresentation that is false or misleading in any material respect and which the consumer either—
> (a) knows to be false or misleading, or
> (b) consciously disregards whether it is false or misleading, and 'fraudulent' or 'fraud' shall be construed accordingly".

Under s.9(2), if a proposer has discharged the duty to answer questions honestly and with reasonable care but where an answer involves an innocent misrepresentation (that is, one that was neither negligent nor fraudulent), the insurer shall be required to pay the claim made and shall not be permitted to avoid the contract on the basis of the misrepresentation.

Under s.9(3), where there has been a negligent misrepresentation that stops short of a fraudulent misrepresentation, the remedy shall reflect what the insurer would have done had it been aware of the full facts. The remedies are based on a compensatory and proportionate test and are listed in s.9(4). For example, if the insurer would have entered into the contract but on different terms than those provided on foot of the misrepresentation, the contract is treated as if it were entered into on those different terms. If the insurer would have entered the contract but would have charged a higher premium, the insurer may reduce proportionately the sum to be paid on a claim. If the insurer would *not* have entered into the insurance contract on *any* terms had it been aware of the full facts, it may avoid the contract and refuse all of the consumer's claims but shall return the premiums paid.

TYPES OF MISREPRESENTATION

In considering what remedies will issue for misrepresentation, one must distinguish between three different types of misrepresentation: fraudulent, negligent and innocent. Different remedies apply depending on the type of misrepresentation arising.

FRAUDULENT MISREPRESENTATION

A fraudulent statement is, according to the House of Lords in *Derry v Peek* (1889) 14 App. Cas. 337, a false statement "made (a) knowingly, [with knowledge of its falsity] or (b) without belief in its truth, or (c) recklessly as to whether it be true or false". In other words, if a person makes a statement that they know or believe is untrue, or where they do not care whether it is true or not, the misrepresentation is fraudulent. Likewise, wilful blindness to certain facts, where a deliberate decision is made to ignore those facts, may amount to fraud. By contrast, if a person honestly believes that their statement is true (whether as a result of negligence or otherwise), the misrepresentation will not be fraudulent.

In practice, it is difficult to prove fraud, though some examples are noted below:

1. In *Pearson v Dublin Corporation* [1907] A.C. 351, an agent for the vendor stated that foundations of a wall were nine feet deep in circumstances where he did not in fact know if this was true or not. This reckless disregard for the truth constituted a fraudulent misrepresentation.
2. In *Fenton v Schofield* (1966) 100 I.L.T.R. 69, the seller of land stated that over the last four years, a river running through the property had yielded 300–350 salmon per year. He also stated that he had spent £15,000 renovating the property. These statements were false and the seller knew them to be false. As such, the purchaser, who bought the land at a price that presumed these statements to be true, was able to recover

damages based on the difference between what the land was actually worth and what the seller represented it to be worth.
3. In *Carbin v Somerville* [1933] I.R. 227, the vendor fraudulently misrepresented that a house was dry when he knew it in fact was not.
4. In *McAleenan v AIG (Europe) Ltd* [2013] 3 I.R. 202, the plaintiff was a solicitor who sought an indemnity from the defendant pursuant to a Professional Indemnity Policy. The proposal form, signed by the plaintiff, contained a misleading statement that she was a partner in the firm she was employed at. The High Court held that although the plaintiff had no intent to deceive the defendant, she had made the statement recklessly, giving the defendant grounds to avoid the policy. In its review of what "recklessness" includes, the court stated:

> "It is clear that 'careless' for this purpose is not the same as when used in relation to the tort of negligence. The carelessness must be something greater to constitute recklessness for the purposes of fraud ... [A] statement may be considered as made recklessly where the circumstances are such that the Court considers the maker can have no real belief in the truth of what he states."

The onus lies on the plaintiff to prove the defendant's lack of honest belief in the truth of their statement. The standard of proof is on the balance of probabilities. However, the court will attach great significance to an allegation of fraud in considering what evidence is sufficient to discharge the burden of proof. The remedies for fraudulent misrepresentation are rescission and damages (as discussed below).

NEGLIGENT MISREPRESENTATION AND NEGLIGENT MISSTATEMENT

It is important to be aware of the differences between negligent misrepresentation and negligent misstatement. The first is a contractual cause of action and requires the plaintiff to prove that the misrepresentation *induced* them into forming a contract. The second is a tort that does not require inducement but does require that the plaintiff prove that a duty of care was owed to them by the representer. Apart from those distinctions, the elements of negligent misrepresentation and negligent misstatement are very similar and they are often pleaded together by a representee—concurrent claims in contract and tort are allowed.

According to *Forshall v Walsh* (unreported, High Court, 18 June 1997), to establish negligent misrepresentation one must show that the representer failed to exercise due care in making the representation and that the representee was induced into entering an agreement on foot of the representation and suffered damage as a result. In *Darlington Properties Ltd v Meath County Council* [2011] IEHC 70, the plaintiff was induced to enter a contract for the purchase of a development site on foot of the defendant's promise that the site could be developed, with permission to construct an access road being central to any such development. This was held to be a negligent misrepresentation given that the defendant had already awarded planning permission to an adjoining site which would make construction of the plaintiff's road impossible. Kelly J. stated that "even if it were necessary to show a special relationship (which it is not), I am satisfied that such special relationship existed having regard to the particular status of the County Council", given that the council was also the planning authority.

In *Stafford v Keane Mahony Smith* [1980] I.L.R.M. 53, an action in contract was brought against an estate agent who had stated to the plaintiff that a property would be a good investment, attracting a resale value of £100,000. The plaintiff entered into a purchase agreement for £70,000 on foot of this advice. He later had to resell the house at a loss. The court noted that in order to establish liability for negligent misrepresentation, there must exist:

(a) a representer to convey the information relied upon;
(b) a representee to whom that information is intended to be conveyed or to whom it might reasonably be expected that the information would be conveyed;
(c) a requirement that the person must act upon such information to their detriment so as to show that they are entitled to damages.

Here, the statements in question were made to the plaintiff's brother and not to the plaintiff. In circumstances where the plaintiff was not the representee, no liability arose.

As regards negligent misstatement in tort, in *Hedley Byrne v Heller & Partners* [1964] A.C. 465, the House of Lords opined that if a reasonable man, knowing that his skills and judgment were being relied on, makes a statement to a representee without the qualification that he accepted no responsibility for it, he must:

> "... be held to have *accepted some responsibility for his answer being given carefully*, or to have *accepted a relationship* with the inquirer which requires him to *exercise such care as the circumstances require*" (emphasis added).

It is therefore important that a "special relationship" exists sufficient to give rise to a duty of care. This principle was subsequently considered by the Irish courts in *Bank of Ireland v Smith* [1966] I.R. 646. Here, an advertisement for the sale of land falsely stated that a portion of the lands was sown with barley and undersown with permanent pasture. The court summarised the test in *Hedley Byrne* as follows:

> "[I]f a person seeks information from another in circumstances in which a reasonable man would know that his judgment is being relied on, the person giving the information must use reasonable care to ensure that his answer is correct, and if he does not do so, he is liable in damages ...".

In *Doolan v Murray* (unreported, High Court, 21 December 1993), the plaintiff purchased property from Mr and Mrs Murray, the first two defendants. The property backed onto another house owned by the third defendant, the mother of Mr Murray. The third defendant had represented to the plaintiff that her property enjoyed a right of way over the land that the plaintiff had purchased, but that it was limited to a pedestrian right of way only. Critically, this statement was not provided by the first or second defendant. When the right of way turned out to be more extensive than she thought, the development works the plaintiff had started had to be removed. The court held that the plaintiff could not recover in either contract or tort as against the first or second defendant. However, liability arose as against the third defendant in *tort* (there being no contractual relationship between the plaintiff and the mother of Mr Murray), given the third defendant's duty to inform the plaintiff of the extent of the right of way when asked.

A duty of care has been held to arise as between:

(a) a solicitor for the vendor of a property and the purchaser of a property to exercise care in answering requisitions on title (see *Doran v Delaney* [1998] 2 I.L.R.M. 1);
(b) *a company and its shareholders (see Securities Trust v Hugh Moore & Alexander Ltd* [1964] I.R. 417);
(c) financial advisers and their clients (see *McSweeney v Bourke* (unreported, High Court, 24 November 1980));
(d) banks and their customers (see *Bank of Ireland v Lennon* (unreported, High Court, 17 February 1998));
(e) estate agents and their clients (see *Dodds v Millman* (1964) 45 D.L.R. (2d) 472).

In *Walsh v Jones Lang LaSalle Ltd* [2017] IESC 38, the defendant misrepresented the floor area of a property to be sold in their sales brochure. The brochure also contained a disclaimer that reserved the right to publish inaccurate measurements and limit liability for errors. As such, the Supreme

Court held that there had been no assumption of responsibility for any negligent misstatements.

Innocent Misrepresentation

Notably, at common law damages are not available for a misrepresentation that is not the result of either negligence or fraud (though some relief may be available under statute). In equity, however, rescission is possible even where the misrepresentation is innocent. An innocently made statement inducing the creation of a contract may, moreover, lead to the repudiation of the contract (allowing the wronged party to regard the contract as terminated) but only if there is a complete failure of consideration as a result of the misrepresentation, and not otherwise.

Remedies

Remedies at Common Law

Traditionally, damages were available for misrepresentation only where it was fraudulently made and not otherwise. Such damages, moreover, lay in tort rather than contract, the court granting relief under the tort of deceit. As a result of the decision in *Hedley Byrne*, however, damages are also available where a negligent misstatement is made, provided that a special relationship existed between the parties, placing a duty of care on the person making the statement. At common law, innocent misrepresentation does not give rise to damages, though the contract may be repudiated by the wronged party if the misrepresentation led to a complete failure in consideration.

Remedies in Equity

Rescission

"Rescission" is an equitable remedy that serves to restore the parties to the position they would have been in had the contract never been made (a remedy also known as *restitutio in integrum*). Where a misrepresentation occurs (be it fraudulent, negligent or innocent), equity may, at the discretion of the court, grant a remedy of rescission. For instance, in *Gahan v Boland* (unreported, Supreme Court, 20 January 1984)), a person buying land was assured that a planned motorway would not affect the land, when in fact it was due to traverse the property. The purchaser was thus entitled to rescind the contract, return the land and recover the money paid. In theory, rescission is available for all types of actionable misrepresentation: fraudulent, negligent and innocent.

Nonetheless, like all equitable remedies, the courts retain discretion to refuse relief. In particular, rescission will not be granted in the following cases:

(a) Where it is not possible to restore the parties to their original position, e.g. where the subject matter being contracted for no longer exists and the person seeking to rescind cannot give or take back what has been transferred under contract. In *Vigers v Pike* (1842) 8 E.R. 220, a mine that was the subject of a voidable contract had been exhausted of minerals.

(b) Where recission would affect the rights acquired by a third party. An example of this is the bona fide purchaser for value without notice. (See *Anderson v Ryan* [1967] I.R. 34.)

(c) Where there has been undue delay in seeking recission (also called "laches"). In *Leaf v International Galleries* [1950] 2 K.B. 86, an innocent misrepresentation that a painting was painted by the artist John Constable was not verified by the plaintiff for five years. The court refused to grant recission due to delay. Where the misrepresentation is fraudulent, however, even a very lengthy delay may not prevent rescission. (See *O'Kelly v Glenny* (1846) 9 Ir. Eq. R. 25.)

(d) Where the contract has been "affirmed", that is, where the innocent party became aware of the misrepresentation but nonetheless continued to act under the contract (though this only applies where the party is aware of the misrepresentation and of their right to rescind).

(e) Where the contract has been executed (performed). Where the duties under the contract have been fully performed, rescission is not possible: *Lecky v Walter* [1914] I.R. 378; *Seddon v North Eastern Salt* [1905] 1 Ch. 326. This is subject to s.44 of the Sale of Goods and Supply of Services Act 1980, discussed below.

Specific performance

Specific performance requires that a contractual obligation be performed by a party. It may be denied where a contract was entered into as a result of a misrepresentation, even if it is innocent. In *Smelter Corp v O'Driscoll* [1977] I.R. 305, specific performance of a contract for the sale of land was denied where the agreement was obtained on foot of an incorrect statement that the land would otherwise be compulsorily purchased by a local authority. In *O'Connor v Potts* [1897] 1 I.R. 534, a statement that a farm was 15% larger than it was led a court to grant specific performance only in respect of the true acreage.

Relief under Consumer Insurance Contracts Act 2019

The Consumer Insurance Contracts Act 2019 provides proportionate remedies for misrepresentation, which are discussed above.

Relief under the Sale of Goods and Supply of Services Act 1980

Part V of the 1980 Act grants certain additional and alternative remedies where a misrepresentation has induced a contract for the sale of goods or supply of services, or alternatively a hire-purchase contract. First, s.44 of the Act allows a contract to be rescinded where it has been induced by misrepresentation notwithstanding the fact that either: (a) the misrepresentation has become a term of the contract, or (b) the contract has been performed. Section 45, moreover, creates a statutory right to damages for misrepresentation causing loss, even where the misrepresentation was not fraudulent. Where the misrepresentation has induced entry into a contract, the source of the misrepresentation will be liable to pay damages for loss unless they can prove that they had reasonable ground to believe, and did believe up to the time the contract was made, that the facts represented were true. This effectively amounts to relief for negligent misrepresentation but with a reverse onus of proof. Additionally, s.45(2) allows a court to grant damages instead of rescission if the court considers it equitable to do so. In other words, if rescission would have been available for non-fraudulent misrepresentation, a court may grant damages if it considers this a more appropriate remedy. Unlike s.45(1), it is not necessarily a defence to establish lack of negligence under s.45(2). If damages are obtained under s.45(2), however, the contract will not come to an end as is the case with rescission, a factor that may render it preferable to rescind the contract. Where damages are sought, the contract remains valid and the parties will still be obliged to perform duties thereunder. Damages will be awarded, moreover, based on principles applicable in tort law, meaning that the wronged party will only be compensated for actual loss sustained, and not for loss of bargain (loss of profit that would have been made had the contract been performed), the usual standard in contract law.

Exclusion for Liability

A contract may exclude liability for misrepresentation unless the misrepresentation was fraudulent, e.g. *Pearson v Dublin Corporation* [1907] A.C. 351. Section 46 of the 1980 Act renders unenforceable clauses purporting to exclude or limit liability for misrepresentation, unless such clauses are shown to be "fair and reasonable".

17 Mistake

Mistake is a complex area of law, the cases on which do not facilitate a particularly coherent summary. In sum, a mistake arises where one or both parties believe that they are consenting to one thing but in fact are consenting to something entirely different. If a clause is included in the contract attesting to the accuracy of a statement or understanding and the statement turns out to be false, relief will be available, but for breach of contract rather than for mistake. Otherwise, where there is no contractual warranty as to accuracy within the contract, a mistake *may* invalidate a contract, in which case the mistake is said to be "operative" or "actionable".

There are basically three different types of actionable mistake (though some caution is required, as the terminology is not always consistently used by the courts):

- *common mistake*, where both parties are mistaken, each making the *same* error (the mistake is said to be "shared");
- *mutual mistake*, where both parties are *mistaken* but do not share the *same* mistake. Since both parties are at cross-purposes, one party believing X, the other Y, the question is whether an agreement has been reached at all;
- *unilateral mistake*, where *only one party* makes a mistake. Relief is available only if the other party either *knows* or *should have known* that the mistake has been made.

As we examine the case law in this area, the following questions will arise:

(a) Did the mistake exist at the time the contract was entered into?
(b) What is the nature of the mistake—fact or law?
(c) Is the plaintiff seeking to invoke common law or equity?
(d) What is the nature of the remedy being sought?

DID THE MISTAKE EXIST AT THE TIME THE CONTRACT WAS ENTERED INTO?

The mistake must have supplied a reason why the party entered into the contract, although it need not have been either the sole or the primary reason for having done so. It logically follows that a mistake made after the contract is entered into is not actionable. For instance, in *Amalgamated Investment & Property Co Ltd v John Walker & Sons Ltd* [1977] 1 W.L.R. 164, a warehouse was sold with a view to being redeveloped, both parties knowing of the plan to redevelop. A day after the agreement was signed, the building was "listed" as a heritage building. As a result, the planned development was severely restricted and the value of the property fell dramatically to 11% of its previous value. Yet, because the mistake arose as a result of factors coming into play *after* the contract was made, the contract was valid. At the time the contract was made, there was no error.

Mistake of Law

In line with the general principle that ignorance of the law is no defence (*ignorantia juris neminem excusat*), traditionally, mistakes (or misstatements) as to the existence or meaning of the law (e.g. a misinterpretation of applicable legislation) have been insufficient to invalidate a contract. Thus, no relief was available when the mistake related to a matter of law as opposed to a matter of fact. In *O'Loghlen v O'Callaghan* (1874) I.R. 8 C.L. 116, for instance, a contract was enforced notwithstanding the fact that it was entered into under a shared mistake relating to local authority rates set by law.

In practice, however, this distinction between law and fact is very difficult to make, and to a significant extent modern case law has mitigated the rule. In particular, equity will permit a contract to be avoided where the mistake relates to the legal consequences of a private transaction or agreement (e.g. the law as it is found in agreements, wills or private Acts of Parliament) as opposed to a general principle of law applicable to the public at large (e.g. a piece of public legislation). For instance, in *Cooper v Phibbs* (1867) L.R. 2 H.L. 149, the plaintiff and defendant contracted to lease a salmon fishery. Both parties were mistaken in their understanding of who owned the fishery, assuming that the defendant's father had owned it and that it had passed to the defendant in a will. In fact, a private Act of Parliament had made the plaintiff tenant for life and he attempted to avoid the contract, in circumstances where he was already the owner. The court held that the contract could be set aside in circumstances where private ownership was a matter of fact that happened to be the result of a matter of law.

The law of restitution has provided a remedy where a mistake of law has been made. Restitution is a remedy that permits money to be repaid where it has been unjustly earned. It is often seen where a local authority charges an excessive rate due to a misinterpretation of the rating legislation. The English decision of *Kiriri Cotton Co Ltd v Dewani* [1960] A.C. 192 was followed in

Dolan v Nelligan [1967] I.R. 247. Here, the court approved the ruling in *Kiriri* where Lord Denning said:

> "The true proposition is that money paid under a mistake of law, by itself and without more, cannot be recovered back ... If there is something more in addition to a mistake of law – if there is something in the defendant's conduct which shows that, of the two of them, he is the one primarily responsible for the mistake – then it may be recovered back."

In other words, the court held that if one party is primarily responsible for the mistake, the payment may be recovered back from him. Subsequently, in *Dublin Corporation v Trinity College Dublin* [1985] I.L.R.M. 283, it was held that local authority rates paid in error by the college could be set off against future rates, notwithstanding the fact that the error was a mistake as to the law. Here, it was held that the responsibility for the mistake was not *pari delicto* (equal fault). Rather, it was the plaintiff that was primarily responsible.

In *Kleinwort Benson v Lincoln City Council* [1998] 3 W.L.R. 1095, the House of Lords appeared to abolish the rule regarding recovery for mistake of law. The plaintiff bank sought to recover monies paid to the defendant over a period of six years under speculative financial agreements. It was thought that these agreements were valid at the time they were entered into. This transpired to be a mistake: they had been held to be illegal by the House of Lords in a 1992 case. The court criticised the traditional rule that no money could be recovered for a mistake in law and held that the rule should no longer be maintained in England. Instead, the court held that there should be a general right to recover monies paid as a result of a mistake of fact or law, subject to the defences available under the law of restitution. In *Re Article 26 of the Constitution and in the Matter of the Health (Amendment) (No. 2) Bill 2004* [2005] 1 I.R. 105, the Supreme Court held that "our law recognises a cause of action for restitution of money paid without lawful authority". This is the case regardless of whether "it was paid under a mistake of law, whether the parties were of equal standing and resources, whether the money was paid under protest and whether it was received in good faith."

COMMON MISTAKE OF FACT

A common mistake arises where both parties share the same mistaken belief regarding a material fact. Such a mistake will only render a contract void if it relates to:

    (a) the *existence* of a thing or survival of a person;
    (b) title to (*ownership* of) the subject matter; or
    (c) in *some limited* cases only, mistakes as to *quality*.

Existence of Subject Matter (Res Extincta)

Where, at the time the contract is made, the subject matter of the contract no longer exists (as might happen where it has been destroyed), or simply never existed, the contract will be void. In *Couturier v Hastie* (1856) 5 H.L.C. 673, a buyer contracted for the purchase of corn that both parties believed was on a ship bound for England. The corn in fact perished and had been sold *before* the contract was made. The contract was thus void.

Section 6 of the Sale of Goods Act 1893 stipulates that a contract for the sale of goods will be void if those goods have perished at the time of the contract (provided the seller is not aware that the goods have perished). Similar results arise in cases where life assurance is taken out in respect of persons mistakenly believed to be alive at the time the agreement is made (see *Scott v Coulson* [1903] 2 Ch. 249; *Strickland v Turner* (1852) 7 Exch. 208), the logic being that the person in respect of whom the insurance was taken out no longer exists. In *Galloway v Galloway* (1914) 30 T.L.R 267, likewise, a separation agreement entered into on the incorrect assumption that the parties were married to each other was deemed void for mistake, as a relationship integral to the contract (the marriage) was absent.

A different conclusion will prevail, however, where, on the facts, one of the parties has knowingly assumed the risk that the item does not exist. In such a case, the contract may not be void, as the parties have agreed that one or other of them will accept that risk. Such a contract is said to be a contract entered into as an "adventure". Thus, where there is "conscious uncertainty" as to the existence of the subject matter, the contract may not be void if the subject matter does not in fact exist.

For instance: Maureen buys a map revealing the location of hidden treasure, on the understanding that the treasure may or may not still be there. More than likely she may not claim that the contract is void if the treasure is not present, as she has accepted that risk.

As a corollary, if one of the parties has warranted, as a term of the contract, that a thing exists, its non-existence will amount not to a mistake but to a breach of contract. In *McRae v Commonwealth Disposals Commission* (1951) 84 C.L.R. 377, the defendant sold the plaintiff a wrecked tanker reported to be lying on "Jourmand Reef". In fact, the plaintiff discovered, having expended large sums of money searching for its purchase, that there was no such shipwreck. The defendant claimed mistake, but the Australian courts concluded that there was an implied condition that the subject matter existed, which term had been breached. The plaintiff was thus entitled to damages for breach of contract, the court most likely being swayed by the defendant's negligence in relation to the matter.

MISTAKE AS TO OWNERSHIP (RES SUA)

As we have seen above, in *Cooper v Phibbs* (1867) L.R. 2 H.L. 149, an agreement to sell a fishery was deemed void for mistake as, under a private Act of Parliament, the buyer already owned (as tenant for life) what he had been sold. Given the common (shared) mistake as to ownership, the contract was set aside.

MISTAKE AS TO QUALITY

As a general rule, a mistake as to the quality or attributes of an item will not render a contract void (see *Fitzsimons v O'Hanlon* [1999] 2 I.L.R.M. 551), though there are some very limited exceptions to this principle. In *Bell v Lever Bros Ltd* [1932] A.C. 161, following a merger, two officers of a company were made redundant, negotiating the redundancy contracts and payments of £50,000 each. In fact, as Lever Brothers subsequently discovered, the two men could have been dismissed without compensation for misconduct. The company claimed that the redundancy contracts were void (and the money refundable) on the basis that the money was paid under a mistake as to the validity of the contracts. The House of Lords ruled, however, that the mistake was not sufficiently fundamental to render the contract void. However, dicta by the House of Lords, particularly Lord Atkin's judgment therein, seems to provide that a common mistake as to the quality of goods *may* render a contract void for mistake in very exceptional cases where the mistake is *fundamental* to the contract "as to the existence of some quality which makes the thing *without the quality essentially different from the thing as it was believed to be*" (emphasis added). This would be enough to render a contract void. In other words, both parties "must necessarily have accepted [something] in their minds as an essential and integral element of the subject-matter."

In *Western Potato Co-Operative Ltd v Durnan* [1985] I.L.R.M. 5, the Irish Circuit Court held that a contract for the sale of seed potatoes was void because both parties thought that the seed potatoes were sound. However, the seed potatoes had physical defects in their genetic structure which meant they would not propagate. This shared mistake as to quality went to the root of the contract.

In *Nicholson & Venn v Smith-Marriott* (1947) 177 L.T. 189, table napkins inaccurately described as having belonged to Charles I were sold at auction. This reassurance was deemed a term of the contract and thus damages were awarded for breach of contract. Nonetheless, it was suggested that the contract might *also* have been treated as void for mistake if the fact that they had belonged to Charles I was "fundamental" to the contract. In *Sherwood v Walker* 66 Mich. 568 (1887), a contract for the sale of a cow believed to be infertile was set aside when it turned out that the cow was pregnant, clearly a very fundamental error as to quality. Nonetheless, it appears that mistakes of quality in common law generally will attract relief only in exceptional cases.

COMMON MISTAKE OF FACT IN EQUITY

Equity is traditionally more flexible when it comes to common mistake, allowing for either the setting aside of the contract (rescission) or the refusal of specific performance (enforcement) of a contract made under a mistaken belief. In equity, however, the contract would be voidable rather than void, the parties being entitled to set it aside, and seek rescission. The leading case of *Cooper v Phibbs* is discussed above. It was held here that in order to rely on common mistake at equity, parties must establish that they made the contract under a fundamental "misapprehension". In *Solle v Butcher* [1950] 1 K.B. 671, a rent of £250 was charged under the common mistaken belief that an apartment was not subject to rent control. In fact, it was subject to such control, the maximum permitted rent being £140. The contract was not void at common law, this being a mistake as to *quality* and *not sufficiently fundamental* to render the contract void. The court nonetheless set the contract aside in equity, giving the tenant the option of leaving the flat or remaining there paying the maximum allowable rent. Lord Denning suggested that if both parties were mistaken either as to facts or to their relative and respective rights, equity would provide relief if the *misapprehension was fundamental* and the party seeking to set it aside was not himself at fault. *Solle* was cited with approval in Ireland in *O'Neill v Ryan* [1991] I.L.R.M. 672 and thus still represents good law in Ireland. (See also *Grist v Bailey* [1967] Ch. 532.) In *O'Neill*, it was suggested that even where relief is not available at common law, equity will set aside a contract entered into under a mistake as to the facts or the rights of the parties, if the mistake is sufficiently fundamental and the party seeking relief is not at fault.

However, the case of *Great Peace Shipping Ltd v Tsavliris Salvage (International) Ltd* [2002] 4 All E.R. 689 seemed to have altered the approach in England. Here, the owners of a ship called "Cape Providence" learned that it was in distress at sea. They engaged another ship called "Great Peace" to provide assistance to the ship. Both parties were under a common mistake as to the proximity of Great Peace to Cape Providence. When the owners of Cape Providence realised this, they tried to rely on common mistake. The English Court of Appeal held that this mistake was not such as to render it impossible for Great Peace to perform its contracted services. The court ruled further that once the mistake was not actionable in common law, it would not be possible to grant equitable relief. In other words, it appears that the doctrine of equitable mistake set out in *Solle v Butcher* has been abolished in English law, though it is still current in Irish law, in lieu of a Supreme Court ruling to the contrary.

Mutual Mistake

Fundamentally, a contract is the result of an agreement between two or more parties. If, objectively speaking, there is no agreement, the contract will be void. Mutual mistake arises where the parties, unbeknownst to either, are not in fact in agreement on a particular point: they have negotiated different things. A contract might therefore be void for mutual mistake. For example, in *Scriven Bros v Hindley & Co* [1913] 3 K.B. 564, the parties had concluded an agreement for the sale of material intended for use in making rope. The plaintiff believed he was selling tow. The defendant, however, believed he was purchasing hemp, hemp being of higher quality than tow. As there was no consensus regarding what was being bought, the contract was void for mutual mistake. Similarly, in *Megaw v Molloy* (1878) 2 L.R. Ir. 530, for instance, the plaintiff offered for sale, by sample, grain being shipped on board one of the plaintiff's ships, the "Emma Peasant". In fact, the sample of grain produced to the defendant was from a superior batch aboard another ship, the "Jessie Parker". The parties were thus deemed not to be in agreement: the plaintiff had intended to sell grain from the Emma Peasant, the defendant to buy different grain from the Jessie Parker. The contract thus was void, the parties having been at cross-purposes. (See also *Raffles v Wichelhaus* (1864) 159 E.R. 375.) Notwithstanding the above, it is important to note the following caveat, which is set out clearly in the judgment of *Smith v Hughes* (1871) L.R. 2 Q.B. 597:

> "If, whatever a man's real intention may be, he so *conducts himself that a reasonable man would believe that he was assenting to the terms proposed by the other party*, and that *other party upon that belief enters into the contract* with him, the man thus conducting himself would be *equally bound as if he had intended to agree* with the other party's terms" (emphasis added).

In other words, if an objective bystander, observing the conduct of the parties, would conclude that a party agreed to the terms proposed by the other party, the agreement will be enforced. This is regardless of the fact that the parties may *subjectively* have expected different conclusions. The question, therefore, is whether the party pleading mistake has a reasonable expectation that the contract would include the terms in question and whether an objective bystander observing the conduct of the parties would agree. In *Wood v Scarth* (1855) 2 K. & J. 33, although the defendant thought he would receive a once-off charge of £500 in addition to rent paid for the lease of a pub, his letter of offer in fact made no reference to this charge. Thus, the contract was (from an objective viewpoint) validly created without the £500 charge. The courts, in other words, will only enforce a party's expectation where it is reasonably well-founded, and not otherwise. In *Mespil Ltd v Capaldi* [1986] I.L.R.M. 373, the plaintiff intended to initiate proceedings against the defendants for the possession of a premises. The parties settled separate litigation, agreeing that the settlement be in "full and final settlement of all matters". The defendants claimed that they had intended this to dispose of all proceedings outstanding, including the possession proceedings. The Supreme Court held that the agreement was void for mutual mistake, outlining that there was a difference between mistake as to the impact of a bargain and a mistake as to the terms of the bargain. The court held that if a person "freely and competently entered into the agreement he will not normally escape being bound by it, by saying that he misunderstood its effect." However, as was the case here, a mutual mistake as to the true nature of the agreement would render the agreement void: "there cannot be said to be the meeting of the minds which is essential for an enforceable contract. In such circumstances the alleged contract is a nullity."

UNILATERAL MISTAKE

A unilateral mistake arises where only one of the parties is mistaken as to the true situation. The basic rule is that if only one party is mistaken, the contract will be void *only if* the other party is *aware* of that mistake, whether or not the mistake was fundamental. If, moreover, the mistaken party can prove that the other party, though not aware of the error, *ought to have been* aware that the former was mistaken, the contract can be set aside in equity. Otherwise the contract is enforceable. In *Hartog v Colin and Shields* [1939] 3 All E.R. 566, for instance, a vendor mistakenly sold hare skins by the pound. The standard practice was to sell by the piece. The vendor was aware of this mistake, which worked out to his benefit. The contract was thus void.

By contrast, in *Centrovincial Estates v Merchant Investors Insurance* [1983] Com. L.R. 158, a landlord mistakenly issued an offer to rent premises at less than half the price he had originally intended. As the tenant was unaware of this mistake, the mistake was not actionable, and the resulting contract was valid.

Errors as to Identity

The question often arises whether a contract is void for mistake where one of the parties has misrepresented their identity for the purpose of defrauding the other party. There is no argument that in such circumstances, the contract would be *voidable* for misrepresentation. A finding of operative mistake, however, will render the contract *void*, thus preventing any title from passing to an innocent third party. With misrepresentation, by contrast, title would pass to an innocent third party unless the contract was avoided beforehand. The real question in many of these cases, then, is which of two innocent parties should be granted relief in cases where a rogue has defrauded one innocent party of property and sold it to another innocent party.

First, the mistake must be as to the identity of the individual rather than the attributes or characteristics of a person. For instance: if Irene agrees to sell shares in her business to Tom believing Tom to be a wealthy investor (when in fact he is not), her mistake will not be operative. If, on the other hand, she sells the shares to Tom and in fact she intended to sell only to his brother Pat, the contract may be void for mistake provided that the identity of the buyer is of fundamental importance to Irene. This latter point is crucial. A mistake as to identity will not be operative and will not render the contract void *unless* it can be proved that the identity of the other was of fundamental importance to the seller.

In practice, this is difficult to prove, the onus being on the person claiming that identity was fundamental. Indeed, where the parties contract face-to-face, it is usually assumed that they each intended to deal with the person who was present, their identity not being relevant. In *Phillips v Brooks* [1919] 2 K.B. 243, for instance, a man who claimed to be "Sir George Bullough" purchased a ring from a jeweller, paying by cheque. He subsequently pledged the ring to the defendant, an innocent person. In fact, the man claiming to be Sir George was an impostor, and the cheque subsequently bounced. On the facts, the court concluded that the contract with the jeweller, though voidable for misrepresentation, was not void for mistake, as the jeweller had "in fact contracted to sell and deliver it to the person who came into his shop". The man's identity was not fundamental, though his characteristics (ostensibly being rich and titled) may have been. Thus, as the contract was not void, and the pledge to the innocent party had been made before the original contract for sale was avoided, the defendant had acquired good title to the ring.

Likewise, in *Lewis v Avery* [1972] 1 Q.B. 198, the plaintiff sold a car to a man who had represented himself to be the famous film actor Richard Greene, showing a movie studio ID card as evidence. Subsequently, the defendant purchased the car from the imposter. The original contract for the sale of the car as between the imposter and the plaintiff was not void for mistake and the plaintiff could not recover the car from the innocent defendant, as the identity of the imposter was not crucial to the plaintiff at the time of the sale. The plaintiff had intended to sell to the person before him. The false claim may have persuaded the plaintiff as to the imposter's creditworthiness, but it was not otherwise relevant.

In *Ingram v Little* [1961] 1 Q.B. 31, by contrast, a conman called to the house of two elderly sisters, offering them a £700 cheque for their car. Although they initially refused, the buyer reassured them that he was a "Mr P Hutchinson", giving them his address. Having checked this name and address in the telephone directory, the sisters agreed to accept the cheque, which subsequently bounced. The English Court of Appeal concluded that the sisters had intended only to sell to Mr Hutchinson. His identity was crucial to the sale, a conclusion that rendered the contract void for mistake. Similarly, in *Cundy v Lindsay* (1878) 3 App. Cas. 459, a Mr Blenkarn sent a letter to the plaintiff asking it to supply him with linen. In the letter, Mr Blenkarn pretended to be representing a reputable company "Blenkiron & Co.", which happened to run a business on the same street where Mr Blenkarn resided. On delivery of the linen, Blenkarn sold it to the defendants, failing to pay the plaintiff. The court concluded that the plaintiff's contract was void, as the identity of the buyer was of crucial importance. *Cundy v Lindsay* is generally taken to be authority for the distinction between contracts made face-to-face (where it is assumed that the wronged party intended to deal with the person before them) and contracts concluded by writing (where the fundamental nature of the writer's identity may be easier to establish). While this distinction was approved by a majority of the House of Lords in *Shogun Finance v Hudson* [2004] 1 All E.R. 215, it does not always hold true. In *King's Norton Metal Co v Edridge, Merrett & Co* (1897) 14 T.L.R. 98, the plaintiff received an order for goods from a writer fraudulently claiming to be "Hallam and Co.". This error, nonetheless, did *not* render the resulting contract void, the court reasoning that the plaintiff had intended to deal with the writer of the letter and not with the particular company that the fraudster claimed to be representing. The identity of the writer was not important, the plaintiff being concerned only that the writer was creditworthy.

Remedies for Mistake

Generally, at common law a contract entered into under an operative mistake is void and thus of no legal effect. Nonetheless, certain remedies may be available to the parties, both at law and in equity.

Rectification

Certain remedies are available specifically where a document does not accurately reflect the intentions of the parties or where there is a mistake as regards the actual nature of the document. A document that purports to be an account of an oral agreement may be rectified where it is found not to reflect the true agreement. In such cases, the document may be altered to reflect the true intention of the parties. It is important to note, however, that this facility is available only where:

- the parties were in agreement at the time the contract was made;
- the written document was intended only as a record or note of this agreement (and not as an agreement in its own right); and
- the document or note failed accurately to reflect the agreement.

Rectification allows the contract to be altered to reflect the true agreement. For instance, in *Craddock Bros v Hunt* [1923] 2 Ch. 136, two parties had orally agreed to exclude a yard from a house being sold, but the written record of this agreement mistakenly included the yard. The document was rectified so as to exclude the yard.

Non Est Factum

A person who signs a document is bound by everything in that document, even if they have not read it. However, where a person is tricked into signing a document, the defence of *non est factum* may be available, rendering a contract void. In sum, this defence arises where a person has been misled by trick or fraud into signing a document under a fundamental mistake as to the nature of the document. The signer must, moreover, be blameless as regards the error. The case of *Ted Castle McCormack and Co v McCrystal* (unreported, High Court, 15 March 1999) set out the test as follows:

> "I am satisfied that a person seeking to raise the defence of non est factum must prove:
> (a) That there was a radical or fundamental difference between what he signed and what he thought he was signing;
> (b) That the mistake was as to the general character of the document as opposed to the legal effect; and
> (c) That there was a lack of negligence, i.e. that he took all reasonable precautions in the circumstances to find out what the document was."

Rescission

A contract entered into under an "operative" or fundamental mistake may be rescinded, allowing the parties to be returned to the positions they were in before the contract was made. In particular, rescission may be available where rectification is refused. As with all equitable remedies, rescission is discretionary and may be declined, for instance, if the party operating under a mistake is wholly responsible for their own state of mind, or where there is delay in seeking relief. (See *Stapleton v Prudential Assurance* (1928) 62 I.L.T.R. 56.)

Damages

Generally, an operative mistake will not attract damages. Damages will only issue if either: (a) the mistake involves a breach of contract, that is, where the contract itself contains a term to the effect that certain facts are true; or (b) the mistake is the result of fraudulent or negligent misrepresentation. Regarding (a), damages are thus available for breach of contract rather than mistake per se.

Specific Performance

Specific performance is again a discretionary remedy. It appears that if a party seeking performance is responsible for the mistake, it will not be granted.

18 Duress, Undue Influence and Unconscionability

Contracts generally arise from an agreement between the parties, the supposition being that the agreement is the product of the parties' free choice. As a general principle, a contract may be voidable where one of the parties acts under illegitimate pressure or undue influence, though certain restrictions apply.

DURESS AT COMMON LAW

Duress is a defence rendering a contract voidable. Duress may basically be defined as illegitimate pressure brought to bear on one of the parties with the result that the latter has no reasonable alternative but to enter into the contract. In some cases, it has been suggested that relief will only issue where the will of one of the parties has been "overborne" by the conduct of the other party. This suggests, misleadingly, that the wronged party does not make any intentional decision. It is suggested that the better view is that the pressure must be such as to foreclose access to any reasonable alternative; in other words, the affected party has no practical alternative but to do what the other party has demanded.

THE TRADITIONAL LIMITS OF DURESS

All sorts of pressure, influence, cajoling and convincing may be brought to bear to induce people to do business. Notably, only certain types of pressure are treated as amounting to "duress". Indeed, historically, duress only arose where there was a threat to "life, limb or liberty", that is, a threat to kill, maim or unlawfully incarcerate a person. For instance, in *Barton v Armstrong* [1975] 2 All E.R. 465, a contract entered into as a result of threats to injure or kill a man and his family members was deemed voidable for duress. In *Lessee of Blackwood v Gregg* (1831) Hayes 277, the relatives of an elderly man abducted him with a view to getting him to execute a deed in favour of one of their number, the resulting contract being deemed voidable as a result of the unlawful incarceration. Generally, the pressure must be of a type that is deemed illegitimate in law. In *ACC Bank plc v Dillon* [2012] IEHC 474,

Charleton J. documented the development of duress from cases of violence and threats of violence to cases of overbearing conduct. The court rejected the argument that the defendants had provided personal guarantees for a loan given to a construction site in Galway under duress. It was claimed that the bank had intimated that it would exercise its rights under the loan agreement to appoint a receiver if the personal guarantees were not obtained.

The court noted that no allegation was made as to any overbearing conduct or "interrogation-type" pressures being brought to bear on the defendants by the bank. The court held that it was legitimate for the bank to offer more time to the defendants to pay their debts in exchange for personal guarantees. While the circumstances of the negotiation were fraught, this did not necessarily amount to illegitimate pressure. All that was done was said to be "within the level of appreciation that must be allowed in commercial bargaining". Critically, Charleton J. stated:

> "The *threat of violence is no longer necessary* to establish that a contract was entered into under duress. *Nor is it necessary that consent to bargain is negatived*; rather that consent must have been *so wrongfully obtained* that it can properly be described as an *illegitimate* and *significant cause of the party ostensibly contracting giving assent*" (emphasis added).

In *Griffith v Griffith* [1944] I.R. 35 (a case involving the validity of a marriage), a marriage was deemed invalid where the groom, falsely accused of paternity in respect of an underage girl, was threatened with prosecution if he did not marry her. The groom had not in fact done anything illegal, though, being innocent in matters sexual, he wrongly believed he was the father nonetheless. The High Court made it clear that if he had in fact broken the law and impregnated the girl, the marriage would have been valid, as the threat to incarcerate would have been justified. Notably, the rules relating to marriages have changed considerably since *Griffith* (see, e.g. *MK (McC) v McC* [1982] I.L.R.M. 277 and *OB v R* [2000] 1 I.L.R.M. 306), though the basic point—that the threat must be illegitimate—remains valid in contract law, as stated above.

Economic Duress and Threats to Breach a Contract

Economic duress is when one party exerts illegitimate economic or similar pressure on another. Although "normal commercial pressure" will not suffice, an illegitimate threat to break a contract, or to commit a tort, may amount to duress if it leaves the party no economic alternative but to submit. For instance, in *North Ocean Shipping Co v Hyundai Construction Co Ltd (The Atlantic Baron)* [1979] Q.B. 705, the parties had entered into an agreement for the purchase of a ship. While the ship was being built, the sellers demanded a 10% increase in the price payable under the contract to compensate for a devaluation in the dollar, or they would break the contract. This constituted duress, the court reasoning that economic pressure could give rise to a voidable contract just as easily as physical force. The contract nonetheless stood, as the buyers had delayed in avoiding the contract.

In *Universe Tankships Inc of Monrovia v International Transport Workers Federation (The Universe Sentinel)* [1983] A.C. 366, the defendant trade union blockaded or "blacked" a ship, refusing to let it leave port until such time as its owners agreed to certain demands made on behalf of the ship's workers. Having agreed under pressure, the ship's owners sought to avoid the contract on the basis of economic duress. The House of Lords concluded that the contract was voidable as it had been entered into as a result of illegitimate pressure. Lord Scarman (although dissenting on the conclusion) laid out a useful series of tests for duress:

1. Did the person alleging duress protest?
2. Was there a feasible alternative to succumbing to the pressure?
3. Was the person alleging duress independently advised?
4. Did the person alleging the duress seek to avoid the contract at the first available opportunity?

This last point, for instance, was not satisfied in *The Atlantic Baron* as the buyer had delayed seeking relief once the pressure was lifted.

In *Atlas Express v Kafco* [1989] 1 All E.R. 641, the defendant won a contract to supply products to Woolworths, a large retailer. It contracted with the plaintiff courier company for the delivery of its products to Woolworths stores. The plaintiff initially quoted a price per product based on its own inaccurate calculation of the number of products it could carry in each of their vans. Upon discovering that the quoted price was less profitable than originally envisaged, the plaintiff threatened not to deliver the products unless an increased price was secured. The defendant reluctantly agreed, but later sought to avoid the contract for duress. Given the proximity to Christmas, the defendant argued that it had no choice but to agree to the increased price, as they were otherwise unlikely to achieve delivery and thus risked losing their contract with Woolworths. Given the illegitimate nature of the threat, the contract was voidable for duress. Similarly, in *B. & S. Contracts v Victor Green Publications* [1984] 1 I.C.R. 419, the defendant's threat not to erect stands at an exhibition for the plaintiff, as agreed, unless extra pay was secured, was also deemed to constitute duress. This threat was made days before the exhibition was due to commence and there was no reasonable alternative but to submit.

In the Irish case of *Carlo Tassara Assets Management SA v Éire Composites Teoranta* [2018] IEHC 182, Costello J., building on earlier cases, considered the distinction between lawful pressure and duress. She indicated that the pressure of keeping employees employed and meeting the expectations of contractors did *not* constitute duress, but rather commercial pressure.

Where money is obtained under duress, restitution may be available (requiring the return of monies unjustly earned), as illustrated by *Great Southern and Western Railway v Robertson* (1878) 2 L.R. (Ir.) 548. Under legislation, railway companies were obliged to transport soldiers at a fixed rate. A railway company that refused to transport soldiers unless a higher rate was paid was required to refund the excess, as it had been extracted under duress. The important point here is that the attempt to charge a higher rate was illegitimate, as it was in breach of legislation.

Duress in Equity

As discussed, specific performance is an equitable remedy, the award of which is subject to the court's discretion. Equity may refuse to grant specific performance of a contract entered into under duress. For instance, in the Supreme Court case of *Smelter Corp of Ireland v O'Driscoll* [1977] I.R. 305, the plaintiff company was given the benefit of an option agreement which gave it the right to purchase the defendant's land. The defendant had only consented to this option agreement because he had been told by the plaintiff's agent that if he did not sell the land to the plaintiff, the local authority would compulsorily purchase his land. As such, he felt like he had no other choice than to agree to the option. In fact, the local authority did not intend to subject the land to a compulsory purchase order. Specific performance of the option agreement was refused by the Supreme Court, given a "fundamental unfairness in the transaction". The misrepresentation by the plaintiff had effectively left the defendant in a position where he felt he had no choice but to sign.

Equity has also allowed contracts to be set aside where they are entered into under a fear of prosecution. (See *Rourke v Mealy* (1879) 13 I.L.T.R. 52.)

Undue Influence

Equity provides some relief in cases where one party to a contract has inappropriately exercised influence over the other party. In *Nature Resorts Ltd v First Citizens Bank Ltd* [2022] UKPC 10, the Privy Council provided the following definition of undue influence:

"[U]ndue influence is concerned with a situation where, by reason of the relationship between them, one party (B) has such influence over the other (A) that A does not exercise a free judgment, independent of B, in relation to the making of a transaction between A and B (or, in a three-party situation, between A and a third party, C)."

This definition is also descriptive of the position in Ireland. The court went on to describe how in law a distinction has been historically made between two different categories of undue influence: actual and presumed.

In *Barclay's Bank v O'Brien* [1993] 3 All E.R. 417, the two different categories were set out as follows: *actual* undue influence occurs where, on the facts, undue influence *has been proved* (e.g. by conduct). Presumed undue influence occurs where undue influence is *presumed to arise from a relationship* in which one party places significant trust and confidence in the other. Where such a presumption arises, the onus is on the person presumed to have exercised undue influence to prove that the contract was the result of an exercise of free will by both parties. This category is further subdivided into two subcategories:

- where the relationship is one that, by its very nature, is *automatically* deemed to attract the presumption (e.g. spiritual advisor and follower, parent and child, solicitor and client);
- where the relationship is one that normally does not attract the presumption but where, *on the facts*, the relationship is one in which one party places significant trust and confidence in the other.

Although in the United Kingdom there is a preference for a more unified approach, Irish law continues to differentiate between actual and presumed undue influence.

Actual Undue Influence

The first category of undue influence is in fact the least commonly invoked. With actual undue influence, the claimant must prove that the wrongdoer actually exerted undue influence on the complainant to enter into a particular transaction (e.g. through conduct). In *Bridgman v Green* (1755) 2 Ves. Sen. 627, a butler was found to have so "completely dominated" his master that a conveyance made by the latter to the former was set aside as having been made de facto (in fact) as a result of undue influence. The master was in such a "state of vassalage" to his servant that he even submitted to the latter's inducement to separate from his wife. In a more modern Irish case, *O'Flanagan v Ray-Ger Ltd* [1963–1993] Irish Co. Law Reports 289 (1983), two businessmen, Messrs Pope and O'Flanagan, were joint shareholders of a company. Knowing that his business partner was close to death, Pope prevailed upon the more impressionable O'Flanagan to agree that, on either's death, the survivor would take full control of the company, free from the claims of the deceased's family. The agreement was made in a pub, at a time when the deceased was seriously ill with terminal cancer.

Upon O'Flanagan's death, Costello P. concluded, on the facts, that undue influence had *in fact* been exercised by Pope, who:

> "... had a strong and forceful personality and had obviously exercised considerable influence amounting to domination of the deceased on previous occasions."

It should be noted, before we explore the category of presumed undue influence, that even in the absence of the presumption, there may be still actual influence. The establishment of actual undue influence will depend on the facts of the case and the evidence proffered.

Presumed Undue Influence

Class 2A: Relationships automatically attracting the presumption

Certain relationships are deemed *automatically* to attract the presumption of undue influence. These include relationships between:

1. Parents and their children. In *McMackin v Hibernian Bank* [1905] 1 I.R. 296, a young woman living with her mother signed two promissory notes securing debts owed by the mother. A presumption arose that the mother had unduly influenced her daughter to sign the notes. As the daughter had not received independent professional advice, the settlement was set aside.
2. Guardians and their wards. In *Mulhallen v Marum* (1843) 3 Dr. & War. 317, a transfer of land from a ward to his guardian was set aside for presumed undue influence.
3. Solicitors and their clients. The presumption is particularly strong in this context (see *Lawless v Mansfield* (1841) 1 Dr. & War. 557).
4. Religious advisers and their followers. In *Allcard v Skinner* (1887) 36 Ch. D. 145, a gratuitous transfer of property from a young nun to her religious order, on the prompting of the mother superior, was deemed subject to the presumption. As the gift had been made without the benefit of external advice, the court was satisfied that the presumption had not been displaced (though, due to delay in seeking relief, the court refused to set the agreement aside). (See also *White v Meade* (1840) 2 Ir. Eq. R.

420.) In *O'Neill v Murphy* [1936] N.I. 16, the presumption arose where a priest asked an architect to forgo his normal fees for building work done for a parish and a local convent.
5. Trustees and beneficiaries.
6. Doctors and their patients.

Class 2B: Relationships that attract the presumption on the facts

Not all relationships will *automatically* give rise to the presumption. However, if the *facts of a case* prove that a person places trust and confidence in a wrongdoer, the presumption will apply to the relationship. For instance, although the relationship between spouses does not automatically attract the presumption, a *particular* spousal relationship may be deemed subject to the presumption if, on the facts, one spouse places a strong degree of trust and confidence in the other. In other words, the facts of a case may justify inferring a presumption of undue influence.

In *Carroll v Carroll* [2000] 1 I.L.R.M. 210, the presumption arose in a case where an elderly father transferred a pub to his son. Although this was not a situation typically attracting the presumption (transactions from child to parent tend to attract the presumption but not vice versa), on the facts, the son had a relationship with the father from which the presumption arose that he had exercised undue influence, the onus being cast on him to prove that the transfer was the result of the father's independent judgment. In *Inche Noriah v Shaik Allie Bin Omar* [1929] A.C. 127, an aged and illiterate woman gifted land to her nephew, who took considerable responsibility for his aunt's financial affairs. In such circumstances, the presumption was deemed to arise and in order to rebut it, evidence had to be adduced that the donor acted freely and not under the influence of her nephew. The nephew was unable to rebut the presumption and the transaction was set aside.

In *Gregg v Kidd* [1956] I.R. 183, the presumption arose in respect of an elderly farmer and his sister, to whose sons he had transferred his farm. Mentally infirm and physically ill, the farmer depended heavily on his sister for care, factors that gave rise to a presumption that she had exercised undue influence in her sons' favour. In *McGonigle v Black* (unreported, High Court, 14 November 1988), the presumption arose from a relationship between an elderly farmer (who was lonely, ill and unable generally to cope) and his neighbour, a relationship that on the facts was one in which the farmer placed considerable trust and confidence in his neighbour.

In *ACC Loan Management Ltd v Sheehan* [2015] IEHC 818, the defendant acted as guarantor for a company of which he and his brother were director and shareholder. The defendant argued that he was under "severe pressure" at the time of executing the guarantee, thinking that if he had not, his brother's business would have failed. Although the evidence suggested that the defendant and his brother were "quite close", there was no suggestion of a "dependent" relationship here. This, and the fact that both brothers were directors and participants in the commercial enterprise, were significant.

Manifest Disadvantage

It has been suggested that for the presumption to arise, the party alleging undue influence must have been placed at a manifest disadvantage by the contract. In other words, one must establish a significant contractual imbalance to the detriment of the party alleging undue influence. This requirement was first proposed in *National Westminster Bank v Morgan* [1985] A.C. 686. (See also *Bank of Credit and Commerce International v Aboody* [1990] 1 Q.B. 923 and *Barclay's Bank v O'Brien* [1993] 4 All E.R. 417.) The House of Lords, however, has since doubted this proposition on several subsequent occasions. In *Royal Bank of Scotland v Etridge (No. 2)* [2001] 3 W.L.R. 1021, the House strongly intimated that manifest disadvantage is at best to be treated as an evidential aid in determining whether there has been undue influence. Although not yet followed in Ireland, *Etridge* suggests that the absence of manifest disadvantage may not be fatal to the raising of the presumption.

That said, as a matter of common sense, it is arguable that evidence of disadvantage will make it easier to shift the onus of proof to the dominant party. In *Goldsworthy v Brickell* [1987] Ch. 378, for instance, Nourse L.J. commented that certain gifts may be so large, or certain transactions so improvident, that standard motives of "friendship, relationship, charity or other ordinary motives" are displaced. "Although influence might have been presumed beforehand", he continues, "it is only then that it is presumed to have been undue". (See also *Allcard v Skinner* (1887) 36 Ch. D. 145.) Indeed, in *Provincial Bank v McKeever* [1941] 1 I.R. 471, Black J. suggests that "the less improvident the bargain, the less strong the presumption." It is clear, of course, that the mere fact of undervalue, without more, will not be sufficient to give rise to an inference of undue influence. In *McCrystal v O'Kane* [1986] N.I. 123, for instance, a sale of land was upheld despite the existence of a substantial undervalue, there being no other factors permitting the court to upset the transaction. The fact of transactional imbalance in itself is not sufficient to trigger the presumption.

How to Displace the Presumption

Where the presumption applies, the onus is on the party alleged to have exercised undue influence to prove that no influence was brought to bear. Unless the presumption is displaced, the contract may be set aside for undue influence. The presumption may be displaced ("rebutted") where the evidence establishes that the alleged victim in fact entered into the contract as a spontaneous act of their free will and not under any pressure. The alleged wrongdoer is required to show that the transaction was the product of a mind unencumbered by influence, that there was a free and informed exercise of independent judgment on the part of the donor.

One of the most obvious ways (though not the only way) to rebut the presumption is to establish that the gift was made after the nature and effect of the transaction has been fully explained to the donor by some independent and qualified person. In *Carroll v Carroll* [2000] 1 I.L.R.M. 210, a solicitor who had acted for both the donor and recipient (but primarily for the recipient) was held not to have been sufficiently independent for these purposes. It may not, however, be necessary to show that the solicitor in question has *never* previously acted on behalf of any of the other parties in other cases. (See *Bank of Nova Scotia v Hogan* [1996] 3 I.R. 239.) It is not necessary that the advice be taken or otherwise heeded.

The advice, however, must be such that the donor is fully and competently informed; any material deficiency in the information conveyed or the competence of the adviser will render the advice insufficient. In particular, the advice must be such that an ordinary reasonable lawyer of adequate skill would have given in the same circumstances. As noted in *Inche Noriah*, the advice "must be given with a knowledge of all the relevant circumstances and must be such as a competent and honest advisor would give if acting solely in the interests of the donor". Thus, in *Inche Noriah* itself, the court set aside the impugned transaction on the ground that, while independent legal advice was given to the aunt, it was so given in ignorance of the fact that the transaction conveyed almost all of her property to the nephew. Similarly, in *Gregg v Kidd* [1956] I.R. 183, advice given in ignorance of the mental deficiencies of the donor did not displace the presumption.

Although the absence of independent advice may be fatal to the validity of a contract (see *McMackin v Hibernian Bank* [1905] 1 I.R. 296), it is not always conclusive. If on the facts the transaction is the result of the spontaneous act of the donor, it may be upheld even in the absence of independent advice (see *Provincial Bank v McKeever* [1941] 1 I.R. 471 and *Kirwan v Cullen* (1856) 4 Ir. Ch. Rep. 322).

Wadlow v Samuel [2007] EWCA Civ 155 considered whether a settlement agreement entered into between the singer Seal and his manager was procured by way of undue influence. The court refused to accept this, given the terms of the settlement contract were actually beneficial to Seal and he had received independent legal advice throughout.

Undue Influence and Third Parties

Many cases concern the effects of undue influence on persons who benefit from a transaction entered into by a person under third party undue influence, e.g. if a person enters into a surety or guarantee agreement with a bank, guaranteeing a debt assumed by their spouse or intimate partner. If that spouse has exerted undue influence on the guarantor, it may be that the guarantee can be set aside as against the bank where the bank was sufficiently aware (had actual or constructive notice) that undue influence had occurred.

This matter was considered by the House of Lords in *Barclay's Bank v O'Brien* [1993] 3 All E.R. 417. In *O'Brien*, Mr O'Brien's company was failing and he agreed with the plaintiff bank to raise the company's overdraft, to be guaranteed by his wife and secured against his family home. Mr O'Brien misrepresented the effect of this transaction to his wife. The plaintiff received but ignored instructions to ensure that Mrs O'Brien understood the extent of the risk and to advise her to obtain independent legal advice. When the husband defaulted, the bank sought to take possession of the family home. Mrs O'Brien sought to avoid the agreement due to the misrepresentation by her husband, of which the bank had notice. The House of Lords held that where a wife offers to stand as surety for the indebtedness of her husband:

- the bank would be liable to having its surety set aside if it had either actual or constructive notice of undue influence, constructive notice being where the bank was aware of a relationship that would put it on inquiry;
- the bank is put "on inquiry" and constructive notice is presumed if the transaction is on its face not to the financial advantage of the wife (unless the bank has taken reasonable steps to satisfy itself that the wife's agreement has been properly obtained).

Reasonable steps might include:

- insisting on the wife's attending a private meeting with a representative of the creditor;
- that at that meeting it be explained to her the extent of her liability and the risks involved;
- that at that meeting it be explained to her the importance of acquiring competent independent legal advice before signing.

These principles were said to apply equally to spouses and cohabitees in an intimate relationship (regardless of sex).

The main principles espoused in *O'Brien* were broadly accepted by the Irish Supreme Court in *Bank of Nova Scotia v Hogan* [1996] 3 I.R. 239. *Hogan* did not concern a claim of third party undue influence. Rather, the defendant argued unsuccessfully that the bank itself had exercised undue influence over her to sign a guarantee for her husband's debts. The subsequent Irish case of *Ulster Bank v Fitzgerald* (unreported, High Court, 9 November 2001) did relate to a claim of third party undue influence, however. Here, a husband and wife had executed personal guarantees in favour of the bank as security for the provision of credit facilities to a company owned by the husband. The wife was neither a director nor shareholder but did rely on the income generated by the business. The wife claimed that her husband had exerted undue influence over her, forcing her to act as surety. She argued that because she had no financial stake in the company, the bank was on notice that there was a risk that she could have been unduly influenced to sign. She also claimed that the bank had failed to ensure she had obtained independent legal advice. The court rejected these arguments, holding that there was nothing in the evidence before it that suggested the bank had constructive notice of any undue influence. Of critical importance was the fact that the wife benefitted from the income generated by the business in this case. The court determined that as a result, she had a financial stake in the business of the company. In the absence of any constructive notice, the court held that there was no obligation to take any steps to ensure the wife obtained independent legal advice. This decision attracted much academic criticism in its aftermath.

In the subsequent case of *Ulster Bank Ireland Ltd v Roche and Buttimer* [2012] IEHC 166, Clarke J. stated that the approach taken by the court in *Fitzgerald*:

> "... offers insufficient protection to potential vulnerable sureties and leaves a lender with no obligations arising from knowledge that the parties are married or otherwise closely connected unless it has some special reason to believe that a wrong has actually taken place."

The controversy surrounding *Fitzgerald* was exacerbated by the fact that it was decided mere weeks after the House of Lords' decision in *Royal Bank of Scotland v Etridge (No. 2)* [2001] 3 W.L.R. 1021. In *Etridge*, the court held that a bank will be put "on inquiry" when faced with a transaction that called for an explanation, e.g. where a wife stands for surety for her husband's debts or vice versa (except where monies are advanced to both jointly). It also stated that shareholding did not reflect the true situation. The court stated that when the bank is put "on inquiry", it must take reasonable steps to satisfy itself that there was no improper influence or misrepresentation brought to bear on the guarantor. It clarified that a personal meeting was not the only way that a bank could discharge its obligation to bring home to the wife the risks she is running. The furthest a bank should have to go, it was held, is to satisfy itself that the wife has had brought home to her by her solicitor, in a meaningful way, the practical implications of the proposed transaction. In this regard:

- The bank should check with the wife the name of the solicitor she wishes to act for her and explain that it will require written confirmation from the solicitor that they have fully explained the nature of the documents and their implications to her.
- The bank should inform her that the solicitor she nominates can either be the same solicitor as is acting for her husband or a different solicitor.
- The bank must provide the solicitor nominated with the financial information they need to advise the wife.
- Exceptionally, there may be a case where the bank believes or suspects the wife has been misled by her husband or is not entering the transaction of her own free will. If this is so, the bank must inform the wife's solicitors of the facts giving rise to its beliefs or suspicions.
- The bank should obtain from the wife's solicitors a written confirmation to the effect mentioned above.

Provided that the lender follows these steps, it will be entitled to rely on a guarantee even if it subsequently transpires that there was undue influence or other wrongdoing.

Despite the judgment in *Etridge*, *Fitzgerald* continued to represent the position in Ireland for several years until the case of *Ulster Bank Ireland Ltd v Roche and Buttimer* [2012] IEHC 166. In this case, the parties were romantic partners. Mr Roche owned a company and Ms Buttimer was a director but not a shareholder of the business. They signed personal guarantees in favour of the plaintiff bank to provide credit banking facilities to the company. Ms Buttimer claimed that at the time the guarantees were entered into, she was subject to undue influence by Mr Roche to sign. The defendants relied on *Etridge* in their attempt to have the guarantees set aside. The court used a two-pronged test, asking: first, whether Ms Buttimer was *in fact* under the undue influence of Mr Roche; secondly, whether there were sufficient circumstances that would allow Ms Buttimer to have the guarantee set aside on the basis of Mr Roche's undue influence. Here, the court held that Ms Buttimer had in fact (based on the evidence available) been acting under undue influence at the time of signing. She had no involvement in the business and was in a dependent and quite abusive relationship. In this regard, Ms Buttimer's clinical psychologist was in a position to give evidence of her mental state. As such, the case came down to whether the undue influence provided a defence to the bank's claim. The court examined the circumstances in which it would be appropriate to attribute to a bank knowledge of undue influence where the bank was not actually aware of its exercise. The court held that constructive knowledge can be broken down into two separate questions:

(a) what factors place a party on inquiry;
(b) the nature of the inquiry or action that might be required.

The court held that in this case, the bank was placed on inquiry when faced with a request for guarantees from business partners who were also in a romantic relationship. In this case, the court found it significant that Ms Buttimer was a director but not a shareholder in the company and had little business acumen. Having been placed on inquiry, the court held that the bank should have taken at least some measures to ensure that the proposed surety was openly and freely agreed to. This case represented a move towards *Etridge*, albeit the court was at pains to highlight that its judgment should not be taken as an acceptance of the precise parameters identified in *Etridge*.

In *Ulster Bank (Ireland) Ltd v De Kretser* [2016] IECA 371, the defendants (who were married persons) were both experienced business people. They sought to defend summary judgment proceedings taken by the plaintiff bank against them on foot of guarantees they had given for loans to a company. Both were directors of this company and so exacted control over it. Mrs de Kretser claimed that her husband had subjected her to undue influence, forcing her to enter the guarantee. The High Court granted summary judgment against the defendants, stating that there was no evidence of undue influence in this case: Mrs de Kretser was very experienced in business and received a monthly salary from the company. In this way, the defendants fell at the first hurdle viz. the two-pronged test set out in *Roche* (i.e. that Mrs de Kretser was not actually suffering under the undue influence of her husband). (See also *Bank of Ireland v Curran* [2016] IECA 399.) Hogan J. dissented, arguing that the spirit of *Etridge* and *Roche* demanded that the bank was under a duty to ensure that the wife was independently advised before signing the guarantee.

In *ACC Loan Management Ltd v Connolly* [2017] IECA 119, a father had guaranteed loans to his son. There was no evidence of undue influence in this case. However, the father argued that even in the absence of undue influence, where the bank was on notice of a familial relationship, they were fixed with an obligation to take steps to ensure that consent to guarantees was freely given. The father claimed that he had been in poor health at the time of signing and had received no independent legal advice as to the transaction. The court rejected this interpretation of recent case law, with Finlay Geoghegan J. noting that it fell at the first hurdle espoused in *Roche*. Hogan J. again dissented, stating that he could not see any reason why the bank was not put on inquiry to ensure that the father had fully understood and freely given consent to the transaction. He considered that broader equitable principles might place a duty on the bank to take steps to ensure that a potentially vulnerable surety is properly advised in a case of this kind. He acknowledged, however, that the Court of Appeal had repeatedly rejected a broader approach to undue influence, and ultimately Hogan J. concurred with the judgment of Finlay Geoghegan J.

In *Barry v Ennis Property Finance DAC* [2018] IEHC 766, Ms Barry executed various guarantees in respect of loans taken out by her son's company. He had assisted her in the running of her deceased's husband's company but had threatened to stop if she did not execute the guarantees in question. The court held that it was clear that a lender would be put on inquiry when it was aware of facts suggesting a significant non-commercial element to a guarantee, e.g. a personal or familial connection or one party having little to no business acumen. Here, Ms Barry had no commercial experience and was dependent on her son's assistance in running her husband's business. The court found that the plaintiff satisfied the first prong of the test in *Roche*. As regards the second prong, the court noted that as of yet, the courts had not provided a list of steps that put a bank's inquiries to rest. Although the court did not wish to provide a list at this juncture, it emphasised that "it is generally considered sufficient if the Bank insisted the influenced party take independent legal advice before executing the agreement".

Unconsciously

A third form of relief arises in the form of unconscionability. This remedy addresses situations where a party under some disadvantage has entered into a contract that, on the whole, is improvident or not to their benefit. Indeed, this type of relief is often described as the doctrine of "improvident bargains". The predominant features of such bargains were set out in the Irish case of *Carroll v Carroll* [1998] 2 I.L.R.M. 218:

- one party is at a serious disadvantage relative to the other (as a result of poverty, ignorance or otherwise) so that unfair advantage could be taken; and
- the resulting bargain was at undervalue; and
- that there was a lack of independent legal advice.

In circumstances where a bargain is said to be unconscionable or unfair because of the above factors, equity will not allow the stronger party to retain a substantial advantage from the bargain. In such cases, equity will set aside the contract, or refuse to enforce it, unless it can be shown that the contract is fair and reasonable overall, and, in particular, that it is the product of the weaker party's free and informed choice. Equity requires that the stronger party was aware, or ought to have been aware, of the weaker party's disadvantaged state (*Hart v O'Connor* [1985] 2 All E.R. 880). While it is important to establish that the bargain itself is unconscionable or unfair in order to secure relief, there are two schools of thought on whether it is also necessary to show fault or *improper behaviour* on the part of the stronger party. In *Keating v Keating* [2009] IEHC 405, the court highlighted the moral culpability of the stronger party in addition to the unconscionability of the bargain itself. However, the test espoused in *Carroll v Carroll* (later upheld by the Supreme Court) did not seem to require unconscionability on the part of the stronger party. Gilligan J. expressly rejected the proposition that moral turpitude was required to be established in *Prendergast v Joyce* [2009] 3 I.R. 519 and this was followed in *MC (A Ward) v FC* [2013] IEHC 272.

The party claiming relief must have been in a position of disadvantage at the time of the agreement, of which, moreover, the stronger party was aware or ought to have been aware. Many earlier cases involved young, impressionable heirs persuaded to sell reversionary interests in land for a pittance, but it is clear that the doctrine goes further. It includes, according to Fullager J. in *Blomley v Ryan* (1956) 99 C.L.R. 362, a situation of "poverty or need of any kind, sickness, age, sex, infirmity of mind or body, drunkenness, illiteracy, lack of education, lack of assistance or explanation". If a claim of unconscionable bargain is made as between family members, the court will examine the actual dynamics within the family. For example, in *Carroll v Carroll*, a father transferred a public house, his only asset, to his son in consideration of natural love and affection subject only to a right to live there for the father's life. At the time, the father was frail and received inadequate legal advice. The transaction was set aside.

Mere disadvantage is not, however, sufficient in itself. There must be an element of unfair advantage/victimisation. This may come in the form of the active extortion of a bargain or the passive acceptance of it in unconscionable circumstances. Relevant factors might include lack of independent legal advice and consideration being at undervalue. In *Fry v Lane* (1888) 40 Ch. D. 312, property had been left to five "poor persons in a humble position". The defendant convinced them to sell the property to him at a discount. This agreement was set aside as unconscionable. In *Grealish v Murphy* [1946] I.R. 35, an elderly illiterate farmer of some wealth but limited mental proficiency agreed to transfer his farm to a younger man, Mr Murphy, who had agreed to work the land in return. Although he retained a life interest in the farm, Grealish assigned the remainder to Murphy in fee simple. The court set this bargain aside, concluding that it was improvident. The farmer lacked competence to look after his own affairs, and he had entered into an agreement under which his interests were not sufficiently protected. He was thus left "for the remainder of his life very much at the mercy of a rather impecunious young man, who had no ties of blood and was still unproved as a friend". In *Filmer v Gott* (1774) 4 Bro. P.C. 230, a transaction under which an elderly woman conveyed her entire estate to her nephew for less than 5% of its market value, was struck down as unconscionable.

In *Prendergast v Joyce* [2009] 3 I.R. 519, the court held that the doctrine of improvidence was not limited to transactions for value and could apply to gifts. If gifts were given in circumstances of improvidence, they could be set aside also.

If, on the other hand, the stronger party can show that the bargain was fair and reasonable, the bargain may stand. This may be proved, for instance, by showing that the weaker party acted of their own free will and with independent expert advice (though the absence of adequate independent advice will not render the contract unconscionable if it is otherwise shown to be a fair transaction).

In *McCormack v Bennett* (1973) 107 I.L.T.R. 127, a contract made by an elderly father, though improvident in certain respects, was upheld as it was entered into of the donor's free and informed will.

Likewise, in *Kelly v Morrisroe* (1919) 53 I.L.T.R. 145, an elderly eccentric woman of limited means sold premises for full value, having received independent advice from her former employer, an experienced businessman. The transaction was upheld.

Independent advice will not, however, be considered sufficient where it is given, as in *Grealish v Murphy*, in ignorance of certain important facts, or where it is otherwise inadequate.

19 Illegal and Void Contracts

Introduction

Despite all that we have said about parties' "freedom to contract", a court will not enforce an agreement that would involve a breach of law or that is regarded as contrary to public policy. Contracts of this type fall into two categories: those that are *illegal* and those that are *void*. At the outset, it is important to keep the following distinction in mind:

(a) An illegal contract is unenforceable in its entirety.
(b) A void contract may be severed by the courts and the offending part(s) removed, leaving the remainder capable of enforcement.

It should be noted that the word "void" is often, unhelpfully, used by the courts and in texts to encompass both circumstances.

Illegal Contracts under Legislation

Statutes (Acts of Parliament) very often declare certain activities to be illegal. As a logical consequence, a contract requiring the performance of an act deemed illegal under statute will generally be unenforceable, unless the statute clearly exempts such a consequence. For example, s.3(1) of the Family Home Protection Act 1976 provides:

> "Where a spouse, without the prior consent in writing of the other spouse, purports to convey any interest in the family home to any person except the other spouse, then [subject to some exceptions] the purported conveyance shall be [unenforceable]."

On the other hand, legislation may expressly provide that notwithstanding the illegality, the entire contract is *not* to be rendered unenforceable. This is often the case when the legislation creates rights for individuals. For instance, s.25 of the Consumer Information Act 1978 used to provide:

"A contract for the supply of any goods or the provision of any services shall not be void or unenforceable by reason only of a contravention of any provision of the [Merchandise Marks Acts 1887–1970] or this Act."

A piece of legislation may also make it a criminal offence to enter an agreement for the performance of particular conduct. In *Gray v Cathcart* (1899) 33 I.L.T.R. 35, an agreement to lease unsanitary premises was deemed unenforceable on the ground that it was an offence under statute to occupy unsanitary lodgings under the Belfast Corporation Acts.

It should be noted, however, that just because conduct is considered a criminal offence under statute, it does not follow that any conduct in which one party acts in breach of that statute will *automatically* make the contract illegal. This would depend on whether the legislation *expressly* states that such conduct would cause the contract to be unenforceable. If the legislation is silent as to its effect on contracts, the courts must ask whether the legislation *impliedly* prohibits a contract from being enforced under the circumstances. To ascertain this, the courts will examine the policy behind or purpose of the statute. In *Smith v Mawhood* (1845) 14 M. & W. 452, for instance, the sale of tobacco without a licence was prohibited by statute. Nonetheless, an unlicensed tobacco seller successfully recovered payment from a purchaser, the purpose of the legislation not being to ban the sale of tobacco but to raise revenue therefrom.

A further distinction may be made between a contract that on its face requires a breach of legislation (illegal in formation), and a contract where the breach arises during the course of the contract's performance. The latter may still be illegal if the statute in question expressly or impliedly bans illegally *performed* contracts, though otherwise the illegal performance may not prevent enforcement. The leading case in this area is *St John Shipping Corp v Joseph Rank Ltd* [1957] 1 Q.B. 267. The plaintiff agreed to transport cargo belonging to the defendant. Contrary to legislative requirements, the plaintiff's ship was deliberately overloaded, the plaintiff reasoning that the excess profit would outweigh any possible fine it might incur. The shipmaster was prosecuted and fined under the applicable Act. The defendant withheld a sum equivalent to the freight on the overall additional cargo by which the ship was found to be overloaded. The plaintiff claimed for the unpaid portion of its fee. The court concluded, on a reading of the particular statute, that the contract was still enforceable. The contract itself was lawful at the time it was entered into. It would be different if the *contract itself* provided for the overloading of the ship. The illegality occurred in the *manner* in which the legal contract was *performed*. Such illegality was not fatal to the enforcement of the contract. Yet it is clear again that such a conclusion depends on the purpose of the relevant legislation, the question being whether the legislation intended expressly or impliedly to ban illegally performed contracts.

In *Quinn v Irish Bank Resolution Corp Ltd (In Special Liquidation)* [2015] IESC 29, the Supreme Court discussed the modern approach to illegal contracts under legislation. The plaintiff argued that certain agreements that were put in place to secure lending from the defendant bank were unenforceable, given that the agreements breached the Market Abuse Regulations 2005 and s.60 of the Companies Act 1963. Clarke J. stated that the first question that should be asked by the court is whether the legislation in question *expressly* states that contracts of a particular class or type are to be treated as void or unenforceable. If so, that is the end of the matter, save that a determination must be made by the court as to whether the contract in question is of this type or category. If the legislation is silent as to whether a contract should be unenforceable or not, the court should assess whether the requirements of public policy and the policy of the legislation (gleaned from its terms) require that (in addition to any penalty for breach provided by the legislation, e.g. a fine) the contract should be treated as being unenforceable. The undesirability of enforcing contracts tainted by illegality should be given appropriate weight unless there exists significant counterweight from the language or policy of the legislation. It should also be taken into account that in drafting legislation, the Oireachtas has the opportunity to specify that certain contracts are to be considered void or unenforceable, the implication being that if the legislature *wanted* to make express provision for the unenforceability of a category of contracts, it would have. This will not necessarily be decisive, however.

In attempting to answer whether the requirements of public policy or the policy of the legislation require that the contract be rendered unenforceable, Clarke J. listed the following factors that the court might consider:

1. whether the contract in question is designed to carry out the very act that the legislation is designed to prevent;
2. whether the wording of the statute implies that the consequences specified therein (e.g. a fine) are sufficient to meet the statutory end;
3. whether the policy of the legislation is designed to apply equally or substantially to both parties to a contract or whether it is designed to place the burden of compliance on one party for the purpose of protecting the other (a good example here would be consumer legislation, which is weighted in favour of consumers—allowing a trader to resile from their obligations under contract with a consumer due to some illegality might be counterproductive to the statutory objective itself);
4. whether the imposition of voidness or unenforceability would be counterproductive to the statute itself;

5. whether, having regard to the purpose of the statute, the range of adverse consequences that are expressly provided therein are to be considered adequate to secure the purposes without holding that the contract is unenforceable;
6. whether holding that a contract is void or unenforceable may be disproportionate to the seriousness of the unlawful conduct in question in the context of the particular statutory regime.

The court noted that this list is not closed and that other factors will come to be defined as the jurisprudence develops.

ILLEGAL CONTRACTS AT COMMON LAW

Certain types of contract are deemed to be *illegal* at common law. The category of contracts illegal at common law is not closed, but included among the most prominent examples are the following.

A CONTRACT TO COMMIT A CRIME OR A TORT

In this context, the principle of *ex turpi causa non oritur actio* arises, suggesting that from the circumstances of a crime, there can arise no action in law. In *Everet v Williams* (1725) (see (1893) 9 L.Q.R. 197), for instance, a contract between two highway robbers to divide the proceeds of their heists was deemed unenforceable. Similarly, in *Beresford v Royal Insurance Co Ltd* [1937] 2 K.B. 197, the heirs of a man who had committed suicide were denied the benefit of a contract of insurance on his life, on the basis that suicide was then an illegal act.

A CONTRACT INVOLVING IMMORALITY

Even if a contract does not promote criminal activity, a contract that promotes immorality may also be illegal. In *Devine v Scott* (1931) 66 I.L.T.R. 107, rent on a premises knowingly let for the purposes of illegal gambling was deemed irrecoverable. Likewise, in *Pearce v Brooks* (1866) 1 Ex. 213, a contract for the hire of a carriage for use by a prostitute was deemed unenforceable. As the owner had been aware of the purpose for which it was hired, he was thus prevented from suing in respect of damage to the carriage.

In former times, any contract involving extramarital sexual relations was liable to be struck down on this ground. Nonetheless, moral standards may evolve and what may have been considered immoral in Victorian times may not be so treated today. For instance, in *Armhouse Lee Ltd v Chappell* (*The Times*, 7 August 1996), a contract under which telephone sex lines were advertised was upheld, the court reasoning that there was no reason of public policy requiring the avoidance of this agreement. Likewise, a contract facilitating a meeting of atheists, deemed illegal in 1867 (*Cowan v Milbourn* (1867) L.R. 2 Exch. 230) was in a subsequent case deemed legal (*Bowman v Secular Society* [1917] A.C. 406), the change undoubtedly reflecting intervening changes in social attitudes.

A Contract Prejudicial to the Administration of Justice

The law generally permits the compromise (settlement) of private and civil claims. However, public law litigation (and in particular criminal law cases) is treated differently. A contract seeking an end to proceedings may be illegal if those proceedings involve criminal matters or matters that have a bearing on the public at large. Thus, in *Keir v Leeman* (1846) 9 Q.B. 371, an agreement not to bring criminal prosecutions in respect of a riot was deemed illegal and thus void. Similarly, in *Nolan v Shiels* (1926) 60 I.L.T.R. 143, an Irish court refused to enforce a contract under which the plaintiff had accepted £50 in exchange for agreeing to drop a prosecution for sexual assault. (See also *Brady v Flood* (1841) 6 Circ. Cases 309.) The situation may be different, however, if the contract is made in circumstances where no prosecution has commenced. Thus, in *Rourke v Mealy* (1879) 13 I.L.T.R. 52, the plaintiff, who had a negotiable instrument that he suspected of having been forged by the defendant's relative, promised not to charge the relative with forgery if the defendant made himself personally liable on the instrument. Here, because no proceedings had been instigated before the promise was given, the plaintiff was entitled to sue the defendant on the instrument.

Maintenance

Maintenance involves "improperly stirring up litigation and strife by giving aid to one party to bring or defend a claim without just cause or excuse". The common law frowns on agreements under which one party attempts to encourage speculative litigation by another party. For instance, in *Uppington v Bullen* (1842) 2 Dr. & War. 184, a solicitor sold land to a Mr Fleming for £400 but agreed to accept £100. The remainder of the proceeds was to be used by the solicitor to take a separate action on Fleming's behalf. The agreement was deemed illegal, as it involved "maintaining" a third party in pursuing litigation.

Champerty

Champerty, like maintenance, concerns agreements to fund speculative litigation, but with an added twist. A contract is champertous if it involves providing financial support for litigation in exchange for a right to share in the winnings. For instance, in *McElroy v Flynn* [1991] I.L.R.M. 294, a contract to share an inheritance in exchange for helping to make a legal claim upon it was deemed illegal. Likewise, in *Fraser v Buckle* [1996] 2 I.L.R.M. 34, the plaintiffs had approached the defendants suggesting that the latter may have been heirs to the estate of a deceased American. The plaintiffs offered to assist in pursuing a claim against the estate, on condition that the plaintiffs would receive one-third of any share the defendants might gain. This being champertous, the contract was deemed illegal and thus unenforceable.

A Contract Encouraging Corruption

In *Lord Mayor, Aldermen and Burgesses of Dublin v Hayes* (1876) 10 I.R.C.L. 226, Hayes had been appointed City Marshal and Registrar of Pawnbrokers. As Registrar he was entitled to certain fees which he had agreed, *as a condition of his appointment*, to pay to the Treasurer of the City of Dublin. This being an agreement to pay money in exchange for appointment to public office, it was illegal as it had the potential to encourage corruption. Likewise, in *Parkinson v College of Ambulance Ltd* [1925] 2 K.B. 1, a contract under which £3,000 was paid in an attempt to secure a knighthood was deemed to be illegal and thus unenforceable. Clearly a contract to pay a member of parliament or a county councillor to vote a particular way would be similarly illegal. (See *Osborne v Amalgamated Society of Railway Servants* [1910] A.C. 87.)

A Contract to Defraud the Revenue

A contract that is created with a view to evading taxes owed to Revenue is illegal in Irish law. This arises most commonly where employment contracts purport to represent salary as "expenses". In *Lewis v Squash Ireland Ltd* [1983] I.L.R.M. 363, for instance, an employment contract under which a salary top-up was misrepresented as "expenses" was deemed unenforceable as it was designed deliberately to evade tax. The result was that the plaintiff was unable to sue for unfair dismissal on foot of the contract. The Employment Appeals Tribunal held that the plaintiff knew his salary was being misdescribed and while it was *technically* feasible to sever the clause from the contract, the fact that both parties knowingly incorporated the term made it impossible to sever. This approach, modelled after the English case of *Tomlinson v Dick Evans "U" Drive* [1978] I.C.R. 638, has received academic criticism for its harsh results. It was followed in *Hayden v Sean Quinn Properties Ltd* (unreported, High Court, 6 December 1993) even though the employer was considered to be the primary mover because the plaintiff had "allowed himself" to contract in a way that would benefit the defendant at the expense of Revenue. After *Lewis v Squash Ireland Ltd*, the Oireachtas provided that a contravention of some Revenue-associated legislation (e.g. Income Tax Acts and Social Welfare Acts) would not preclude an employee from suing on foot of the contract for unfair dismissal. There seems to have been some relaxation of the illegality test in England in more recent years (see *Hall v Woolston Hall Leisure Ltd* [2001] 1 W.L.R. 225) which may provide persuasive authority to shift towards a more flexible test in Ireland.

A CONTRACT LIABLE TO ENDANGER DIPLOMATIC RELATIONS WITH A FRIENDLY COUNTRY OR TO ATTACK A FRIENDLY STATE

For instance, a contract involving a breach of foreign law will not be enforced. Thus, in *Foster v Driscoll* [1929] 1 K.B. 470, a contract to smuggle whisky into the United States during Prohibition was deemed illegal.

CONSEQUENCES OF ILLEGALITY

The consequences of illegality depend on whether the contract is:

- illegal in itself, or "on its face"; or
- illegal as performed.

ILLEGAL IN ITSELF OR "ON ITS FACE"

A contract illegal in itself is null and void and unenforceable. This is the case even if the illegality is confined to part of the contract only; nonetheless, the contract as a whole is deemed unenforceable. For instance, in *Murphy & Co v Crean* [1915] 1 I.R. 111, the defendant leased a pub from the plaintiff, agreeing as part of the contract to source all its stout from the plaintiff. A covenant in the lease permitted the plaintiff to nominate a person to whom the pub licence should be transferred. Such transfer, however, was illegal under licensing law. Notwithstanding the fact that the bulk of the contract was otherwise in compliance with the law, the contract was unenforceable in its entirety. Likewise, in *Re Mahmoud and Ispahani* [1921] 2 K.B. 716, a buyer falsely stated that he was licensed to buy linseed oil (as required by law), but subsequently refused to accept such oil under a contract for its purchase. As the contract contemplated a sale in breach of the law, it could not be enforced.

As a general rule, any property that passes under an illegal contract cannot be recovered. The general rule in this regard is summarised in the Latin phrase *in pari delicto, potior est conditio possidentis*. Roughly translated, this means that where the parties are equally at fault in respect of the illegality, the loss will lie where it falls. The courts, thus, will generally not come to the aid of a party to an illegal contract, where both parties are equally guilty of wrongdoing. There are, however, certain exceptions to this rule:

1. Where the parties are, however, not *in pari delicto*, i.e. not equally at fault, the court may intervene on behalf of the party bearing less of the blame, in particular by restoring to the less guilty party property transferred under the agreement (see *Martin v Galbraith* [1942] I.R. 37).
2. A party may be able to recover if she "repents" before the illegal purpose has been carried out.
3. Property may be recovered if there is another cause of action available that does not concern the illegal contract. For instance, in *Tinsley v Milligan* [1993] 3 All E.R. 65, two women, both of whom had provided money for the purchase of a house, agreed to put the house in the name of Tinsley only, so that Milligan could continue (unlawfully) to claim social welfare. Nonetheless, an understanding existed that ownership of the house would be shared. Although the agreement was illegal, the House of Lords concluded that, independently of the contract, a trust arose in favour of Milligan on foot of her payments towards the purchase (in Ireland, this would arise on foot of a "resulting trust").

Illegal in Performance

A contract that is legal on its face but illegal as *performed* may be unenforceable if *both parties* intended the illegal performance. For example, a contract for the sale of a car may be perfectly legal on its face. However, if the car is to be robbed from a third party in order for the contract to be carried out, that contract for sale will be deemed unenforceable. However, where one of the parties is innocent of any wrongful intent, the contract may be enforced by that party, provided they took steps to repudiate the contract on discovering the illegal performance. For instance, in *Marles v Philip Trant & Sons Ltd (No. 2)* [1954] 1 Q.B. 29, the defendant sold a quantity of seeds to the plaintiff. These seeds were thought to be spring wheat seeds but were actually winter wheat seeds. When the defendant delivered the seeds to the plaintiff, it did not provide a statement of particulars, which was required of them by statute. The court held that this omission did not make the contract itself unlawful, but rather the performance of it. As such, the contract was unenforceable by the defendant but was not rendered illegal. Likewise, in *Whitecross Potatoes v Coyle* [1978] I.L.R.M. 31, the defendant farmer, from Co. Meath, agreed to sell potatoes to the owner of a chain of English fish-and-chip shops. Both parties anticipated that certain issues with cross-border trade in potatoes would arise. If this happened, the contract provided that a higher than normal price would be paid. The plaintiff anticipated that performance of this clause would take the form of the defendant purchasing potatoes in Northern Ireland and delivering these to it. The defendant, however, intended to illegally smuggle the potatoes across the border. As the defendant alone intended to act illegally through performance, the plaintiff was allowed to sue on foot of the contract, the potatoes not having been delivered.

When it comes to statutory illegality, *Quinn v Irish Bank Resolution Corporation Ltd (In Special Liquidation)* (discussed above) provides some interesting guidelines. Here, Seán Quinn had entered into certain share transactions with Anglo Irish Bank which were allegedly illegal, being contrary to s.60 of the Companies Act 1963 and the Market Abuse Regulations. The Quinn children, who were seemingly unaware of the illegality, signed guarantees and share charges in relation to these transactions, which they sought to have set aside on the grounds of statutory illegality. The Supreme Court noted, amongst other things, that the regulations were intended to counteract the manipulation of markets by way of false or misleading practices and to protect shareholders. The court was therefore not prepared to deprive shareholders of the value of the children's guarantees and share charges as this would be counterproductive to the policy behind the regulations. This was despite any innocence from the children's perspective.

Void Contracts

Terms in contracts may be void under statute or at common law. Many examples of such terms arise under consumer legislation (as, for instance, where an exclusion clause unlawfully purports to exclude certain statutory terms from consumer contracts). Though the remainder of any such agreement will be valid, the specific clause attempting to oust this right will not be enforceable. An example is s.74 of the Land and Conveyancing Law Reform Act 2009, which replaced the Statute of Fraudulent Conveyances of 1634. It states that any conveyance of property made with the intention of defrauding a creditor or any other person is voidable by any person thereby prejudiced.

Contracts void at common law broadly fall into three categories.

Contracts that Oust the Jurisdiction of the Courts

A contract that seeks to deny the courts their ordinary jurisdiction in resolving legal disputes will be void at common law.

For instance: if Ailbhe, a member of a particular professional body or organisation (e.g. the Law Society, the Engineering Council, the Medical Council) is stopped from accessing the courts due to a clause in her contract which states that said organisation has final say in the event of a dispute, this provision will be considered void.

In *Baker v Jones* [1954] 1 W.L.R. 1005, a contract that sought to give an association exclusive power to interpret the law was deemed void, as it excluded the possibility of judicial review or other recourse to the courts. In this regard, a distinction must be made between rules that seek to prevent access to the courts in matters of law (which are void) and those that nominate an independent arbitrator (arbitration clause) or tribunal to officiate on factual matters in cases of dispute (which are valid). In *Scott v Avery* (1856) 5 H.L.C. 811, for instance, a clause that referred contractual disputes to an arbitrator was deemed acceptable as the contract still allowed for ultimate access to the courts. In short, the parties should always have access to the courts in order to clarify matters of law. It is worth bearing in mind that the right of access to the courts is a constitutionally protected right.

Contracts that "Subvert" Marriage

Marriage brokerage contracts, where a fee is paid to a brokerage to find a wife or husband for the customer, are considered void (see *Hermann v Charlesworth* [1905] 2 K.B. 123). Similarly, unilateral contracts where one person promises to not marry any person *other than* the promisee are considered to be void (see *Lowe v Peers* (1768) 4 Burr. 2225).

It is well established in Irish law that an agreement made in contemplation of the potential future separation of spouses (for example, in a pre-nuptial contract) will not be enforced (see *Marquess of Westmeath v Marquess of Salisbury* (1830) 5 Bli. (n.s.) 339; *Cohane v Cohane* [1968] I.R. 176). The (rather unconvincing) reasoning is that such agreements tend to destabilise marriages, and moreover may incentivise the parties to split. By contrast, an agreement that is made where the parties intend to separate with immediate effect will be enforced. Case law in the United Kingdom (e.g. *Radmacher v Granatino (No. 4)* [2010] UKSC 42) takes a more progressive view, holding that there is no difference between an agreement entered into the day before a wedding and the day after it. Irish law has yet to catch up to *Radmacher*.

Cohabitation agreements

In *Ennis v Butterly* [1997] 1 I.L.R.M. 28, a couple (who were married to other people, but not to each other) lived together for years before their relationship ended. The plaintiff claimed that during their relationship, the defendant had promised to support her for her life if she moved into the house bought by the parties, forgo employment and become a home-maker. It was also agreed that the pair would marry upon a grant of divorce being secured by both of them. Kelly J. held that the portion of the contract relating to the promise to marry was no longer enforceable in Irish law, as a result of the Family Law Act 1981. The court also held that contracts to cohabit were contrary to public policy given "the special place of marriage and the family under the

Irish Constitution". The court stated that to uphold the contract would be to give cohabitation agreements "a similar status in law as a marital contract".

It should be noted that s.202 of the Civil Partnership and Certain Rights and Obligations of Cohabitants Act 2010 now provides that the proprietary and financial affairs of cohabitants may be the subject of a cohabitation agreement and that such agreements may be given effect to in the event that the relationship comes to an end. In allowing such agreements, s.202 seems to depart from *Ennis*, in that cohabitation agreements are no longer regarded as contrary to public policy.

CONTRACTS IN RESTRAINT OF TRADE

A contract may be deemed void where it unreasonably restricts the right of a person to trade, or to carry out a business or profession. Similar principles apply where a contract purports unreasonably to limit an employee's right to work after an employment contract is terminated. The basic principle is that such restraints will be void as a matter of public policy unless they can be justified as being:

(a) reasonable having regard to the interests of the parties; and
(b) reasonable having considered the interests of the public (see *Nordenfelt v Maxim Nordenfelt & Co* [1894] A.C. 535).

In this regard, the courts essentially seek to strike a balance between a number of competing rights:

- On the one hand is the right of the business/employer to protect its legitimate interests. An allied concern is the issue of freedom of contract: if a party has freely agreed to a particular restraint, arguably that party should be held to the bargain.
- On the other hand, one must consider the right to earn a livelihood (which is, after all, a constitutional right) as well as the interest of society as a whole in the promotion of free trade and competition and the benefits derived therefrom.

It is worth bearing in mind, of course, that these rules are now supplemented by competition legislation and other measures governing restrictive practices as well as the competition obligations under EU law.

The modern common law rule is set out in *Esso Petroleum v Harper's Garage* [1968] A.C. 269. The court held that restraints on trade would be upheld only if the impugned measure:

(a) is reasonably required to protect the legitimate interests of the beneficiary (the business/employer);
(b) goes no further than is necessary to protect those interests (if so, the restraint is prima facie void);
(c) is reasonable having regard to the rights of the restricted party; and
(d) is not inconsistent with the public interest (a point emphasised in *Macken v O'Reilly* [1979] I.L.R.M. 791).

The onus of proof differs depending on whether the interests of the parties or those of the public are being considered. The onus of proving that the restraint is reasonable having regard to the parties is on the person wishing to rely on the restraint. On the other hand, the onus of proving detriment to the public interest lies on the person seeking to avoid the restraint. In considering such matters, the courts will have regard to:

- *The scope of the restriction*: the wider the restraint, the more extensive the range of tasks to which it refers, the less likely it is that it will be upheld.
- *The duration of its application*: the longer the restraint is scheduled to last, the less likely it is that it will be upheld. For instance, in *Esso* the defendant owned two petrol stations. Both were subject to an "exclusivity agreement" requiring that the defendant only purchase petrol from Esso for 4.5 years (viz. the first garage) and 21 years (viz. the second garage). While the exclusivity agreement was deemed reasonable in respect of the first garage, it was void in respect of the second, as it went much further than was required to protect Esso's legitimate interests.
- *The geographical scope of the term*: a clause preventing a former employee from setting up a business in the same street as the former employer might be reasonable. A clause that extended to the entire of Ireland might not be.

Established commercial practice is relevant in this context. The courts have upheld long-standing practices within particular trades, for instance, exclusivity contracts involving pubs and brewers (*Murphy & Co v O'Donovan* [1939] I.R. 457, where a contract to source stout exclusively from the plaintiff was upheld) and contracts involving oil companies and petrol stations (solus agreements). For example, in *Continental Oil v Moynihan* (1977) 111 I.L.T.R. 5, a garage owner's five-year agreement to source oil only from the plaintiff was upheld as reasonable. It is clear, however, that such agreements may not go further than is required to protect the interests of the parties, as in *McEllistrem v Ballymacelligott Co-op* [1919] A.C. 548, where the House of Lords struck down an agreement restricting members of the co-op from selling their milk to any other creamery or from unilaterally leaving the co-op.

SEVERABILITY

Where a contract is void at common law, it is nonetheless possible to sever the offending portion from the remainder of the contract, thus upholding the rest of the contract. This does not give the courts carte blanche to redesign a contract. Rather, as stated in *Attwood v Lamont* [1920] 3 K.B. 571, the doctrine of severance is:

> "... permissible in a case where the covenant is not really a single covenant but is in effect a combination of several distinct covenants. In that case and where the severance can be carried out without the addition or alteration of a word, it is permissible but in that case only."

For instance, in *Skerry's College v Moles* (1907) 42 I.L.T.R. 46, a contract restricting a teacher from teaching within seven miles of Dublin, Cork and Belfast for three years was upheld insofar as it related to Belfast but struck down in relation to Dublin and Cork. Severance thus allows the offending portion of the contract to be "extracted". Provided that the remainder of the contract is not unreasonable, it can still be enforced absent the offending provision.

Discharge of a Contract

Introduction

This chapter concerns how a contract is terminated; in other words how it is "discharged". Where a contract is discharged, the parties are deemed free of any further obligations towards each other. There are four different ways in which a contract can be discharged: agreement, performance, frustration and certain types of breach. Each of these options will be considered in turn.

Agreement

A contract may be terminated where the parties agree that it should come to an end. A distinction must be made, however, between an agreement to terminate under which both parties benefit ("bilateral discharge") and an agreement under which only one benefits ("unilateral discharge"). While a bilateral discharge will generally be valid (as consideration has been provided, both giving a benefit under the contract), a unilateral discharge will only be upheld if it is either contained in a deed or separately supported by consideration. Thus, it is said that there must be "accord and satisfaction", the "accord" referring to the agreement to terminate and the "satisfaction" alluding to the consideration required. Where certain formal requirements may have applied to the original contract (such as a requirement of written evidence in respect of a contract for the sale of land), an agreement to discharge will not necessarily need to follow the same formalities. Where the discharge is intended to be complete (that is, to terminate all obligations thereunder), an oral agreement will suffice. On the other hand, if the parties wish to *alter* the agreement (rather than completely terminate it), any relevant formal requirements will need to be met. Similar requirements apply if the parties wish to replace their old agreement with a new one: the new contract will only replace the old one if the formal requirements are complied with.

Performance

Where all obligations under a contract have been performed, the contract is deemed to come to an end. At common law, if a contract is an "entire contract", it was said that the contract was not discharged until every element thereof was completed exactly as anticipated by the contract. Thus, in strict theory, even very minor deficiencies in performance of an entire contract may prevent the contract from being deemed "performed".

In *Nash & Co v Hartland* (1840) 2 Ir. L.R. 190, a definition was provided for the concept of an "entire contract": if the contract expressly or impliedly provides that exact performance must be completed of certain duties before any obligation arises for the other party to act, the contract is an entire contract. In *Cutter v Powell* (1795) 6 Term Rep. 320, a sailor contracted to serve on a voyage from Jamaica to Liverpool. He was given a promissory note of 30 guineas to be paid 10 days after the voyage was completed. He died during the voyage and his widow tried to claim part payment of the sum promised for the time that he had served before his death. The court concluded that the contract was an "entire contract" and, as such, payment was not to be made unless it was performed in its entirety. Here, the sailor was deemed to have accepted the perils of the journey and the risk that he might not perform the contract in full. In exchange, he was offered a wage at some four times the average rate, should he complete. Likewise, in *Coughlan v Moloney* (1905) 39 I.L.T.R. 153, a builder who had agreed to build a house was deemed to be entitled to nothing when he failed to complete work on the partly built house some nine months after the agreed deadline. In *Re Moore & Co v Landauer* [1921] 2 K.B. 519, the parties had agreed that tins of fruit to be supplied to the buyer would be packed in boxes of 30. Some of the tins were packaged in boxes of 24. The buyer was thus entitled to repudiate the contract as, although the buyer had received the correct number of tins, the contract had not been performed as agreed.

There are, however, some exceptions to this rather harsh rule.

Substantial Performance

Equity may require payment where the contract is substantially performed, subject to a clawback in respect of the unperformed portion of the work. This exception, arising from *Boone v Eyre* (1779) 1 Hy. Bl. 273n, stipulates that where a contract is performed with minor deviations, payment will be due, less the amount needed to address the deficiency. In *Hoenig v Isaacs* [1952] 2 All E.R. 176, a builder completed all but a small portion of redecoration work on the defendant's home. The parties had agreed a fee of £750, which the defendant refused to pay as a book shelf remained incomplete. The court nonetheless ordered payment of the full fee, less £55, being the amount of money required to finish the book shelf. The court reasoned that unless the breach went to the root of the contract, it could order payment, subject to a deduction in respect of the incomplete portion of the work. Lord Denning added that even where a lump sum was agreed, the courts would lean against requiring complete performance as a condition precedent to payment.

However, this exception applies only where what has been received is in fact of substantially the same value as what was promised. For instance, in *Bolton v Mahadeva* [1972] 2 All E.R. 1322, a central heating system that cost £560 emitted fumes and ran inefficiently. It was estimated that it would cost £124 to fix the system, in which circumstances the court concluded that there had not been sufficient performance to justify even part payment of the agreed fee. Another way of putting this is that the substantial performance exception only applies where the breach is relatively minor in the context of the whole contract.

Likewise, where the contract has been *abandoned* prior to completion, it may not be possible to exact payment. In *Kincora Builders v Cronin* (unreported, High Court, 5 March 1973), a builder refused to complete insulation work agreed on the attic of a house he was building for the defendant. Although this represented a relatively minor deviation from the agreement, the court refused to find that substantial performance had occurred, on the ground that the plaintiff builder had abandoned the work, refusing to complete it.

Severable/Divisible Contracts

To a large extent, the harsh results in cases like *Cutter v Powell* turn on the interpretation of the relevant contract. If the contract requires that payment only be made on entire performance, partial performance will not suffice. If, on the other hand, the parties can be said explicitly or implicitly to have agreed that partial performance would attract partial pay, the courts may grant some relief. A contract may thus be interpreted as divisible such that payment will be required for the performance of discrete obligations thereunder. If the contract can be regarded as involving a series of separate obligations, it may be possible to order payment in respect of the performance of those obligations that have been performed, even if other obligations remain outstanding.

Consider the following example: Sarah agrees to supply strawberry jam on a monthly basis to David for a year. She would arguably be entitled to payment for each month's supply that she has delivered, even if she were to withdraw from the contract after a couple of months.

This is the case, for instance, with most employment contracts and tenancy agreements. Thus, if a contract of employment is terminated before it is due to end, the employee is still entitled to a proportionate payment of salary. (See *Treacy v Corcoran* (1874) I.R. 8 C.L. 40.) Likewise, if a tenancy ends prematurely, the landlord is entitled to recover for the period during which the tenancy lasted. As stated, it is often a matter of interpretation whether the contract is an "entire agreement" requiring performance of every element, or whether it is divisible. In *Brown v Wood* (1864) 6 Ir. Jur. 221, the plaintiff agreed to take the defendant's yarn and weave cloth from it, delivering the cloth as it was completed. Some consignments of cloth were delivered; however, the defendant failed to utilise all the yarn. The court concluded that the plaintiff was nonetheless entitled to be paid for the cloth that was delivered, subject to the defendant's right to recover for the yarn not processed. In *Verolme Cork Dockyard Ltd v Shannon Atlantic Fisheries Ltd* (unreported, High Court, 31 July 1978), the defendant alleged that repair works due to be completed by the plaintiff to its fishing boat were not completed in full and that the contract was entire. The court held that the contract contained a term requiring substantial payment to be made when a reasonably high proportion of the work had been carried out.

Prevention of Performance

Where an entire contract needs to be completed precisely and the other party is deliberately preventing completion, the former may be entitled to part payment in respect of what has been completed to date. In *Arterial Drainage v Rathangan River Drainage Board* (1880) 6 L.R. (Ir.) 513, the defendants asked the plaintiffs to drain land. The contract required that this be performed with "due diligence" or the defendants could terminate the contract. The work did not progress as quickly as planned, and the defendants attempted to terminate. However, as the delay had been considerably contributed to by the defendants (having failed to grant prompt access to the land and plans), the court concluded that the plaintiffs were entitled to part payment for work already completed. In *Planché v Colburn* (1831) 8 Bing. 14, the plaintiff agreed to write one of a series of books, but before he had finished, the publisher decided to stop publishing the series. In circumstances where the plaintiff's entire performance had been precluded by the publisher's decision, the plaintiff was entitled to £50 for work done: half the agreed price for the completed book.

Tender of Performance

Where a person's attempts to perform under a contract are rebuffed by the other party, this may relieve the former of any further obligation. A so-called "tender of performance" is an attempt at performance and even if rejected, may result in discharge.

In *Startup v MacDonald* (1843) 6 Man. & G. 593, the defendant ordered oil from the plaintiff with a stipulation that it be delivered by 31 March. The plaintiff attempted to deliver on 31 March at 8.30 p.m., but the defendant did not accept this delivery, alleging that the delivery was too late. The court held that as performance had been tendered, the plaintiff had done everything it could to fulfil its obligation. It was entitled to be paid notwithstanding the failure to accept.

Where a tender is made, however, it must comply with the terms of the contract. For instance, if a contract requires payment in cash, an offer to pay by cheque or credit card will not amount to an adequate tender of performance.

TIME

Generally speaking, a contract may be successfully completed even where performance occurs after a stipulated deadline has passed. In short, unless time is deemed to be of the essence, a failure to perform on time will not discharge the contract. In *United Scientific Holdings v Burnley Borough Council* [1978] A.C. 904, the plaintiff claimed that the defendant, as landlord to the plaintiff, had lost the right to pursue a 10-yearly rent review, as the defendant had sought such a review two months after the deadline stipulated in the lease. The court nonetheless allowed the review to proceed on the basis that, unless otherwise agreed, time generally is presumed not to be "of the essence".

There are, however, three ways in which time may be deemed to be "of the essence", such that a failure to perform on time will discharge the contract, entitling the wronged party to sue for damages:

1. If the parties have expressly agreed in the contract that the time of performance is crucial, the failure to meet a deadline will result in discharge of the contract. In *Crean v Drinan* [1983] I.L.R.M. 82, the plaintiff specifically earmarked a completion date for the purchase of property. It was also agreed that an assignment of interest would be obtained from a third party by the closing date. While failure to close on the proposed day was not enough to discharge the agreement, failure to obtain the deed of assignment by that date did discharge the contract.
2. Even if there is no express agreement on the point, the nature of the contract's subject matter may necessarily imply that time is of the essence where, for instance, the subject matter is perishable (such as food) or subject to sharp price fluctuations (e.g. oil).
3. Even where the parties did not initially agree that time is of the essence, a contracting party may, after the deadline has passed, notify the other party of a further deadline, compliance with which is deemed to be essential. In such a case, provided the time for completion is reasonable, a failure to complete by the stipulated date will result in discharge. In *Nolan v Driscoll* (unreported, High Court, 25 April 1978), for example, the plaintiff had agreed to buy the defendant's house but some 15 months later, the sale remained outstanding. Although time was originally not

deemed to be of the essence, the defendant served notice requiring completion of the sale within a month of the notice. The court ruled that failure to complete within the month served to terminate the contract.

FRUSTRATION

As a general rule, contractual liability is absolute: a person who agrees to do something is bound by their agreement, even if they are unable, and never were able, to perform. This latter rule is exemplified in the rather extreme case of *Paradine v Jane* (1647) Aleyn 26, where rent paid under a lease was deemed payable notwithstanding the fact that the tenant had been ejected from the land by the military during the English Civil War.

The doctrine of frustration, however, deals with cases where a contract cannot be performed as a result of circumstances beyond the control or responsibility of the parties. Said contracts may be deemed as discharged and the parties are thus relieved of their obligations under the contract. This occurs where one of the following conditions is met.

IMPOSSIBILITY OF PERFORMANCE

If due to an intervening event the performance of a contract is rendered impossible, the contract will be deemed frustrated. A classic example arose in *Taylor v Caldwell* (1863) 3 B. & S. 826. A music hall, hired for use as a concert venue, was destroyed in a fire six days before the first concert was due to take place. The destruction of the hall rendered the parties unable to perform, thus frustrating the contract. The licensor was therefore excused from failing to provide the music hall and the licensee was excused from having to pay the rental fee. In so deciding, the court drew an analogy between the case before it and a contract involving someone who dies after agreeing to write a book: the death would, if it entirely prevented performance, render the contract frustrated.

Likewise, if the *method* of performance stipulated in the contract subsequently becomes impossible, the contract may be frustrated, though not if the agreement can be interpreted as permitting an alternative mode of performance. It is important in this regard to distinguish between events that make performance impossible and those that render it more onerous or difficult to perform. Put simply, mere hardship or inconvenience is not enough to frustrate a contract. For instance, in *Tsakiroglou & Co Ltd v Noblee Thorl GmbH* [1962] A.C. 93, a contract was made to ship ground nuts from the coast of Sudan to Hamburg. It was originally envisaged that the goods would travel via the Suez Canal (the shortest route), but due to an outbreak of war, the canal was closed, necessitating a much lengthier journey around the southernmost tip of Africa. Despite the added time and cost involved (the cost in fact doubled), frustration was held to have *not* occurred. The House of Lords ruled that the fact that performance was rendered more difficult did not mean that frustration had occurred. Notably, there was no implied term that the canal was the *only* permissible route and the extra time did not cause any deterioration of the goods shipped. Similarly, in *Davis Contractors v Fareham UDC* [1956] A.C. 696, the plaintiff had agreed to construct 78 houses for £94,000. Severe problems involving the supply of materials and labour disputes resulted in a 14-month delay in completion and a final bill that exceeded the contract price by £21,000. These factors nonetheless were deemed *not* to have frustrated the contract, the key point being that although the performance was rendered more difficult, it was not made impossible: the houses were still built.

Frustration of Purpose

A contract entered into for a specific reason may also be discharged if, due to intervening events, the reason or purpose for the contract no longer applies. In *Krell v Henry* [1903] 2 K.B. 740, the plaintiff hired his flat to the defendant *specifically* because it overlooked the route of King Edward VII's planned coronation procession. The procession having been cancelled due to the King's illness, the contract was deemed to have been frustrated. Although the defendant still had the use of the room, the specific purpose of the contract was to watch the procession, and this was now postponed. Watching the procession, the court concluded, went to the "root of the contract" and the cessation of the procession thus led to its discharge. Contrast this with *Herne Bay Steam Boat v Hutton* [1903] 2 K.B. 683. Hutton hired a steam boat. His plan was to use the boat to watch a naval review. When Edward fell ill, the review was cancelled. Nonetheless, the court concluded that the contract remained valid and enforceable, as it was still possible to take trips on the boat and to view the fleet. The distinction between these two cases seems to be that, in *Krell*, the thing contracted for was a view of the coronation procession, whereas in *Herne Bay*, the thing contracted for was the hire of the steamship, though the distinction seems remarkably difficult to justify.

Intervening Illegality

A contract that is legal when entered into may be frustrated due to the fact that the performance contracted for is subsequently deemed illegal. For instance, in *Fibrosa Spolka Akeyjna v Fairbairn Lawson Combe Barbour* [1943] A.C. 32, a contract between an English firm and a Polish company was deemed frustrated when Poland was invaded by Germany. Because at common law it is illegal to contract with citizens of an enemy state, the contract was deemed to have been frustrated. (See *Ross v Shaw* [1917] 2 I.R. 367 for a similar Irish example.) By the same token, where an Act of Parliament invalidates a contract, this may be deemed a frustrating event. For instance, in *Ó Cruadhlaoich v Minister for Finance* (1934) 68 I.L.T.R. 174, the plaintiff had been appointed a judge in the first Dáil. This was an appointment for life. This position was subsequently revoked by a statute of the Irish Free State. The contract was deemed to have been discharged by the intervening statute.

WHERE FRUSTRATION WILL NOT OCCUR

Frustration will not occur in certain circumstances:

- Where the contract has been rendered simply more difficult or onerous by a change in circumstances, but not impossible.
- Where the conduct of one of the parties has caused the change in circumstances (self-induced frustration). In *Herman v Owners of S.S. Vicia* [1942] I.R. 304, a ship was unable to dock in Britain, as planned, due to its owners' negligence in not obtaining the requisite documentation for this purpose. As the failure of the contract was self-induced, no frustration arose. Similarly, in *Maritime National Fish Ltd v Ocean Trawlers Ltd* [1935] A.C. 524, Maritime National Fish Ltd hired a trawler from Ocean Trawlers Ltd. Maritime National Fish Ltd applied to the Minister for a licence to use the vessel for fishing. The Minister granted three licences and Maritime National Fish Ltd applied these licences to three of its other trawlers. The failure to obtain a licence for the vessel in question was not a frustrating event, as the absence of a licence was the result of a choice made by Maritime National Fish Ltd to apply the licences received to its other ships.
- If a contract makes specific provision for a particular event (for instance, by assigning the risk of its occurrence to one or other party), the occurrence of such an event will not constitute frustration. In *Mulligan v Browne* (unreported, Supreme Court, 23 November 1977), a doctor's contract of employment at a Donegal hospital was made expressly conditional on the availability of funds for the running of the hospital. As this eventuality was foreseen by the parties, and provided for in the contract, the hospital's subsequent funding crisis was not deemed to be a frustrating event.
- If the event was actually foreseen, its occurrence will not amount to frustration. In *McGuill v Aer Lingus and United Airlines* (unreported, High Court, 3 October 1983), the first defendant had booked passengers on board a partner airline despite being aware of an imminent strike at the latter airline. As predicted, the strike went ahead, but because it had been foreseen, the contract was not frustrated. It is clear, then, that the frustrating event must be unexpected.

Effects of Frustration

The effects of frustration are relatively stark and sometimes quite unfair. Put simply, the contract is deemed discharged, with both parties being relieved of all future obligations. In *Appleby v Myers* (1867) L.R. 2 C.P. 651, a contract to install a machine and maintain said machine for two years after installation was frustrated by a fire destroying the building in which the machine was being installed (the installation being almost but not fully complete). The manufacturers of the machine were deemed unable to recover for work already done on the machine, as the obligation to pay fell on a date that fell after the frustrating event.

However, an obligation that falls due *before* the frustrating event occurs will stand: in other words, if a payment is due, or an obligation arises prior to the event in question, such payment or obligation may still be enforced. For instance, in *Krell v Henry*, the owner of the flat could not pursue the balance owed in respect of the hire of the flat as the obligation to pay this arose after the frustrating event. On the other hand, in the same case the obligation to pay a deposit arose *before* the frustrating event. Similarly, where a payment is made under the contract prior to the frustrating event occurring, such payment is not recoverable—the loss essentially "lies where it falls". Nonetheless, where no consideration at all is received under the contract (i.e. no tangible benefit has resulted from the contract), it may be possible to get relief. In *Fibrosa*, for instance, under a contract to provide machinery to a Polish factory, £1,000 was paid in advance to an English firm. However, because of the outbreak of World War II, the machine could not legally be delivered. Because the Polish company received no benefit at all, the £1,000 had to be returned.

Recent Events and Frustration

Two major recent world events have inspired a slew of frustration cases. The first is Brexit. In *Canary Wharf (BP4) T1 Ltd v European Medicines Agency* [2019] EWHC 921 (Ch), after the United Kingdom sought to leave the European Union, a 2018 EU Regulation was passed stipulating that the European Medicines Agency had to relocate its headquarters from London to Amsterdam. The defendant argued that its lease of its London headquarters at Canary Wharf was therefore frustrated by Brexit. It was held that the lease had not been frustrated by a supervening illegality, as the EU had the power to keep the headquarters of its agencies in third countries if it wished to under law. The court held that any frustration here was self-induced. Given the lead-in time to Britain's departure from the EU, the defendant could have avoided or mitigated its issues by subletting the property.

The dispute in *Foot Locker Retail Ireland Ltd v Percy Nominees Ltd* [2021] IEHC 749 took place during the Covid-19 pandemic. The plaintiff tenant and the defendant landlord could not reach agreement on rent arrears that had accrued as a result of the pandemic. The plaintiff sought a declaration from the court that the lease for the premises was frustrated and that it had no liability for rent given that it was required to close its premises during lockdown. Initially, the plaintiff pleaded that the lease was entirely frustrated, but later it claimed "partial frustration" of the contract, arguing that it should be free from any duty to pay rent under its lease but should otherwise be entitled to continue to occupy the premises. In other words, the plaintiff's argument was that it should be freed from its liabilities but that it should continue to benefit from the defendant's duties. The court described this as a "violence to the fundamentals of the doctrine". The court also noted that while a pandemic may not have been anticipated at the time when the contract was drafted, the lease was drafted at a time when the possibility of closure connected with violence in Northern Ireland would have been anticipated and the lease made no provision for the suspension of rent in such circumstances.

FORCE MAJEURE CLAUSES

Many commercial contracts will include an express force majeure clause that pre-empts an event (e.g. a strike, a natural disaster, a pandemic) and dictates what might happen if said event comes to pass. Often, it is agreed that the contract may be terminated or the parties' obligations suspended in such circumstances. Whether the clause applies will depend on the precise wording thereof and it should be noted that the courts tend to construe said clauses strictly (i.e. in the event of ambiguity, the clause may be said not to apply). Indeed, too general a force majeure clause may be found to be void for uncertainty.

DISCHARGE BY BREACH

Although a breach of contract normally entitles a party to damages, there are certain types of breach that may additionally permit the innocent party to treat the contract as being discharged. It is important to note that the party in breach may not rely on their *own* breach as discharging the contract. If the breach is sufficiently serious, however, the innocent party may opt either to have the contract discharged or to let it stand.

BREACH OF A CONDITION

As discussed in Chapter 12, there is a distinction between conditions and warranties. A breach of a warranty does not permit discharge: the contract stands, though the wronged party is entitled to damages for breach. Breach of a condition, on the other hand, or of an innominate term in circumstances where the effects of the breach are serious, will entitle the wronged party to regard the contract as having been terminated. However, even in such a case, the innocent party may alternatively elect to allow the contract to stand, and seek damages for breach.

Repudiatory Breach

Where a party repudiates a contract or threatens to do so, the innocent party may choose to discharge the contract. A "repudiatory breach" involves a decision by a party, clearly intimated by words or conduct, that they intend not to be bound by the contract's terms and will not perform their obligations thereunder. For instance, in *Athlone RDC v A.G. Campbell and Son (No. 2)* (1912) 47 I.L.T.R. 142, contractors were half-way through the performance of a contract for excavation services when the local authority wrote to them indicating that their services were no longer required. This was a repudiatory breach. The contractors were allowed to treat the contract as having been discharged.

A repudiatory breach may be committed even before performance falls due, as where a person indicates in advance that they do not intend to perform an obligation under the contract. This is called an "anticipatory breach". It may entitle the innocent party to seek discharge, as shown by *Hochster v De La Tour* (1853) 2 E. & B. 678. A courier was due to start work on 1 June with the defendant. The agreement was struck on 12 April. On 11 May, the defendant indicated that it would not be employing the courier after all. This was deemed to amount to repudiation. Although the date on which the obligation commenced had not yet passed, the courier was deemed entitled to discharge the contract for breach. This case has been accepted in Ireland (see *Leeson v North British Oil and Candle Co* (1874) 8 I.R.C.L. 309).

Fundamental Breach

A "fundamental breach" (which, confusingly, is totally different from the type of fundamental breach described in Chapter 14) is a breach of an essential term of the contract. In other words, the breach of such a term will have serious consequences that go to the root of the contract. Such a breach will entitle the innocent party to choose to regard the contract as being discharged. For instance, in *Dundalk Shopping Centre v Roof Spray Ltd* (unreported, High Court, 21 March 1979), a contract requiring that a roof be made watertight was deemed to have been fundamentally breached in circumstances where the defendant failed, within a reasonable time, to eliminate leaks.

Effects of a Breach

As noted above, only certain types of breach lead to the discharge of a contract, and even then, only at the instance of the innocent party. The latter may, moreover, choose to waive this right and allow the contract to stand (in which case the contract is "affirmed"). Similarly, the right may be lost through delay, as in *Bord Iascaigh Mhara v Scallan* (unreported, High Court, 8 May 1973). That said, the innocent party, even where the right to discharge is lost or waived, does not lose the right to sue for damages. It is also important to note that a discharge in case of breach releases the parties from the obligations under the contract only with *prospective* effect. In other words, the innocent party may still sue for damages in respect of a breach prior to discharge. Additionally, the parties may still rely on certain terms in the contract insofar as they relate to events that occurred before discharge. For example, in *Doyle v Irish National Insurance Co plc* [1998] 1 I.L.R.M. 502, it was held that an insurance company could rely on an arbitration clause in a policy for motor insurance that had been repudiated for non-disclosure of a material fact. The arbitration clause survived for the purpose of determining the mode of settlement.

Remedies   21

Where a breach of contract occurs, certain remedies are available to the innocent party. Although one might think that the most obvious remedy would be enforcement of the contract (a remedy termed "specific performance"), in practice the most common remedy available is damages.

Damages

It is important to distinguish between the purpose of damages in the context of tort (for civil wrongs) and the purpose of damages in contract law:

- In *tort law*, an award of damages generally addresses only the actual loss sustained as a result of the tort. In this context, damages seek to restore the injured party to the position they would have been in had the tort not occurred.
- In *contract law*, by contrast, judges generally seek to address the "expectation loss". The purpose of damages, therefore, is to place the wronged party in the position they *expected to be in* had the contract been performed as agreed.

In order for damages to issue, a number of matters must be considered.

Causation

A party in breach must have *caused* the loss in question. It is not necessary that their breach be the only cause of the loss suffered, provided that it contributed in some manner to the loss.

Remoteness of Loss

The ramifications of a breach may be significant. However, while a breach may have caused a particular consequence, it may not be compensable in contract law. Similar to the "reasonable foreseeability" test in tort law, contract law places a limit in the chain of consequences beyond which a party cannot be held liable. In other words, contract law will not provide compensation for losses that are too "remote". For instance, if a passenger is "bumped" from a flight due to overbooking, they would arguably not be entitled to compensation for the loss of a major business contract that occurred as a result of the missed flight if this was neither a typical result of such an event nor within the contemplation of the airline.

In the main case on this point, *Hadley v Baxendale* (1854) 9 Exch. 341, the Court of Exchequer explained that a loss would only result in damages where:

- the loss may fairly and reasonably be considered as arising naturally (i.e. according to the usual course of things) as a result of the breach; or
- the loss would not arise in the usual course of things, but may reasonably be supposed to have been in the contemplation of both parties at the time they made the contract, as the probable result of the breach; or
- where *special circumstances* under which the contract was actually made were communicated by the plaintiff to the defendant (and thus known to both parties) and the loss in question could be said to ordinarily follow from those special circumstances communicated.

In *Hadley*, the owners of a flour mill sued in respect of the late delivery of a crank shaft. Here, the crank shaft broke and was dispatched by the plaintiff to Gloucester to serve as a pattern for a new crank shaft. The plaintiff used the defendant carriers to transport the crank shaft to Gloucester. The carriage was delayed due to the negligence of the defendant. This caused a knock-on delay in the plaintiff receiving the new crank shaft. The mill had stopped all operations pending receipt of the new crank shaft and the owners sued for the loss of profit they would have made had the shaft been delivered on time. This loss, however, was considered to be too remote. It was not a natural consequence of the breach. It was not within the contemplation of both parties at the time the contract had crystallised. It had also not been communicated to the defendant that if the shaft was delivered late, the mill would cease operations. Similarly, in *Victoria Laundry v Newman Industries* [1949] 2 K.B. 528, a laundry lost a lucrative state contract as a result of a five-month delay in the delivery of a boiler. Although the laundry was awarded damages for loss of normal profits (deemed to be a natural consequence of the breach), the loss in respect of the government contract was deemed too remote, as this was neither a natural consequence of such a breach nor was the defendant informed that such a contract was at stake. (See also *The Heron II* [1969] 1 A.C. 350.)

In *Maye v Merriman* (unreported, High Court, 13 February 1980), the defendant delayed in fulfilling his contractual obligation to sell land to the plaintiff. The plaintiff had intended to stock his land with cattle and the price to purchase said cattle increased during this delay. As a result, the plaintiff argued that he suffered a loss of £19,400, being the extra amount paid by him in stocking the said lands. This loss, however, was deemed not to be a natural consequence of the breach of contract. The price of cattle could have risen or fallen during the period.

In *Kemp v Intasun Holidays* [1987] 2 F.T.L.R. 234, due to an overbooking of holiday accommodation, a woman was placed in dusty accommodation that brought on an asthma attack. As this was a reaction particular to sufferers of asthma (and not the public at large), it was not deemed to arise in the ordinary course of things. Further, the condition had not been brought to the defendant's attention beforehand. As such, damages for the consequences of the asthma attack were deemed too remote.

In *Wilson v Dunville* (1879) 6 L.R. (Ir.) 210, a court concluded that injury to animals was a natural consequence of supplying feed containing lead pellets to cattle. Similarly, in *Stock v Urey* [1955] N.I. 71, damages were awarded where a smuggled car, sold under a contract, was seized by the customs authorities (this being a natural consequence of the breach: smuggling).

In *Lee and Donoghue v Rowan* (Unreported, High Court, 17 November 1981), a failure to complete a shed to be used for drying potatoes prompted a court to order payment of damages for the cost of finishing the shed and compensation for what it would have cost to transport the crops to storage in another shed (both eventualities being foreseeable). However, in this case, the farmer was unable to source alternative storage facilities, with the result that the crop was completely destroyed. The farmer was unable to secure damages for the crop as a whole as this was neither foreseeable nor within the contemplation of the parties at the time the contract was made.

The English case of *Transfield Shipping Inc v Mercator Shipping Inc (The Achilleas)* [2009] 1 A.C. 61 represented a shift in approach from the strictures of the classic *Hadley v Baxendale* test. In this case, Transfield Shipping Inc was a charterer that hired Mercator's ship, "The Achilleas". Transfield were supposed to deliver a ship back to Mercator by 2 May 2004. Due to a delay, the ship was not delivered until 11 May 2004. Unbeknownst to Transfield, Mercator had contracted to let the ship to another charterer on 8 May 2004 for $39,500 a day. When Mercator failed to deliver the ship to the new charterer on time, the new charterer renegotiated the daily rate at a cost of $8,000 to Mercator, given the volatile freight market condition. The question for the court to determine was how much Transfield had to pay Mercator for returning the ship late.

Mercator claimed that Transfield should pay the amount they had lost on the new chartering account. Transfield argued that the company should be liable for lesser damages calculated for the nine days they were in default, predicated on the market rate for daily hire of the ship. The Court of Appeal held with Mercator. However, the House of Lords reversed this decision and found that the loss of profits from the next charter was not within the scope of *Hadley v Baxendale*. The reasoning for this decision was unclear, with Lord Rodger and Baroness Hale following the "conventional" or "orthodox" remoteness test as set out in *Hadley v Baxendale* and Lords Hoffmann and Hope taking a more nuanced approach.

- *Lord Rodger and Baroness Hale*: Both Lords held that it was not in the reasonable contemplation of Transfield when it had entered into the contract that Mercator would lose money on a follow-on time charter if the ship was returned late, due to volatile market conditions. Further, this result could not be said to occur in the ordinary course of things. Lord Rodger stated that the situation might be different if Mercator drew Transfield's attention to the new charter and informed it of the risks associated with Transfield's delay (special knowledge). In this way, the Lords focused on the "orthodox" approach as espoused in *Hadley v Baxendale*.
- *Lords Hoffmann and Hope*: Both Lords considered whether Transfield, at the time it entered the contract, could reasonably have expected to have assumed responsibility for losses due to the volatile market. Lord Hoffmann looked at the "background of market expectations" in this regard and noted that in the shipping industry, it was understood that charterers were only liable for loss during the overrun period. The Lords considered that liability for the next contract would be "completely unquantifiable" by Transfield at the time of contracting and that Transfield had no knowledge or control over what contract Mercator might be making next at the time of contracting. Given the expectations in the shipping industry, the volatile nature of that market, and the fact that Transfield had no visibility of the extent of loss or control over the follow-on contract meant that to impose liability on it for the loss sought was inappropriate. This approach extended the principle of *Hadley v Baxendale* to include a consideration as to the intention of parties in relation to assumed responsibility for a particular risk.

The decision in *The Achilleas* proved to be controversial. Notwithstanding this perceived departure from the orthodox approach, Clark in *Contract Law in Ireland*, 9th edn (Dublin: Round Hall, 2022) at para.19-48 notes that "later cases have, so to speak, steadied the ship by emphasising that their Lordships were divided and that Lord Hoffmann's perspective was a minority view on this point." He cites *The Amer Energy* [2009] 1 Lloyd's Rep. 293 as authority here. However, he also points to *Supershield Ltd v Siemens Building Technologies FE Ltd* [2010] EWCA Civ 7, where the court held:

> "*Hadley v Baxendale* remains a standard rule but it has been rationalised on the basis that it reflects the expectation to be imputed to the parties

in the ordinary case, i.e. that a contract breaker should ordinarily be liable to the other party for damage resulting from his breach if, but only if, at the time of making the contract a reasonable person in his shoes would have had damage of that kind in mind as not unlikely to result from a breach. However, *South Australia [Asset Management Corp v York Montague Ltd* [1997] A.C. 191] and *Transfield Shipping* are authority that there may be cases where the court, on examining the contract and the commercial background, decides that the standard approach would not reflect the expectation or intention reasonably to be imputed to the parties."

That being said, Clark states: "[i]t is arguable that an Irish court should decline to follow *The Achilleas* on the basis that greater predictability and ease of application are facilitated by following earlier decisions."

Mitigation

Where a party stands to lose as a result of a breach of contract, that party is not permitted to stand idly by. The innocent party is required to do everything reasonably within their power to mitigate or reduce the loss, though only where the loss has actually been sustained and not where the breach is "anticipatory". For instance, if a butcher refused to accept meat supplied by a farmer under a contract for supply, the farmer would be obliged to find another buyer to mitigate his losses. The farmer would not be compensated if he let the meat rot simply because the butcher would not accept it, as required. Thus, in *Brace v Calder* [1895] 2 Q.B. 253, a manager who was wrongfully dismissed on the dissolution of a partnership declined an offer by two of the partners to re-employ him. As the manager had failed to mitigate his losses, he was deemed unable to recover damages for dismissal.

In *Malone v Malone* (unreported, High Court, 9 June 1982), damages were not awarded to compensate the plaintiff for additional interest being charged on a loan that he had taken out to buy property, notwithstanding the defendant's breach of the sales contract. The court held that he should have repaid the money to mitigate his losses once the breach transpired. Similarly, in *Bord Iascaigh Mhara v Scallan* (unreported, High Court, 8 May 1973), the plaintiff was deemed unable to recover for damage sustained by a ship abandoned by its hirers, as the plaintiff had failed to take steps to recover the ship again upon its abandonment.

Types of Damages

Expectation Loss and Speculative Damages

The general measure of damages is the amount that the wronged party stood to make if the contract was carried out as planned. Notably, this includes the projected (*expected*) profit that would have been made had the contract been fulfilled. In many cases, however, it may not be possible to tell whether a profit or loss would have been made. *Afton v Film Studios of Ireland* (unreported, High Court, 12 July 1971) appears to be authority for the proposition that damages for loss of expectation will not issue where it is unclear whether a particular contract would result in a profit or loss.

The courts will nonetheless show a willingness to estimate the probable loss, provided that it is established that a particular event was likely to occur. For instance, in *Hawkins v Rogers* (1951) 85 I.L.T.R. 129, in breach of contract, a racehorse was prevented from taking part in a series of races. Despite the fact that it might never have won a race, the court granted damages based on an assessment of the horse's general performance in past competitions. In *Blackpool and Flyde Aero Club v Blackpool Borough Council* [1990] 3 All E.R. 25, the plaintiff won damages in respect of the council's omission to consider the club's tender, even though there was no guarantee that the club would have won the tender, if considered.

Where loss is so uncertain that damages cannot be recovered as expectation loss, they may be recovered as reliance loss.

Reliance Loss

This allows the innocent party to sue for damages in respect of losses incurred due to their reliance on the contract, that is, to recover damages in respect of expenses incurred that would not have arisen had the contract not been made.

For example: Deborah hires a van to courier goods. The goods become unavailable. The cost of hiring the van might be said to be reliance loss.

Damages for reliance loss are usually awarded where it is not possible to award the expectation interest, e.g. where it is difficult to quantify the expectation. For instance, where a top actor is contracted to appear in a film, but in breach of contract withdraws therefrom, it may not be possible to determine the extent of expectation loss (the film might have been a box office success or a flop). In *Anglia Television v Reed* [1972] 1 Q.B. 60, a famous actor (Oliver Reed) who had agreed to star in a film withdrew from production at a late stage, with the result that the film was not completed. As it would have been difficult to establish the likely profit lost (if any), the television company sued based on reliance loss. The court thus allowed it to recoup any losses sustained making the film on the basis that it had relied on its contract with the actor. It was also deemed, however, to be entitled to claim for pre-production costs including those sustained in advance of the contract with Reed. The court reasoned that the latter costs would have been within Reed's contemplation when he entered into the contract.

There is a limit as to when reliance interest may be available. It is not possible to choose to pursue recovery of reliance interest over expectation interest when the recovery of the reliance loss would exceed the value of the expectation of the contract. In other words, the plaintiff should not be protected from a bad deal and put in a better position than if the contract had been performed. In *Bowley Logging v Domtar* (1982) 135 D.L.R. (3d) 179, a haulier hired to transport logs succeeded in establishing that its breach of agreement actually *lowered* the losses that the logging company would have expected to incur had the contract been fulfilled. The logging company had contracted to sell the logs at a significant undervalue, and actually stood to make a greater loss if the haulier had fulfilled its side of the bargain.

Restitution Loss and Consequential Loss

Less commonly, damages may be awarded in the form of restitution loss, in order to prevent a party from deriving an unjust enrichment from the contract.

In the case of *Hickey & Co Ltd v Roches Stores (Dublin) Ltd (No. 1)* (unreported, High Court, 14 July 1976), the parties had entered into a contract that permitted the plaintiff to sell fabric in the defendant's shop. The defendant broke the contract after calculating that even if they had to pay damages for doing so, they would make more money if they sold the fabric themselves. In obiter, the court stated that such conduct should lead the courts to look at both the injury suffered and the profit gained by the wrongdoer. If the wrongdoer would still obtain a profit, the damages may be increased to deny the wrongdoer the profit.

It appears also that provided the damage is not too remote, damages may issue for consequential loss (a separate head of loss to restitution loss). For instance, in *Stoney v Foley* (1897) 3 I.L.T. 165, in consequence of the purchase of diseased sheep, the land on which they were grazed was deemed unfit for use for four months (including the Spring and early Summer). The buyer was permitted to recover for his inability to use the land as well as for the loss of the sheep. In *Leahy v Rawson* (unreported, High Court, 14 January 2003), the defendant undertook to build an extension but did an insufficient job. The extension the defendant built therefore had to be demolished. In addition to the compensation awarded in respect of the demolition and rebuilding, the plaintiff was permitted consequential loss in the form of loss of income that would have been acquired by using the premises as a B&B.

Performance Interest

Some case law has recognised "performance interest" or "loss of amenity" as a legitimate head of loss. This acknowledges that the performance of some contracts provides more than just financial rewards. If the injured party has an interest in seeing the contract performed, damages can be awarded to protect this. In *Ruxley Electronics v Forsyth* [1995] UKHL 8, the defendant was able to recover £2,500 from the plaintiff builder who had built a swimming pool in his garden that should have been constructed slightly deeper than it was. This miscalculation did not affect the value of the pool. It was still safe for diving. However, because the defendant's contractual preference had not been satisfied, he was able to recover damages for performance interest/loss of amenity. The court held that "the law must cater for those occasions where the value of the promise to the promisee exceeds the financial enhancement of his position which full performance will secure". To award nothing would have been to say that the promise was illusory.

Compensation for Non-financial Loss/Disappointment and Distress

Generally, contract law is concerned only with financial loss and not damages for hurt feelings, disappointment and mental distress flowing from a breach of contract (see *Addis v Gramophone Co Ltd* [1909] A.C. 488). In *Kelly v Crowley* (unreported, High Court, 5 March 1985), for instance, owing to the negligence of his solicitor, a man purchased what he thought was a pub licence. In fact it was a drinks licence for a hotel. While this error caused him some considerable upset, he was unable to recover for mental distress, only for financial loss. The injured sensibilities of a business person, it seems, cannot be the subject of compensation in contract law at least (though a remedy may be available in tort).

Nonetheless, in more recent cases the courts have granted relief in respect of non-financial losses, such as mental distress, in cases where the provision of recreation or peace of mind is at the root of the contract. The rule appears to be that where the parties reasonably expect some enjoyment or relaxation to arise from the contract, a loss of enjoyment may be the subject of damages. If, for instance, the owner of a health spa insisted on constant powerdrilling in one of its treatment rooms while clients were present, one might feasibly claim that compensation should be available for the resultant stress, the purpose of attending a health spa being to relax and unwind. In *Jarvis v Swan Tours* [1973] 2 Q.B. 233, travel agents failed to deliver on promises made in a holiday brochure relating to a holiday package. Although the plaintiff was transported to and accommodated in a Swiss holiday resort, specific entertainment events promised as part of the package fell far short of what was promised and in some cases did not materialise at all. Damages were awarded for the plaintiff's disappointment. Similarly, in *Dinnegan v Ryan* [2002] 3 I.R. 178, the distress and humiliation arising when a bride and groom and their guests were turned away from a planned reception on their wedding day resulted in an award of damages. In *Scaife v Falcon Leisure Group* [2007] IESC 57, the Supreme Court held that hotels owe a duty to exercise reasonable care and skill (under both common law and under the Package Holiday Directive) regarding the facilities to be provided under contract, and if this is not executed the consumer is entitled to sue.

It appears that this principle is not confined to contracts involving travel or entertainment so long as the contracts in question have as their "very object" the provision of "pleasure, relaxation, peace of mind or freedom from molestation" (per *Watts v Morrow* [1991] 1 W.L.R. 1421).

In *Johnson v Longleat Properties* (Unreported, High Court, 19 May 1976), for instance, damages were awarded for the inconvenience and loss of enjoyment arising from the defective performance of a contract to build a house. To put the defects right, the homeowner would have to put up with considerable disruption, including the presence of builders in his home for a considerable period, as well as the lifting of carpets and tiles and the excavation of the concrete sub-floor. The homeowner was awarded damages in respect of the inconvenience arising. Similarly, in *Farley v Skinner* [2001] 3 W.L.R. 899, a pensioner bought a house for his retirement. A surveyor secured by the pensioner failed to advise of the high levels of noise emanating from a nearby airport. The pensioner succeeded in claiming damages for distress arising from this error. The House of Lords reasoned that a major objective of the contract was to confer pleasure and relaxation through the provision of comfortable accommodation for the pensioner's retirement. In *Browne v Iarnród Éireann (No. 2)* [2014] IEHC 117, the defendant breached an agreement to allow the plaintiff early retirement. He suffered no economic loss but experienced inconvenience as a result of his being deprived of a "restful and less stressful life" associated with early retirement. The court awarded him €20,000 per year for each of the three years in question. In *Da Silva v Miranda* [2017] IECA 252, the Court of Appeal found that accommodation services provided by the defendants to their employees did not meet minimum standards. Although the plaintiffs in this case did not expect or anticipate that they were going to enjoy the same personal comforts as the plaintiffs in *Jarvis*, they were entitled to basic comforts including hot water, appropriate furniture and leisure facilities. The fact that the plaintiffs were denied these brought this case within the exception to the rule in *Addis*.

Punitive or Exemplary Damages

Although there is a public interest in holding people to their bargains, it is not the function of contract law to punish people for breaking contracts. In fact, it would be extremely unusual for an Irish court to award punitive or exemplary damages (damages that seek to punish a party for a particularly flagrant and "high-handed" breach of contract). *Garvey v Ireland* (1979) 113 I.L.T.R. 61 provides a rare Irish example, where punitive damages were awarded in respect of the wrongful dismissal of a Garda, the process being in breach of constitutional principles of natural justice. Nevertheless, the courts tend to regard punitive damages as inappropriate in contract cases (a point underlined by the courts' dislike for penalty clauses noted below). The Law Reform Commission in its *Report on Aggravated, Exemplary and Restitutionary Damages* (LRC 60-2000) has stated that it does not recommend the use of punitive or exemplary damages in breach of contract claims.

Liquidated Damages and Penalty Clauses

In some cases, the contract itself may attempt to stipulate the amount of damages that will be payable in cases of breach (termed "liquidated damages"). On the one hand, this can be useful in providing clarity and reducing litigation on the quantification of damages, as well as limiting liability in cases of breach. In particular, in cases where damages may be difficult to estimate, the courts will appreciate the efforts of the parties in agreeing a fixed sum in advance. On the other hand, the courts will not enforce even an agreed sum where the purpose or effect of the imposition of damages is to penalise a party for breach of contract. Such "penalty clauses" are frowned upon by the courts, contract law not having as its purpose the penalisation of parties in breach of contract.

Lewison in *The Interpretation of Contracts*, 6th edn (London: Sweet & Maxwell, 2015) at para.17.01 defines a penalty clause as:

> "... a clause which, without commercial justification, provides for payment or forfeiture of a sum of money, or transfer of property by one party to the other, in the event of a breach of contract, the clause being designed to secure performance of the contract rather than compensate the payee for the loss occasioned through the breach."

In *Dunlop Pneumatic Tyre v New Garage and Motor Co* [1915] A.C. 79, Lord Dunedin espoused a four-factor test that summarised the presumptions to be applied in ascertaining whether a clause will be deemed to be a penalty clause:

1. If the clause requires payment of a sum that is "extravagant and unconscionable" when compared to the greatest actual loss that could conceivably occur in respect of the breach, it will be held to be a penalty clause. In *Durkan New Homes v Minister for the Environment, Heritage and Local Government* [2012] IEHC 265, Charleton J. held that a provision in a contract that required the vendor to pay damages on an ascending scale from the closing date to the date of actual transfer infringed this first principle.
2. The breach consists only of a failure to pay a sum of money, and the stipulated penalty exceeds this former sum. In *O'Donnell v Truck and Machinery Sales* [1998] 4 I.R. 191, for instance, the Supreme Court ruled that a failure to pay a fixed sum cannot result in damages exceeding that sum with interest. This situation must be distinguished from situations where, on failure to pay an instalment, an entire debt falls due under what is called an "acceleration clause". Such acceleration clauses are valid provided that the sum claimed does not exceed the entire sum due with interest.
3. There is a presumption that a clause is penal when the amount of damages stipulated for is the same regardless of the nature and extent of the damage caused by the breach. In *Schiesser International (Ireland) v Gallagher* (1971) 106 I.L.T.R. 22, the plaintiff had paid to train the defendant as a textile cutter. In return, the defendant committed to working for the plaintiff for three years. A clause in the contract stated that if he left their employment within three years, he would have to reimburse the plaintiff for the cost of the training. As it applied equally regardless of the departure date (i.e. whether he left within a day or two years), the clause was considered a penalty clause and was therefore unenforceable.
4. There is no issue with a sum stipulated being a genuine pre-estimate of damage. If the consequences of the breach are difficult to estimate in financial terms, the courts will skew in favour of upholding a clause that seeks to operate as a genuine pre-estimation of damage. The courts take the view that it is better for the parties themselves to estimate the damages that will result.

Other Matters Relating to Damages

As a general rule, the date by reference to which damages are assessed is the date on which the contract is breached, though there are exceptions to this rule. Interest may be awarded by the court in respect of the period between the date of breach and the date of the judgment.

Remedies other than Damages

Although damages are the most common type of remedy available where a breach of contract occurs, other remedies are available and are summarised below.

Specific Performance

In exceptional cases, the court may, exercising its equitable jurisdiction, order the party in breach to perform their contractual obligations. The terms of the contract need to be sufficiently certain to allow for an order of specific performance and the remedy will not be appropriate in every instance. In particular, the courts will not generally order performance in respect of contracts involving *personal* performance by a party, for instance, employment contracts (see *Lumley v Wagner* (1852) 1 De G.M. & G. 604 and *Warner Bros Pictures Inc v Nelson* [1937] 1 K.B. 209). It will also not be appropriate where the contract requires supervision by the courts, e.g. where the party's obligation is a continuous act. Specific performance will only be granted where damages are not adequate to provide relief (see *O'Neill v Ryan* [1992] 1 I.R. 166). It is open to a party to argue against specific performance on the basis that it will cause them significant hardship. Because specific performance is a discretionary remedy, delay may defeat it. Further, there are certain doctrines of contract law, such as mistake or illegality, that preclude the existence of an enforceable contract. Specific performance of said contract could therefore not be granted.

Injunctions

A prohibitory injunction may be granted to enforce a negative promise, e.g. to not play music earlier than 9am on a Saturday. A mandatory injunction is restorative and forces a party to reverse the effects of a breach of contract. If the injunction will have the same effect as specific performance of a contract involving *personal* performance (e.g. of an employment contract), it will likely not be granted. For instance, in *Page One Records v Britton* [1968] 1 W.L.R. 157, an injunction was refused where the manager of a rock band sought to prevent the appointment of his replacement. The court reasoned that to grant the injunction would effectively force the band to keep their manager, and would thus require specific performance of a contract involving personal performance. Because injunctive relief is a discretionary remedy, it may be defeated by delay.

Restitution

Where money is paid under a contract and nothing is received in return, an action for restitution may be available. This permits the donor to recover monies paid, on the basis that a failure to recover would result in the recipient being unjustly enriched. Restitution will generally only be granted, however, where there has been a total failure of consideration (i.e. nothing of value has been received in exchange for the payment).

Quantum Meruit

The remedy of *quantum meruit* (literally meaning "as much as is deserved") permits a person, who has performed duties under a contract, to be paid a reasonable price for performance in circumstances where the parties have not agreed a fee, or where the fee is unclear. Provided that the parties intended that the performance would be remunerated, the court may order such payment as it considers reasonable in the circumstances.

Rescission

Rescission is an equitable remedy requiring that a contract be terminated and the parties restored to the position they were in before the contract was made. It is different to "discharge", in that discharge treats the contract as having ended and relieves parties of further obligations. In this way, rescission is backward-looking and discharge is forward-looking. Rescission is not a general remedy and is only available in a limited number of circumstances, e.g. misrepresentation, mistake, duress or undue influence as well as in certain cases of breach, though usually only where the breach is serious. Rescission will only be awarded at the discretion of the court. It can be defeated by delay. Further, rescission cannot be ordered if events have occurred (that the injured party has participated in) that make it impossible to restore the parties to their previous position.

APPENDIX
Answering Exam Questions

GENERAL POINTS TO NOTE

TAKE A HOLISTIC APPROACH

Contract law is not a subject that is easily severable. Exam questions tend to borrow from disparate aspects of the course, as opposed to focusing on one or two bulky topics. Students that attempt to study only some aspects of the course or rely on "banker" questions tend not to perform well on contract law exams. If faced with time constraints, it is better to focus on having a breadth of knowledge of contract law rather than a depth of knowledge on fewer topics.

CASES

Some cases are seminal, e.g. *Carlill v Carbolic Smoke Ball Co* as it pertains to unilateral offers. It is essential to include said seminal cases in an exam answer when dealing with the relevant topic. Other cases may prove useful when elaborating upon a point made, but do not do much else. Priority should be given in any exam answer to the seminal cases: more time and detail should be paid to a discussion of these cases over cases that merely add to established precedent.

FOR (NEARLY!) EVERY RULE THERE IS AN EXCEPTION

One should be careful not to engage in sweeping generalisations in exam answers. For virtually every rule in contract law, there is at least one exception. Use phrases like "generally", "ordinarily" or "in most cases" when outlining general principles of law to which there may be exceptions.

ESSAY QUESTIONS

The basic purpose of an essay question is to give you an opportunity to demonstrate your understanding of the law on a particular topic. Hence, a typical question might ask you to "discuss", "outline and comment upon", "evaluate" or "critique" the law.

Analyse the Prompt

It is critical to carefully read the essay question to identify the legal issues involved and what you have been asked to discuss, e.g. are you being asked to compare two concepts (e.g. an offer and an invitation to treat)? Are you being asked to critically analyse a topic or a line of case law?

Plan Your Essay

If time permits, you should create a skeleton outline of the essay you propose to write before you start writing. This can be jotted down in the margins of the exam paper or on scrap paper provided.

Introduction

Your introduction should include a "thesis statement". This represents the main argument of your essay, your position on the question posed or the central issue that you will discuss. For example, if an exam question asks you to discuss recent changes in the law as they pertain to consumer protection and contract law, your thesis statement might begin:

> "The Consumer Rights Act 2022 has introduced sweeping reforms in the area of consumer protection and contract law in Ireland ..."

Your introduction should also signpost what you intend to discuss in the body of the essay to prove the thesis statement, for example:

> "This essay will examine the new statutory rights and remedies in contracts for digital content provided for by the Consumer Rights Act 2022. It will also examine ..."

Body

Each paragraph in the body of your essay should focus on a single idea that supports your thesis statement. Start each paragraph with a topic sentence that clearly sets out this idea and then provide evidence to support it. When using case law as evidence:

(a) give the *name* of the case (the year and place where the case is reported generally do not have to be provided in exam answers), e.g. *Dickinson v Dodds*;
(b) outline the *basic facts* of the case;
(c) state the *decision* in the case; and
(d) explain the *reasons* given by the judges for their decision(s).

Good students do not provide evidence for consideration without analysis. Don't be afraid to discuss the implications of the case law or the effectiveness of the legislation you are citing as evidence. Were there any dissenting opinions of note in the judgment, for example? Are there recent trends that forecast a departure from this approach? If there are potential counterarguments to your argument, it is also important to address these in the body of the essay and refute them with reasoned evidence. End each paragraph with a sub-conclusion that summarises the main idea discussed in that paragraph. Ensure that the sub-conclusion links back to the thesis statement. For example, in the case of a paragraph dealing with digital content contracts and digital service contracts, a sub-conclusion might read:

> "Consumer contracts for the supply of digital content and digital services have not previously been the subject of legislative protection. As seen above, the 2022 Act has introduced impactful change by establishing safeguards that specifically apply to these categories of contract."

Conclusion

Reference should be made to the original thesis statement in your conclusion. You should also revisit the sub-conclusions that you have used throughout the body of the essay to provide a summary of the key points you have made that have proved this thesis statement.

Problem Questions

Problem questions are a common and useful tool of assessment. The purpose of this type of question is to assess your ability in applying legal principles to new fact scenarios. These questions usually pose a hypothetical legal problem that the candidate is expected to solve. Very often, such problem questions quite closely replicate or mirror the facts of a seminal case(s) that you have studied as part of the course. In such a case, the purpose of the exercise would be to discuss the case(s), apply the precedent to the new fact scenario and to suggest a likely outcome to the problem posed. The suggested approach for tackling such questions is known as the "ILAC" method:

1. *Identify the legal issue*: The key to answering this type of question lies in identifying the problem generated by the specific fact scenario.
2. *State and discuss the applicable law*: The next step is to outline the applicable law clearly and concisely. If there are any relevant cases (especially if they involve a very similar fact scenario), the facts should

be briefly outlined, followed by a summary of the decision in the case. In particular, remember to explain the reasoning of the court in such cases. Applicable legislative provisions should also be set out in this section of your answer. Resist the urge to apply the law to the factual matrix at this point. You will do so in the "Application" section of your answer.

3. *Apply the law to the problem*: In this section of your answer, you should imagine that you are a lawyer advising a client: take the law that you have set out in the preceding paragraphs and apply it to the factual matrix provided, discussing the implications of the legal situation for the hypothetical party. There may not be one definitive legal solution to a problem. The law may be uncertain, or there may be no direct precedent on the point. The job of a lawyer in such cases is simply to give an educated assessment of what a court is most likely to do, based on more indirect precedents, on the merits of the case and on one's general knowledge of the legal principles.

4. *Conclude*: Arrive at a considered conclusion.

When answering a problem using the ILAC method, students often use the following sub-titles to delineate effectively: *Issue, Law, Application, Conclusion*.

Index

Abandonment of contract, 219
Acceleration clause, 239
Acceptance
  definition, 19
  by person to whom offer made, 19
  communication, 27–28
  electronic communication, 100
  exceptions to communication rule, 28
  express acceptance, 24
  implied acceptance, 24–25
  in ignorance of offer, 19–20
  indication, 24–26
  method stipulated, 27
  modern communication methods, 31–32
  postal rule see Postal rule
  silence as, 25–26
  time limit, 17–18
  unconditional acceptance, 20–23
  unilateral offer, 5, 16–17, 23–24, 28
Accord and satisfaction, 217
Additional payments under contract, 55–56
Adhesion contract, 129
Administration of justice, contract prejudicial to, 208
Advertisement, 6–8
Age of majority, 77
Agency, 73–75
Agreement, contract as, 1
Airline strike, 224
Ambiguous term, 46, 112–113
Anticipatory breach, 227
Arbitration clause, 46, 47, 137–138, 213, 228
Atheism, 208
Auction, 10

Bad bargain, 2
Band manager, 240
Bank guarantee, undue influence, 197–201
Bargain, contract as, 1
Battle of the Forms, 21–23
Bilateral offer, 4
Black list of terms, 158–159
Bona fide purchaser, 174
Boxing, 75, 82–83
Breach of contract
  anticipatory breach, 227
  breach of condition, 226–227
  damages see Damages
  discharging contract, 226, 228
  effects, 228
  fundamental breach, 140–141, 227
  mitigation of loss, 233
  other remedies see Remedies for breach
  repudiatory breach, 227
  threat, as duress, 189–191
  waiver or loss of innocent party's rights, 228
Brexit, 225
Building contract, 47, 50–51, 71, 113, 218–219, 223, 235, 237
Business efficacy test, 47, 124–125

Capacity to contract
  concept, 77
  convicts, 86
  infants see Infancy
  intoxication, 85–86
  mental incapacity, 84–85
  onus of proof, 77
Car park, exclusion clause, 134–135
Carbolic smokeball, 7–8, 38

Casino chips, 51
Cattle, 109, 114, 164, 165–166, 180–181, 231
Caveat emptor, 2–3, 142
Certainty
    examples of uncertain terms, 45
    methods of clarification, 46–47
    requirement, 45–46
Champerty, 208–209
Click-wrap, 31, 103
Cohabitation agreement, 213–214
Collateral contract, 75–76, 116–118
Commercial agreement, 36–38
Common mistake *see* **Mistake**
Competition winnings, 36
Composition with creditors, 58
Concert ticket, 7, 102–103
Conditions of contract, 119–120
Conditions precedent/subsequent, 118
Conduct, as misrepresentation, 164–165
Confidentiality clause, 75
Conformity with contract, 143, 145–148
Consequential loss, 235
Consideration
    definition, 48–49
    act of forbearance, 49
    adequacy and sufficiency, 50–51
    example, 48
    insufficient consideration, 52–58
    must move from promisee, 49
    need not move to promisor, 49–50, 56–57
    nominal sum, 51
    one-sided benefit, 50
    parol evidence proving amount, 115–116
    part payment of debt, 57–58
    past consideration is no consideration, 52–53
    privity of contract distinguished, 71
    promise to do what one is already obliged to do by law or contract, 53–57
    requirement, 47
    tangible value, 50–51
Constitution, terms implied by, 128
Constructive notice of undue influence, 197–201
Consumer contract, 72
Consumer rights
    acceptance of deviation from conformity, 148
    background/history, 142, 143–144
    cancellation of distance or off-premises contracts, 158
    collective legal action, 159
    conformity with contract, 143, 145–148
    Consumer Rights Act 2022, 103–104, 142, 144
    cooling-off period, 104, 158
    delivery and risk, 151
    digital content/service contracts, 103–104, 152–153, 159
    digital elements, 145, 147–148
    distance contracts, 103–104, 154–155
    durability of goods, 147
    EU Directives, 143–143
    exclusion of liability, 151
    gifts, 72, 152
    inertia selling, 25–26
    information requirements, 146, 155–158
    intermediary services, 159
    motor vehicle, lack of conformity, 72, 152
    off-premises contracts, 154
    on-premises contracts, 154
    privity, changes to rule, 76, 152
    public statements regarding goods, 147
    quantity, quality etc of goods, 146–147
    recent developments, 159
    remedies for non-conformity
        final right to terminate, 149–150

proportionate reduction in price, 149–150
repair or replacement, 148–149
short-term right to terminate, 148
trader's obligations where contract terminated, 150–151
withholding of payment, 151
right to terminate where trader has no right to sell, 145
Sale of Goods Act 1893, 143
Sale of Goods and Supply of Services Act 1980, 143
sales contract for goods defined, 144–145
service contracts, 153
trade-ins, 145
unfair terms, 158–159
updates to goods with digital elements, 147–148
Contra proferentem rule, 138–139
Contract for services
implied contract, 26
infant's contract, 81–83
Cooling-off period, 104, 158
Corruption, 209
Council housing, 126–127
Counter-offer, 13–14, 20–23
Covenants pertaining to land, 75
Covid-19 pandemic, 225–226
Creamery, 37, 215
Crime or tort, contract to commit, 207
Custom, 47, 113–114, 125–126

Damages
breach of contract, 229–233
causation, 229
consequential loss, 235
date for assessing, 239
expectation loss, 229, 234
liquidated damages and penalty clauses, 238–239
misrepresentation cases, 173
mistake cases, 187
mitigation of loss, 233
non-financial loss/disappointment and distress, 236–237
performance interest, 236
pre-estimation, 239
punitive or exemplary damages, 238
reliance loss, 234–235
remoteness of loss, 229–233
restitution loss, 235
speculative damages, 234
tort and contract distinguished, 229
Death of offeror or offeree, 14–15
Debt of another, contract to pay for, 88–90
Deceit, tort, 173
Deed under seal, 48
Defrauding the Revenue, 209–210
Delay
breach cases, 228
economic duress cases, 190
exclusion clause, 139
preventing rescission, 174, 187
remoteness of damage, 230–232
time of the essence, 221
undue influence cases, 193
Delivery of goods, 151
Demolition and rebuilding, 235
Deposit, 94
Detrimental reliance, 65–66
Digital content/service contract, 103–104, 152–153, 159
Digital elements, 145, 147–148
Disappointment and distress, 236–237
Discharge of contract
agreement to terminate, 217
bilateral and unilateral discharge, 217
breach of contract *see* Breach of contract
concept, 217
frustration *see* Frustration
performance of contract *see* Performance
Disclosure, and misrepresentation *see* **Misrepresentation**

Discrimination, 13, 15
Display of goods for sale, 8–10
Distance contract, 103–104,
  154–155
Duress
  definition, 188
  common law, 188
  economic duress, 189–191
  equitable remedies, 191
  invalidity of marriage, 189
  overbearing conduct by bank, 189
  refusal to grant specific performance,
    191
  test, 190
  threat of prosecution, 189
  threat to breach contract, 189–191
  threat to life, limb or liberty, 188–189
Duty of care, 170–172

Economic duress, 189–191
Electronic commerce
  concept, 100
  consumer rights, 103–104
  electronic signature, 101–102
  incorporate of terms, 102–103
  offer and acceptance, 100
Email, postal rule, 31–32
Employee accommodation, 237
Employment contract
  implied terms, 127
  injunctive relief, 240
  proportionate payment of salary, 219
  restraint of trade, 214–215, 216
  salary misrepresented as expenses,
    209–210
  specific performance, 240
Enemy state, 223–224
Entire contract, 217–218
Equitable estoppel *see* **Promissory
  estoppel**
Essential elements of contract, 1
Estoppel by representation, 59, 68
Ex turpi causa non oritur actio, 207
Exaggerated statement, 38–39,
  161

Exclusion clause
  adhesion/standard form contracts,
    129
  concept, 129
  consumer contracts, 151
  excluding liability for
    misrepresentation, 175
  interpretation
    contra proferentem rule,
      138–139
    core obligation, 140–141
    main purpose rule, 139
    risk covered, 139
  misrepresentation as to terms, 131,
    141
  oral assurance negating, 141
  past dealings incorporating, 137–138
  reasonable notice
    classic test, 132
    form of notice, 135
    onerous nature of term, 135–136
    prominence of notice, 135
    red hand rule, 135
    reference to conditions
      obtainable elsewhere, 133,
      136
    ticket cases, 132–134
    timing of notice, 134–135
  signature incorporating, 130–131
Exemplary damages, 238
Exemption clause *see* **Exclusion
  clause**
Expectation loss, 229, 234
Expenses, salary misrepresented as,
  209–210
Express acceptance, 24
Express terms
  concept, 105
  conditions and warranties
    distinguished, 119–120
  conditions precedent/subsequent,
    118
  incorporation of oral statements
    see **Statements during
    negotiations**

innominate terms, 120–121
parol evidence, where written and oral terms conflict *see* Parol evidence

Failure of precondition, 18
Failure to read contract, 130
Fair procedures, 128
Family arrangements, 34–36
Family home, conveyance without consent, 204
Family relationships, undue influence, 194–195
Fax, 30, 31–32
Fiduciary relationship, 166
Film star, withdrawal from contract, 234–235
Final right to terminate, 149–150
Fire frustrating contract, 222, 225
Fishing licence, 224
Fishing rights, 91
Fitness for habitation, 126–127
Fitness for purpose, 143, 146
Flu remedy, 7–8, 38
Foolish bargain, 2
Football contract, 83
Football violence, 54
Force majeure **clause**, 226
Formalities
 concept, 87
 part performance, 96–99
 signature, 93, 95–96
 writing *see* Writing
Franchise renewal, 17
Fraudulent misrepresentation, 168, 169–170
Free flights for life, 49
Fructus naturales and *industriales*, 91
Frustration
 Brexit, 225
 circumstances not constituting, 224
 Covid-19 pandemic, 225–226
 discharging contract, 225
 doctrine, 222

 effects, 225
 impossibility of performance, 222–223
 intervening illegality, 223–224
 obligation falling due before frustrating event occurs, 225
 of purpose, 223
 self-induced, 224
Fundamental breach, 140–141, 227

Gambling, 207
Gender of person accepting offer, 8
Gentleman's agreement, 39–40
Gift, 72, 152
Grey list of terms, 158–159
Guarantee
 bank guarantee, undue influence, 197–201
 concept, 88
 illegal share transactions, 212
 indemnity distinguished, 88–89
 writing requirement, 88–90

Hadley v Baxendale **principles**, 230–233
Half-pay, 8, 23
Half-truths, 165
Handshake agreement, 3
Hardship or inconvenience, 222–223
Harrier Jet, 38–39
Health spa, 236
Hedley Byrne **principle**, 171–172
Heritage building, 177
High Trees **principle**, 59–61
Holiday package, 236–237
Holiday pay, 126
Honour clause, 39–40
Horse, soundness, 52, 106, 107–108, 110
Hyperlink, 103

Identity, error as to, 184–185
Ignorance of law is no defence, 177

Illegal contract
   common law, 207–210
   consequences, 210–212
   contract prejudicial to administration of justice, 208
   corruption, contract encouraging, 209
   crime or tort, contract to commit, 207
   defrauding the Revenue, 209–210
   endangering foreign relations or attacking friendly state, 210
   ex turpi causa non oritur actio, 207
   illegality in performance, 205–206, 211–212
   illegality on the face, 210–211
   immorality, contract promoting, 207–208
   in pari delicto, potior est conditio possidentis, 210–211
   intervening illegality, 223–224
   legislative provisions, 204–207
   maintenance and champerty, 208–298
   public policy behind legislation, 206–207
   recovery of property transferred, 210–211
   resulting trust, 211
   void contract distinguished, 204
Illiteracy, 131
Immorality, 207–208
Implied acceptance, 24–25
Implied terms
   business efficacy test, 47, 124–125
   common law, 126–127
   concept, 123
   constitutional basis, 128
   consumer legislation, 128
   custom or trade usage, 47, 125–126
   in fact, 123–125
   officious bystander test, 47, 123–124
   reasonableness principle, 46–47
   statutory terms, 46
   types of terms, 123

Impossibility of performance, 222–223
Imposter, 184–185
Improvident bargain, 201–203
In pari delicto, potior est conditio possidentis, 210–211
Inconvenience, 222, 237
Indemnity, 88–89
Independent legal advice, 196, 197–198, 200–201, 202
Inducement to enter into contract, 162–164
Inertia selling, 25–26
Infancy
   age of majority, 77
   binding contracts, 81–83
   categories of contracts, 77
   contracts for necessaries, 78–80
   contracts valid unless repudiated, 80–81
   contracts void under 1874 Act, 78–80
   Law Reform Commission proposals, 83–84
Informal arrangements, 37–38
Injunctive relief, 240
Innocent misrepresentation, 173
Innominate terms, 120–121
Insurance contract
   duty of disclosure, 166–169
   life insurance *see* Life insurance
Intention to create legal relations
   commercial agreements, 36–38
   exaggerated statements, 38–39
   example, 33
   family arrangements, 34–36
   honour clauses/gentleman's agreements, 39–40
   joke offer, 39
   letters of comfort, 40–41
   letters of intent, 41
   presumptions, 33
   subject to contract, 41–44
Intermediary services, 159

Internet transaction *see* **Electronic commerce**
Interpretation of contracts
 exclusion and limitation clauses, 138–141
 five rules/general principles, 122
 objective approach, 3
 parol evidence *see* Parol evidence
Intervening illegality, 223–224
Intoxication, 85–86
Invitation to treat, 6–10

Joinder of documents, 94–96
Joke, 3, 39

Laches, 174
***Lampleigh v Braithwait* exception**, 52–53
Lapse of offer, 17–18
Late payment of instalments, 64
Legislation, as source of law, 2
Legitimate expectation, 26, 69
Let the buyer beware, 2–3
Letter of acceptance *see* **Postal rule**
Letter of comfort, 40–41
Letter of intent, 6, 41
Letter of revocation, 15–16
Life insurance
 infant's contract, 80–81
 widows' and children's right to sue, 72
Limitation clause *see* **Exclusion clause**
Limited stock theory, 7
Liquidated damages, 238–239
Loan facilities, oral assertions, 117–118
Loss lies where it falls, 225
Loss of amenity, 236
Loyalty points, 38–39

Maintenance and champerty, 208–209
Maintenance payments, 55, 62
Mandatory injunction, 240
Market manipulation, 212

Marriage
 agreements between spouses, 34
 bank guarantees, undue influence, 197–201
 contract subverting, 213–214
 contracts required to be in writing, 90
 duress, 189
 legal age, 77
 payments upon, 49, 70
 right to sue on life policy, 72
Meadowing, 91–92
Memorandum of agreement *see* **Writing**
Mental incapacity, 84–85
Merchantable quality, 143
Mere representation, 106
Mining strike, 54
Minor *see* **Infancy**
Misrepresentation
 definition, 160
 conduct of parties, 164–165
 contract makes disclosure mandatory, 166
 effect on exclusion clause, 131, 141
 essential elements, 160
 exclusion of liability, 175
 fiduciary relationship, 166
 fraudulent misrepresentation, 168, 169–170
 half-truths, 165
 inducement to enter into contract, 162–164
 innocent misrepresentation, 173
 insurance contracts, 166–169
 must be statement of fact, not law, 162
 negligent misrepresentation/misstatement, 170–173
 property contracts, 165
 remedies
  common law remedies, 173
  consumer insurance contracts, 175
  damages, 173
  equitable remedies, 173–174

rescission, 173–174
Sale of Goods and Supply of
Services Act 1980, 175
specific performance, 174
silence as misrepresentation, 164
statements of fact vs. intention,
161–162
statements of fact vs. opinion,
160–161
statements of fact vs. trader's puff,
161
subsequent falsity, 165
unusual defects, 165–166
Mistake
definition, 176
common mistake
definition, 176
existence of subject matter, 179
in equity, 181–182
ownership, 180
quality, 180–181
voidance of contract, 178
errors as to identity, 184–185
existence at time of contract,
176–177
mutual mistake, 176, 182–183
of law, 177–178
operative mistake, 176, 184, 185,
187
remedies
damages, 187
non est factum, 186
rectification, 186
rescission, 187
specific performance, 187
unilateral mistake, 176, 183
Mitigation of loss, 233
Motor vehicle, lack of conformity,
72, 152
Mutual mistake, 176, 182–183

Natural justice, 128, 238
Necessaries, infant's contract, 78–80
**Negligent misrepresentation/
misstatement**, 170–173

Noise, 237
Non est factum, 130–131, 186
Non-financial loss, 236–237

Objective approach to interpretation, 3
Odyssey Millennium project, 65
Off-premises contract, 154
Offer
definition, 4
acceptance *see* Acceptance
advertisement/invitation to treat, 6–8
auction, 10
bilateral offer, 4
counter-offer, 13–14, 20–23
cross-offers, 27
death of offeror or offeree, 14–15
display of goods for sale, 8–10
electronic communication, 100
failure of precondition, 18
lapse of time, 17–18
letter of intent/statement of intention, 6
oral, written or by conduct, 4
other concepts distinguished, 5–12
price quotation, 5–6
rejection, 12–13
revocation, 15–17
statement of opinion, 5
tender, 11–12
termination, 12–18
unilateral offer, 5, 16–17, 23–24, 28
world at large, 4
Officious bystander test, 47, 123–124
**One year, contract not to be
performed within**, 90–91
Operative mistake, 176, 184, 185, 187
Oral contract, 87, 105
Ordinary reasonable person, 3
Ousting jurisdiction of courts,
212–213
Overbooking
flights, 229–230
holiday accommodation, 231
Overdrawn bank account, 14
Overloading of vessel, 205–206
Owner's risk *see* Exclusion clauses

Pardon, 53
Parol evidence
   custom or trade usage, 113–114
   impact of rule, 118
   interpretation of ambiguous terms, 46, 112–113
   oral statement giving rise to collateral contract, 116–118
   oral statement limiting operation of contract, 115
   proving amount of consideration, 115–116
   rectification purposes, 112
   rule against, 111–112
   written document not recording totality of contract, 114–115
Part payment of debt, 57–58
Part performance, 96–99
Parties
   errors as to identity, 184–185
   identification, 93
Past consideration is no consideration, 52–53
Past dealings
   exclusion clause, 137–138
   implied terms, 47
   silence as acceptance, 26
Payment under mistake of law, 177–178
Penalty clause, 238–239
Peppercorn rent, 50, 51
Performance
   as acceptance of unilateral offer, 5, 16–17, 23–24, 28
   discharging contract, 217–218
   hardship or inconvenience, 222–223
   illegal performance, 205–206, 211–212
   impossibility of performance, 222–223
   prevention of performance, 220
   rescission not possible, 174
   severable/divisible contracts, 219–220
   substantial performance, 218–219
   tender of performance, 220–221
   time for, 221–222
Performance interest, 236
Petrol station, 161, 215
Pinnel's Case, **rule in**, 57
Police services, 54
Postal rule
   lost or delayed letter, 29
   non-application
      another method stipulated, 30
      express exclusion, 30
      instantaneous communication, 31
      letter of revocation, 16, 29–30
      manifest inconvenience and absurdity, 30
      modern communication methods, 31–32
   operation/examples, 15–16, 28–29
Postal strike, 30
Prayers, as consideration, 50
Pre-nuptial contract, 213
Prevention of performance, 220
Price
   memorandum of agreement, 93–94
   proportionate reduction, 149–150
   quotation, 5–6
   reasonable price for services, 153
Prior dealings *see* **Past dealings**
Prisoner, 86
Privity of contract
   definition, 70
   consideration distinguished, 71
   essential elements, 70
   examples, 70–71
   exceptions
      agency, 73–75
      collateral contracts, 75–76
      confidentiality clauses, 75
      covenants pertaining to land, 75
      equitable, 72–73
      legislative, 72
      sale of goods, 76, 152
   Law Reform Commission proposals, 76
   subcontractors, 71

Prohibitory injunction, 240
Promise to do what one is already obliged to do by law or contract, 53–57
Promissory estoppel
  conditions giving rise to, 61–62
  equitable concept, 59
  High Trees principle, 59–61
  legitimate expectation distinguished, 69
  liberal view, 63
  orthodox view, 61–62
  other concepts distinguished, 68–69
  pre-existing legal relationship, 62–63
  proprietary estoppel distinguished, 68
  reliance (and possible detriment), 65–66
  remedy a matter for court, 67
  shield, not sword, 62, 67
  test/essential elements, 60, 61–62
  unambiguous representation, 63–65
  unfairness or unconscionability, 67
  waiver distinguished, 68
Proprietary estoppel, 68
Prosecution
  agreement not to prosecute, 208
  threat, as duress, 189
Prostitution, 207
Publishing contract, 83, 220
Punitive damages, 238
Purpose, frustration, 223

Quantum meruit, 241
Quotation, 5–6

Railway season ticket, 83
Reasonable time, 17
Reasonableness principle, 46–47
Recovery of mistaken payments, 177–178
Rectification, 112, 186
Redundancy contract, 180
Referential tender or bid, 11–12
Rejection of offer, 12–13

Reliance loss, 234–235
Religious adviser, undue influence, 193–194
Remedies for breach
  damages *see* Damages
  injunctions, 240
  quantum meruit, 241
  rescission, 173–174, 187, 241
  restitution, 177–178, 241
  specific performance, 174, 187, 191, 240
Remoteness of loss, 229–233
Rent reduction, during war, 59–60
Repair or replacement, 148–149
Representative action, 159
Repudiatory breach, 227
Request for more information, 21
Res extincta, 179
Res sua, 180
Rescission, 173–174, 187, 241
Reserve price, 10
Restitutio in integrum, 173–174
Restitution loss, 235
Restitution, remedy, 177–178, 241
Restraint of trade, 214–215, 216
Resulting trust, 211
Revenue, defrauding, 209–210
Revocation of offer, 15–17
Reward, 5, 19–20
Rezoning of land, 55
Right of disassociation, 128
Risk
  exclusion or limitation of liability *see* Exclusion clause
  occurrence does not constitute frustration, 224
  sale of goods, 151

Sailor
  death during voyage, 218
  extra wages to perform duty, 54–55
Sale of goods
  definition, 144–145
  consumer rights *see* Consumer rights

misrepresentation, remedies, 175
no writing requirement, 92
privity of contract, exceptions, 76, 152
Sale of land
  electronic signature, 102
  part performance, 96–99
  subject to contract, 41–44, 96
  writing requirement, 91–92
Seaworthiness, 121
Self-induced frustration, 224
Service contract, 153
Severance
  partial performance, 219–220
  void parts of contract, 204, 216
Shield, not sword, 62, 67
Short-term right to terminate, 148
Signature
  acts constituting, 93
  electronic, 101–102
  exclusion clause, 130–131
  series of documents, 95–96
Silence
  as acceptance, 25–26
  as misrepresentation, 164
Small print, 130
Smartphone, 145
Solus agreement, 215
Sources of contract law, 2
Spare parts/after-sales service, 146
Specific performance, 174, 187, 191, 240
Speculative damages, 234
Speculative litigation, 208–209
Sponsorship deal, 264
Sports management/representation contract, 75, 82, 83
Spouse see **Marriage**
Standard form contract, 129
Statement after contract, 110
Statement during negotiations
  belief or fact, 107–109
  collateral contracts, 116–118
  crucial to conclusion of contract, 109
  emphasis in statement, 110

expressly stipulated to be part of contract, 109
parol evidence, where written and oral terms conflict see Parol evidence
special skill or knowledge, 106–107
time between statement and conclusion of contract, 110
warranties and representations distinguished, 105–106
whether part of contract, 105
written contract intended to be conclusive, 111
Statement of fact vs. opinion, 107–109, 160–161
Statement of intention, 6, 161–162
Statute of Frauds, 87–88
Stevedore, 74–75
Stock in trade, 117
Subcontractor, 71
Subject matter of contract, 94
Subject to contract, 41–44, 96
Substantial performance, 218–219
Subverting marriage, 213–214
Supermarket purchase, 3
Swimming pool, 236

Tax evasion, 209–210
Telephone acceptance, 16, 27, 30, 31–32, 114
Telex, 31–32, 92, 95
Tender of performance, 220–221
Tendering, 11–12
Termination of offer, 12–18
Three Ps, 45
Third party, undue influence, 197–201
Ticket cases, 132–134
Time of the essence, 221
Timesheet, 130–131
Tobacco sale, 205
Tort
  contract to commit, 207
  damages in tort and contract distinguished, 229
Trade-in, 145

Trade usage, 47, 113–114, 125–126
Trader's puff, 38–39, 161
Trust concept, 72–73
Tuition contract, 82

Uberrima fides, 166–167, 168
Unconditional acceptance, 20–23
Unconscionability, 51, 67, 201–203
Undue influence
 definition, 191–192
 actual undue influence, 192–193
 bank guarantees, 197–201
 independent legal advice, 196
 manifest disadvantage, 195
 onus of proof, 192, 195–196
 presumed undue influence
  concept, 192
  relationships automatically
   presumed to be, 193–194
  relationships presumed on the
   facts to be, 194–195
  rebutting presumption, 195–196
 third party influence, 197–201
Unfair terms in consumer contracts,
 158–159
Unilateral mistake, 176, 183
Unilateral offer, 5, 16–17, 23–24, 28
University place, deferral, 61
Unjust enrichment, 235, 241
Unsanitary premises, 205

Vehicle mileage/age, 106–107
Vienna Convention, 22
Voidable contract with infant, 80–81
Void contract
 illegal contract distinguished, 204
 examples under statute, 212
 ousting jurisdiction of courts,
  212–213

restraint of trade, 214–215,
 216
severability, 204, 216
subverting marriage, 213–214

Waiver, 68
Warranty
 breach of warranty, 226–227
 condition distinguished, 119–120
 meaning, 105–106
 mere representation distinguished,
  105–106
Website transaction *see* **Electronic
 commerce**
Wedding dress, 131
Wedding reception, 237
Writing
 definition, 87
 contract not to be performed within
  one year, 90–91
 contract the consideration for which
  is marriage, 90
 electronic representation, 87
 guarantee, 88–90
 joinder of documents, 94–96
 memorandum of agreement
  other essential features, 94
  overview, 92–93
  parties, 93
  price, 93–94
  signature, 93, 95–96
  subject matter, 94
 part performance, 96–99
 requirement generally, 3, 87
 sale of goods (repealed), 92
 sale of land or interest, 91–92
 Statute of Frauds, 87–88
 subject to contract, 96
Wrongful dismissal, 238

5 reasons to choose ProView eBooks

1. Always Have Your Publications On Hand
Never worry about an internet connection again. With ProView's offline access, your essential titles are always available, wherever your work takes you.

2. The Feel of a Real Book
ProView's book-like features, including page numbers and bookmarks, offer a seamless transition to digital without losing the touch of tradition.

3. Effortless Library Management
Access previous editions, transfer annotations to new releases, and automatically update your looseleaf materials—all in one place.

4. Tailor Your Reading Experience
With ProView, customize your reading with adjustable display settings, font sizes, and colour schemes. Read your way, effortlessly.

5. Find Information in a Flash
Cut through the clutter with ProView's advanced search. Pinpoint the information you need across your entire library with speed and precision.

Scan the QR code to find out more or contact us at proviewtrial@tr.com for a free trial

Sweet & Maxwell